THE PERSIAN METRES

BY THE SAME AUTHOR

Colloquial Persian (Routledge and Kegan Paul)

Modern Iran (George Routledge)

The Wonderful Sea-Horse and Other Persian Tales (Geoffrey
Bles)

A Guide to Iranian Area Study (American Council of Learned
Societies)

Persian Proverbs (John Murray)

Persian Oil: A Study in Power Politics (Lawrence and
Wishart)

Elementary Persian Grammar (Cambridge University Press)

Payambar: The Messenger (Translation) (Sh. Muhammad Ashraf,
Lahore)

In Search of Omar Khayyam (Translation) (George Allen and
Unwin)

THE PERSIAN METRES

L.P. ELWELL–SUTTON

Reader in Persian in the
University of Edinburgh

WITHDRAWN
FROM
UNIVERSITY OF PENNSYLVANIA
LIBRARIES

Cambridge University Press
Cambridge
London · New York · Melbourne

Published by the Syndics of the Cambridge University Press

The Pitt Building, Trumpington Street, Cambridge CB2 1RP

Bentley House, 200 Euston Road, London NW1 2DB

32 East 57th Street, New York, NY 10022, USA

296 Beaconsfield Parade, Middle Park, Melbourne 3206,

Australia

© Cambridge University Press 1976

Library of Congress Cataloguing in Publication Data

Elwell-Sutton, Laurence Paul.
    The Persian metres.

    Bibliography: p.
    Includes indexes.
    1. Persian language--Versification. I.   Title.
PK6353.E4   891'.5   75-39392
ISBN 0 521 21089 5

First published 1976

Printed in Great Britain by Kingprint Limited,
Richmond, Surrey

Contents

For quick reference a table of the thirty commonest metres
is given on page xiv.

Introduction

For more than one thousand years the study of the metres of Persian verse has been dominated by the theories and principles devised by the analysts of Arabic poetry, and thereafter applied without discrimination to the classification of the compositions of the Persian poets. So complete has this domination been that this use of the traditional Arabic terminology has actually misled many scholars, both eastern and western, into assuming an intimate relation between the two systems, and even into asserting that Persian verse is derived from Arabic. In fact, as this book sets out to show, there is no support for such a belief. It is true that the Arabic terminology may (with some stretching of its legitimate use) be employed to describe the Persian metres; but this does not mean that the latter, as used by the poets, were copied from Arabic poetry – any more than the fact that Shakespeare wrote in what we choose to call iambic pentameters means that he copied this metre from the Greeks.

It is not the purpose of this book to criticise this traditional Arabic terminology insofar as it has been applied to Arabic verse. There must however be general agreement that, particularly in the failure to isolate and

identify the syllable as the unit of speech and therefore
of scansion, the prosodic theories of traditional eastern
scholarship fall far short of those of the Greeks in
simplicity and clarity, and it is indeed surprising that
such a clumsy system should have survived so long. This is
not however to suggest that the Greek or any other alien
system should be applied to Persian. The aim of the
present book has been to analyse afresh the metres actually
used by the Persian poets, and to work out, primarily for
the benefit of students of Persian poetry, a new and
simplified set of rules for their recognition and identification. At the same time it is recognised that some knowledge of the traditional laws of prosody and of the
technical terms used is often necessary for an understanding
of allusions in Persian poetry and prose. The first
chapter is therefore devoted to a full description of these,
which it is hoped may be of value to students of Arabic as
well as Persian.

It was very quickly apparent that the lists of metres
provided by the classical prosodists gave little or no
indication of the relative frequency of different metres,
and indeed it was by no means uncommon for the prosodist to
compose his own verses in some obscure or unknown metre
required to fill a gap in the theoretical system erected by
him. A proper basis for such a classification could only
be a "field" study of the metres in which poets actually
wrote, and this involved the examination of the dīwāns of

poets of all periods, together with a variety of anthologies, ta<u>dk</u>irāt, etc., amounting in all to some 20,000 poems and fragments ranging from the 3rd/9th century to the present day.   It was thought that such a study might indicate certain historical trends in the use and development of Persian metres; but in fact it soon became clear that the metrical system in universal use up to the present day (until the monopoly was broken by the introduction of "free verse") differs in no essential respects from that already in existence when Islamic Persian poetry emerged into the light of written record.   The very fact that this system has lasted unchanged for so long is in itself evidence that it is closely bound up with the genius of the Persian language, and is unlikely to owe anything to the influence of an alien tongue.   But it is one of the frustrating aspects of the situation that virtually no Persian poetry has survived from before that date, so that it is extremely difficult to suggest the stages by which the metrical system developed into its present form.   The last chapter glances briefly along some of the avenues that remain to be explored in the direction of prose patterns, popular verse, and normal speech, and of Middle Iranian and Avestan verse, and thence into the ocean of Sanskrit, Greek and Indo-European metres generally.

A work of this nature must draw on a great many sources, and these are acknowledged in the bibliography.   My special thanks are due to my one-time colleagues Mr. Ḥasan Balyuzi

and Mr. Abolqasem Ṭaheri for recording samples of Persian
verse, and to the British Broadcasting Corporation for
providing facilities for this; to Dr. P.N. Xanlari,
Prof. Masᶜud Farzad, and Mr. Amir Feridun Moᶜtamed, both
for their stimulating studies in this field, and for
helpful and suggestive conversations and letters; and to
numerous colleagues in the University of Edinburgh,
especially in the Departments of Turkish, Arabic, Sanskrit,
and Phonetics, for illuminating discussions and the use of
technical facilities.   Finally, my particular gratitude
goes to Mrs. Pat Williams for the patience and accuracy
with which she typed a very difficult and complicated text.

                              L. P. Elwell-Sutton

Edinburgh, October, 1975

Transcription

To assist the investigation of what are primarily phonetic
questions, and to avoid the ambiguities involved in using
scripts running in opposite directions, transcription has
been used throughout. It is hoped that the unfamiliar
appearance thus produced will not prove too great a
stumbling block.

Generally speaking, Persian words and names are trans-
literated according to the Persian table, and Arabic
according to the Arabic. This rule has been followed even
when the Persian word or name is of Arabic origin or Arabic
in form. In the case of book titles, the transcription
shows the language of the book. An exception to this
general rule is made in the case of the technical terms of
prosody, which are all transcribed according to the Arabic
system, even in the few cases where they are actually
Persian (dū-pāra, tarāna, etc.). hamza at the beginning of
words is generally omitted, except in verse, where it affects
the scansion. For the sake of consistency the modernised
spelling of Persian is used throughout, except where special
reference is being made, e.g. to intervocalic d for modern d,
ō, ē for modern u, i, etc.

In addition to the two main systems, variations are

employed in two cases:

(a) In verse, where the scansion is to be shown, the colon (:) has been substituted for the macron (̄) as an indication of length.

(b) Where the emphasis is on the <u>letters</u> of the original script (as in discussing traditional methods of scansion), the Arabic system is adhered to for both languages, and capital letters are used to represent the ḥurūf (letters) and lower case for the ḥarakāt (vowel signs).

Persian	Arabic	Letter	Persian	Arabic	Letter
Consonants					
ʔ		ا	q̇		غ
b		ب	f		ف
p	–	پ	q		ق
t		ت	k		ك
s̱	ṯ	ث	g	–	گ
j		ج	l		ل
c	–	چ	m		م
ḥ		ح	n		ن
x		خ	v	w	و
d		د	h		ه
ẕ	ẕ	ذ	y		ى
r		ر		Vowels	
z		ز	a		◌ٔ
ž	–	ژ	α	ā	ا◌ٔ
s		س	e	i	◌ٕ
š		ش	i	ī	ى◌ٕ
ṣ		ص	o	u	◌ٗ
ż	ḍ	ض	u	ū	و◌ٗ
ṭ		ط		Diphthongs	
ẓ		ظ	ei	ay	ى◌ٔ
ʕ		ع	ou	aw	و◌ٔ

Code No.	Basic Scansion	Arabic _baḥr_
1.1.11	⏑ – – ⏑ – – | ⏑ – – ⏑ –	mutaqārib
1.1.12	⏑ – – ⏑ – – ⏑ – – ⏑ – –	"
2.1.11	⏑ – – – ⏑ – – – | ⏑ – –	hazaj
2.1.16	⏑ – – – ⏑ – – – ⏑ – – – ⏑ – – –	"
2.3.16	– – ⏑ – – – ⏑ – – – ⏑ – – – ⏑ –	rajaz
2.4.11	– ⏑ – – – ⏑ – – – ⏑ –	ramal
2.4.15	– ⏑ – – – ⏑ – – – ⏑ – – – ⏑ –	"
2.4.16	– ⏑ – – – ⏑ – – – ⏑ – – – ⏑ – –	"
3.1.11	⏑ ⏑ – – ⏑ ⏑ – – | ⏑ ⏑ –	ramal
3.1.15	⏑ ⏑ – – ⏑ ⏑ – – ⏑ ⏑ – – ⏑ ⏑ –	"
3.1.16	⏑ ⏑ – – ⏑ ⏑ – – ⏑ ⏑ – – ⏑ ⏑ – –	"
3.3.14	– – ⏑ ⏑ – – ⏑ ⏑ – – ⏑ ⏑ – –	hazaj
3.3.07(2)	– – ⏑ ⏑ – – – | – – ⏑ ⏑ – – –	"
3.4.11	– ⏑ ⏑ – – ⏑ ⏑ – – ⏑ –	sarīʿ
3.4.16	– ⏑ ⏑ – – ⏑ ⏑ – – ⏑ ⏑ – – ⏑ ⏑ –	"
4.1.15	⏑ – ⏑ – ⏑ ⏑ – – | ⏑ – ⏑ – ⏑ ⏑ –	mujtatt
4.1.16	⏑ – ⏑ – ⏑ ⏑ – – ⏑ – ⏑ – ⏑ ⏑ – –	"
4.4.13	– ⏑ ⏑ – – ⏑ – ⏑ – ⏑ ⏑ – –	munsariḥ
4.4.07(2)	– ⏑ ⏑ – – ⏑ – | – ⏑ ⏑ – – ⏑ –	"
4.5.11	⏑ ⏑ – – ⏑ – ⏑ – ⏑ ⏑ –	xafīf
4.7.11	– – ⏑ – ⏑ – ⏑ ⏑ – – –	mudāriʿ
4.7.02/09	– – . . . . ⏑ ⏑ – – ⏑ – ⏑ – –	qarīb
4.7.14	– – ⏑ – ⏑ – ⏑ ⏑ – – ⏑ – ⏑ –	mudāriʿ
4.7.07(2)	– – ⏑ – ⏑ – – | – – ⏑ – ⏑ – –	"
5.1.10	– – ⏑ ⏑ – ⏑ – ⏑ | – –	hazaj
5.1.11	– – ⏑ ⏑ – ⏑ – ⏑ – – –	"
5.1.13 }	– – ⏑ ⏑ {– ⏑ – ⏑ – – ⏑ ⏑ –	"
3.3.13 }	{ – ⏑	
5.2.16	– ⏑ ⏑ – ⏑ – ⏑ – – ⏑ ⏑ – ⏑ – ⏑ –	rajaz
5.3.16	⏑ ⏑ – ⏑ – ⏑ – – ⏑ ⏑ – ⏑ – ⏑ – –	ramal

A full list of Persian metres with examples will be found in Chapter III.

The above table lists those most commonly met with.

I. The traditional analysis of Arabic and Persian prosody

Writers on Persian and Arabic prosody are legion, but few of
them add much to what their predecessors have written.   We
cannot do better than to go back to the beginning, to the
"Father of Arabic Prosody", al-Xalīl b. Aḥmad al-Farhūdī (or
al-Farāhīdī) of Baṣra, who was born about 100/718 and died
in 170/786 (175/791 or 190/806, according to other
authorities).   The earliest extant work to contain a statement of al-Xalīl's ideas is the ʕiqd al-farīd of Ibn ʕabd
Rabbih of Cordoba (246/860-328/940).   His most important
successors were al-Axfaš (215/831 or 221/836) and Abu'l-Ḥasan
ʕalī b. Saʕda of Balx (d. 376/986).   The earliest named
writer on Persian prosody is Moulana Yusef of Nišapur (d. c.
390/1000), and other early theorists were Bozorjmehr Qommi (or
Qasemi) and Bahrami of Saraxs, author of the Xojaste-name.
Nothing has survived of the works of these writers, while two
important books of the 5th/11th and 6th/12th centuries, the
Tarjoman ol-balaǧe of Raduyani and the Ḥadayeqos-sehr of
Rašidoddin Vaṭvaṭ deal rather with the art of poetics,
rhetoric, metaphor and allusion, poetic conceits, and so on.
It is not until the seventh/thirteenth century that we get
the first serious work devoted primarily to the Persian

1

metres.   This is <u>al-Moꞓjam fi maꞓayire aš̌ꞓarel-ꞓajam,</u> by
Šamsoddin Moḥammad b. Qeis Razi, written in 614/1217.   It was
quickly followed by Naṣiroddin Ṭuṣi's <u>MeꞓyaroI-aš̌ꞓar</u>, written
in 649/1251.   Of innumerable later works, one of the most
useful is the <u>ꞓaruẕ-e Seifi</u>, written by Seifi of Boxara in
896/1491, and reference should also be made to the <u>Resale-e
ꞓaruẕ</u> of Abdorraḥman Jami, completed about 885/1480, as an
example of a work by a practising poet.

European works that reproduce the theories of the
oriental scholars without significant change are those by
Samuel Clarke (1661), Ewald (1825) and Freytag (1830) for
Arabic; and Gladwin (1801), Rückert (1827), Garcin de Tassy
(1848), and Blochmann (1872) for Persian.   The following
account of the traditional system is a résumé of all these
sources, and is applicable equally to Arabic and to Persian,
though the technical terms are given throughout in their
Arabic form.

Generally speaking, any given poem in Arabic or Persian
is composed throughout in lines (hemistich - <u>miṣrāꞓ</u>) of
constant length and metre (<u>wazn</u>) (with permissible variations).
These hemistichs are paired in couplets (<u>bayt</u>, pl. <u>abyāt</u>),
this being the unit of verse.   The classical system of
prosody is based on the assumption that there are a certain
number of basic (sound, <u>sālim</u>) metres (<u>baḥr</u>, pl. <u>buḥūr</u>), a
certain number of sub-divisions of each of these categories
that constitute distinct metres (and so cannot be used in the
same poem), and a certain number of variations that are

permitted within the same metre.

One of the surprising blind spots of the Muslim prosodists
was their failure to recognise the syllable.   Indeed they
failed ever to isolate the vowel except as a function of the
consonant or letter, a failure all the more surprising since
they must have been familiar not only with Greek works on the
subject, but also with the ideas of the Zoroastrian priests
who devised the Avestan alphabet.   Be that as it may,
scansion (taqtī٩) is based on the written form, and is
carried out by a process of counting letters (ḥarf, pl.
ḥurūf), the general rule being that each line of a poem contains the same number of letters (with the permissible addition of one at the end).   The letters are classified into
vowelled (moving, mutaḥarrik pl. mutaḥarrikāt) and unvowelled
(resting, silent, sākin pl. sawākin).   Included in the
latter are the three letters ʔ, w, and y, whether they represent consonants, long vowels or diphthongs.   In Arabic
verse two sākin letters may never come together (except
rarely at the end of a bayt), and though in Persian this
juxtaposition is common, there is no place for it in the
prosodic system, and in such cases the second sākin letter
is assumed for scansion purposes to be mutaḥarrik.   So
much a part of the system has this become that Turkish and
Indian readers, when reciting Persian poetry, actually insert
a short a-sound (nīm-fatḥa) after the second sākin, though
of course no such vowel-sound is to be found in the original
language.   All sākin letters after the second are ignored.

Muslim prosodists use the symbol o for mutaḥarrik letters and
| for sākin, but while occasional reference will be made in
this survey to these symbols, for the most part use will be
made of the rather simpler Western signs ◡ - (though their
significance is quite distinct).

It must be borne in mind however that few lines of Arabic
or Persian verse can be scanned in this way at sight. First
of all it is necessary for the "spelling" of the line to be
adjusted so as to include all letters that are sounded but
not written, and to eliminate all those that are written but
have no phonetic value.   In Arabic the number of such
adjustments is comparatively restricted; it includes, among
letters to be added, the tanwīn, the tašdīd, alif in words
like allāh, hadā, dālika, and short vowels at the end of a
bayt, and among letters to be omitted the alif standing for
ḥamzat al-waṣl.[1]   The range in Persian is very much wider,
as the following table shows:

A. Letters always omitted

 1. Silent v after x.

 2. n after a long vowel (ɑ, i, u) (ḍ:ına).   خان ٢

 3. Third and subsequent of a cluster of sākin letters, e.g.
ni:st = NiYS[T], ɑnjɑ:st = ʔaʔNJaʔS[T].

B. Letters that may be omitted

 1. Initial alif (ḥamza), especially in Persian words but
commonly also applicable to Arabic:

bani: ʔɑ:dam aʕzɑ:y-e yakdi:garand

                    ke dar ʔɑ:fari:neš ze yak gouharand

                                         (Saʕdi)

(a) Straightforward transcription:

min ʕa:šiqin ṣabbin yusirru'l-hawa:

                 qad šaffahu'l-wajdu ʔila: kaltami

                  (ʕumar b. Abī Rabīʕa)

molḥed-e: gorsone dar xɑ:ne-ye xɑ:li: por xˇɑ:n

           ʕaql bɑ:var nakonad kaz ramaẓɑ:n ʔandi:šad

                  (Saʕdi)

(b) Letter by letter transcription (the Arabic ḥurūf represented by capitals, vowels and other letters not shown in
the script by lower case):

MiN ʕaʔŠiQin ṢaBbin YuSiRru ʔLHaWaY   (16 letters)

QaD ŠaFfaHu ʔLWaJDu ʔiLaY KaLṮaMi   (17 letters)

       - - - - - - - -

MuLḤiDi GuRSuNaH DaR XaʔNaHi XaʔLiY PuR XWaʔN (25 letters)

ʕaQL BaʔWaR NaKuNaD KaZ RaMaẒaʔN ʔaNDiYŠaD   (24 letters)

(c) Letter by letter transcription after "adjustment" (short
vowels omitted and sākin and mutaḥarrik letters indicated by
symbols):

M N ʕ ʔ Š̌ Q N Ṣ B B N Y S R R L H W Y (11 mutaḥarrik, 8 sākin)

Q D Š̌ F F H L W J D . ʔ L Y K L Ṯ M Y (11 mutaḥarrik, 7 sākin)

o ǀ o ǀ o o ǀ o ǀ o(ǀ)o o ǀ o ǀ o o ǀ

       - - - - - - - -

M L Ḥ D Y G R S N D R X ʔ N H X ʔ L Y P R Xʔ(14 mutaḥarrik,

                              9 sākin)

ʕ Q L B ʔ W R N K N D K Z R M Ẓ ʔ ʔ N D Y Š̌ D (14 mutaḥarrik,

o ǀ o o ǀ o ǀ o o o ǀ o ǀ o o o ǀ o ǀ o ǀ o ǀ   9 sākin)

     A Persian verse composed by a prosodist provides a more
extreme example:

(a) nešast sarvar-e ʔahl-e karam be-majles-e xɑ:ṣ

    do xᵛɑ:n se xᵛɑ:n do se xᵛɑ:n xᵛɑ:st xɑ:n ce xᵛɑ:n ke
                       naxᵛɑ:st

(b) NiŠaST SaRWaRi ʔaHLi KaRaM BiMaJLiSi Xaʔṣ (22 letters)

    DuW XWaʔN SiH XWaʔN DuW SiH XWaʔN XWaʔST XaʔN CiH
             XWaʔN KiH NaXWaʔST (42 letters)

(c) N Š S T S R V R ʔ H L Y K R M B M J L S X ʔ Ṣ
                  (15 mutaḥarrik, 8 sākin)

    D X ʔ S X ʔ D S X ʔ X ʔ S X ʔ C X ʔ K N X ʔ S
                  (15 mutaḥarrik, 8 sākin)

    o o | o o | o o o | o | o o | o o | o o o

Particular metres are distinguished according to the sequence of mutaḥarrik and sākin letters (which can be re-interpreted in practice into the sequence of short and long syllables - see below). To facilitate identification (and for other reasons that will become clear), the sequence of letters is broken up into units (aṣl, pl. uṣūl) as follows:

(i) sabab (pl. asbāb), "rope"

    (a) sabab xafīf = one mutaḥarrik and one sākin, e.g.

        (Arabic) Ku-N = kun

        (Persian) ʔa-Z = az

    (b) sabab taqīl = two mutaḥarrikāt, e.g.

        (Arabic) La-Ka = laka

        (Persian) Sa-Ri = sar-e

(ii) watad (watid, pl. awtād), "peg".

    (a) watad mafrūq = one mutaḥarrik, one sākin, one
                mutaḥarrik, e.g.

        (Arabic) Qa-B-La = qabla

        (Persian) Ku-W-Yi = kuy-e

(b) <u>watad majmūⵒ</u> (<u>maqrūn</u>) = two mutaḥarrikāt, one
sākin, e.g.

(Arabic) La-Qa-D = laqad

(Persian) Bi-Ku-N = bekon

(iii) <u>fāṣila</u> (pl. <u>fawāṣil</u>), "section".

(a) <u>fāṣila ṣuḋrā</u> = three mutaḥarrikāt, one sākin (i.e.
sabab ṯaqīl + sabab xafīf), e.g.

(Arabic) Qa-Da-Mi-Y = qadamī

(Persian) Bi-Ra-Wi-Y = beravi

(b) <u>fāṣila kubrā</u> = four mutaḥarrikāt, one sākin (i.e.
sabab ṯaqīl + watad majmūⵒ), e.g.

(Arabic) Ḍa-Ra-Ba-Hu-M = ḍarabahum

(Persian) Na-Gu-Ḏa-Ri-Y = nagoẕari

The <u>Dorre-e Najafi</u>[2] adds the following:

(i) (c) <u>sabab mutawassiṭ</u> = one mutaḥarrik, two sawākin,
e.g.(Arabic) Ḍa-ʔ-L(-LuN) = ḍāllun

(Persian) Ya-ʔ-R = yⲁr

(ii)(c) <u>watad kuṯrā</u> = two mutaḥarrikāt, two sawākin, e.g.

(Arabic) Ta-Ḍa-ʔ-L(-La) = taḍālla

(Persian) Fi-Ra-ʔ-Z = ferⲁz

(iii)(c) <u>fāṣila ⵒuẕmā</u> = five mutaḥarrikāt, one sākin (i.e.
sabab ṯaqīl + fāṣila ṣuḋrā), e.g.

(Arabic) Ḥa-Ra-Ka-Tu-Ha-ʔ = ḥarakatuhā

(Persian) Bi-Na-Di-Ha-Ma-Š = benadihamaš

Of the above, (i)(c) and (ii)(c) are peculiar to Persian
verse, while (iii)(b) and (c) are only found in Arabic verse.
In general the fawāṣil are of little practical value, since
they are merely combinations of uṣūl from the other two

categories.

It may help to illuminate this somewhat puzzling scene if
the various figures in it are represented also in the guise
of European notation.   For this purpose a mutaḥarrik
consonant (i.e. consonant + short vowel) is to be regarded as
a short syllable (ᵕ), and a mutaḥarrik plus sākin (i.e.
consonant + short vowel + consonant, or consonant + long
vowel) as a long syllable (-):

   (i)(a) o | -

     (b) oo   ᵕ ᵕ

     (c) o|| —ᵛ

  (ii)(a)o|o   - ᵕ

     (b)oo| ᵕ -

     (c)oo|| ᵕ —ᵛ

 (iii)(a)ooo| ᵕ ᵕ -

     (b)oooo| ᵕ ᵕ ᵕ -

     (c)ooooo| ᵕ ᵕ ᵕ ᵕ -

Equipped with these units, we are now in a position to
form the feet (rukn, pl. arkān, or juz?, pl. ajzā?) that go
to make up a line of verse.   In order to avoid repetition of
the clumsy terminology, formulae (afāʕĪl) were devised to
represent the feet, using the three letters familiar for this
kind of purpose throughout Arabic grammar - f, ʕ, and l.

Ten basic feet are recognised, two consisting of five
letters (two uṣūl), known as xumāsī, and eight of seven
letters (three uṣūl), known as subāʕī:

(a) <u>xumāsī</u>

1. Faʔʔ-ʕiLuN = faːʕilun : sabab xafīf + watad majmūʕ - ◡ -

2. FuʕuW-LuN = fuʕuːlun : watad majmūʕ + sabab xafīf ◡ - -

(b) <u>subāʕī</u>

3. MaFaʔ-ʕiY-LuN = mafaːʕiːlun : watad majmūʕ + sabab xafīf
   + sabab xafīf ◡ - - -

4. MuS-TaF-ʕiLuN = mustafʕilun : sabab xafīf + sabab xafīf +
   watad majmūʕ - - ◡ -

5. MuFaʔ-ʕaLa-TuN = mufaːʕalatun : watad majmūʕ + sabab
   ṭaqīl + sabab xafīf ◡ - ◡ ◡ -

6. MuTa-Faʔ-ʕiLun = mutafaːʕilun : sabab ṭaqīl + sabab xafīf
   + watad majmūʕ ◡ ◡ - ◡ -

7. Faʔ-ʕiLaʔ-TuN = faːʕilaːtun : sabab xafīf + watad majmūʕ
   + sabab xafīf - ◡ - -

8. MaF-ʕuW-LaʔTu = mafʕuːlaːtu : sabab xafīf + sabab xafīf +
   watad mafrūq - - - ◡

9. Faʔʕi-Laʔ-TuN = faːʕilaːtun : watad mafrūq + sabab xafīf
   + sabab xafīf - ◡ - -

10. MuS-TaFʕi-LuN = mustafʕilun : sabab xafīf + watad mafrūq
    + sabab xafīf - - ◡ -

The following table compares the arrangement of the uṣūl
within the arkān:

	1st aṣl	2nd aṣl	3rd aṣl
1.	Faʔ	ʕiLuN	
	<u>sabab xafīf</u>	<u>watad majmūʕ</u>	
2.	FuʕuW	LuN	
	<u>watad majmūʕ</u>	<u>sabab xafīf</u>	

3.	MaFaʔ	ʕiY	LuN
	<u>watad majmūʕ</u>	<u>sabab xafīf</u>	<u>sabab xafīf</u>
4.	MuS	TaF	ʕiLuN
	<u>sabab xafīf</u>	<u>sabab xafīf</u>	<u>watad majmūʕ</u>
5.	MuFaʔ	ʕaLa	TuN
	<u>watad majmūʕ</u>	<u>sabab taqīl</u>	<u>sabab xafīf</u>
		(<u>fāṣila ṣuɋrā</u>)	
6.	MuTa	Faʔ	ʕiLuN
	<u>sabab taqīl</u>	<u>sabab xafīf</u>	<u>watad majmūʕ</u>
	(<u>fāṣila ṣuɋrā</u>)		
7.	Faʔ	ʕiLaʔ	TuN
	<u>sabab xafīf</u>	<u>watad majmūʕ</u>	<u>sabab xafīf</u>
8.	MaF	ʕuW	LaʔTu
	<u>sabab xafīf</u>	<u>sabab xafīf</u>	<u>watad mafrūq</u>
9.	Faʔʕi	Laʔ	TuN
	<u>watad mafrūq</u>	<u>sabab xafīf</u>	<u>sabab xafīf</u>
10.	MuS	TaFʕi	LuN
	<u>sabab xafīf</u>	<u>watad mafrūq</u>	<u>sabab xafīf</u>

It will be seen that every foot consists of one watad and one or two asbāb.   The significance of this, as also of the distinction between Nos. 7 and 4 on the one hand and Nos. 9 and 10 on the other, will be discussed later.

Nos. 5 and 6 are found only in Arabic verse.

The basic feet are not sufficient to account for all the variations that are found in Arabic and Persian metres, and it is therefore necessary to postulate a considerable number of "derived" feet.   For this purpose the basic arkān are

known as the uṣūl, and the derived feet as the furūʕ (sing.
farʕ). This terminology must not be confused with the other
use of the term aṣl referred to above. Of the ten uṣūl, the
following six are found only as "basic" feet:

  mufa:ʕalatun, mutafa:ʕilun, fa:.ʕila:.tun,

  mafʕu:la:tu, fa:ʕi.la:.tun, mus.tafʕi.lun.

(exceptionally, fa:.ʕila:.tun may be derived from fa:ʕilun by
tarfīl, as indicated in the tables below). The other four
are regarded as uṣūl in certain metres, and occur as furūʕ
in others:

  fuʕu:lun - aṣl in the metres tawīl and mutaqārib

            farʕ in all others

  fa:ʕilun - aṣl in the metres madīd, basīṭ, and mutadārik

            farʕ in all others

  mustafʕilun - farʕ in the metre kāmil

            aṣl in all others

  mafa:ʕi:lun - farʕ in the metre wāfir

            aṣl in all others

Apart from the above ten feet (whether aṣl or farʕ), 37 other
feet are found which are regarded as being derived from one
or other of the basic or "sound" (sālim) feet. Such feet
are known as ḍayr sālim ("unsound"). Modification may take
the form of

  (a) addition of one or more letters.

  (b) "silencing" of one or more letters (i.e. elision of
      vowel).

  (c) elision of one or more letters (with accompanying

vowel).

These modifications fall into two categories:

(i) ziḥāf (pl. ziḥāfāt): generally speaking, the ziḥāf
is a modification applicable to any or all of the feet in a
hemistich (miṣrāʕ), and affects only the asbāb.   In Arabic
verse the ziḥāfāt are permissible variations within the frame-
work of a given metre.   This is not the case in Persian
verse, in which many ziḥāfāt are used to account for basic
differences in the metre, which must be maintained throughout.

A ḍayr sālim foot, if it has been modified by a ziḥāf,
is called muzāḥif.

(ii) ʕilla (pl. ʕilal):   the ʕilla is a modification
applied (in Arabic verse) only to the awtād in the first or
last feet of a miṣrāʕ (in Persian also to the foot before a
mid-line caesura).   It generally alters the length of the
foot and so of the line, and thus forms a new metre.   A foot
thus modified is called maʕlūl.

Of the forms of modification listed above, (a) is found
only in the ʕilal;   (b) and (c) may occur in either category.

The lists of ziḥāfāt and ʕilal differ in various
authorities, and there are some inconsistencies in
terminology.   Forty-eight (14 ziḥāfāt and 34 ʕilal) seem to
be generally recognised, and these are set out in full in the
following tables.   Table A lists all the ziḥāfāt (marked
with an asterisk) and ʕilal, arranged in the sequence of the
Arabic alphabet, together with their definitions, the arkān

to which they apply, and the effect they have on them.   This
effect is also described in terms of Western notation, and
this part should be read in conjunction with Chapter III.
Table B breaks the arkān down into their component uṣūl, and
shows the ziḥāfāt and ʕilal applicable to these according to
their category and position in the rukn.   Appended tables
give the same information in terms of syllables, and list the
various classifications of ziḥāf and ʕilla.   Table C shows
the ziḥāfāt and ʕilal applicable to each of the ten sālim
feet, and the feet thus derived.   Table D gives a complete
list of feet, both sālim and ḍayr sālim, arranged in
descending order of length, together with the sālim feet from
which they are derived and the relevant ziḥāf or ʕilla.   This
shows that there are 47 such feet - six regarded only as uṣūl,
four serving as either uṣūl or furūʕ, and the remaining 37
serving only as furūʕ.   It should be noted that, in arriving
at the formula for the derived foot, the immediate result of
applying a ziḥāf or ʕilla to a basic foot is re-expressed in
one of the recognised forms.   For instance, if we apply
taxlīʕ to the basic foot MuSTaFʕiLuN, we find that we are
required by definition to drop the second sākin of the initial
sabab xafīf (S), to elide the sākin of the final watad majmūʕ
(N), and to "silence" the preceding letter - i.e. elide the
vowel (u).   This leaves us with MuTaFʕiL, which must be re-
expressed by its equivalent FuʕuWLuN (fuʕu:lun, ﹀ - -).

TABLE A

Arabic term		Significance in Arabic terminology				Significance in Western terminology		
Noun	Adj.	Meaning	sālim foot	muzahif foot	Equivalent	Meaning	Basic	Modified
iḍāla or taḍyīl	muḍāl muḍayyal	Insertion of sākin letter in final watad majmūʕ	mustafʕilun fa:ʕilun mutafa:ʕilun	mustafʕila:n fa:ʕila:n mutafa:ʕila:n		Final long syllable becomes overlong		
isbāʁ v. tasbīʁ	musbaʁ							
*iḍmār	muḍmar	Silencing of 2nd mutaharrik of sabab taqīl	mutafa:ʕilun	mutfa:ʕilun	mustafʕilun	Initial two shorts become one long		
batr	abtar	jabb + xarm haḍf + qatʕ or Elision of watad majmūʕ	mafa:ʕi:lun fuʕu:lun fa:ʕila:tun	fa: fuʕ or lun fa:tun or fa:ʕil	faʕ faʕ faʕlun	Elision of ᴗ – or of ᴗ – –		
taxlīʕ	muxallaʕ	xabn + qatʕ	mustafʕilun fa:ʕilun	mutafʕil faʕil	fuʕu:lun faʕal	Shortening of first long, elision of final long, and lengthening of penultimate short		
*taxnīʁ	muxannaʁ	Elision of 1st mutaharrik of watad majmūʕ (in middle of misraʕ – cf. xarm)	mafa:ʕi:lun	fa:ʕi:lun	maʕu:lun	Elision of first short syllable		
taḍyīl v. iḍāla	muḍayyal							
tarfīl	muraffal	addition of sabab xafīf to final watad majmūʕ	mustafʕilun fa:ʕilun mutafa:ʕilun	mustafʕiluntun fa:ʕiluntun mutafa:ʕiluntun	mustafʕila:tun fa:ʕila:tun mutafa:ʕila:tun	Addition of final long syllable		

tasbīẖ / isbāẖ	musabbaẖ or musbaẖ	insertion of sākin in final sabab xafīf	fa:ʕila:tun / fa:ʕi.la:ta:n / fuʕu:lun / mafa:ʕi:lun / mustafʕi.lun	fa:ʕila:ta:n / fa:ʕi.la:ta:n / fuʕula:n / mafa:ʕi:la:n / mustafʕi.la:n	Final long becomes overlong
tašʕīt / šaʕt or	mušaʕʕat or	Elision of 1st mutaharrik of watad majmuʕ	fa:ʕila:tun	fa:la:tun	mafʕu:lun	Elision of (2nd) short syllable
tatwīl	mutawwal	Addition of watad mafruq to final sabab xafīf	mustafʕilun	mustafʕilunta:n	mustafʕila:ta:n	Addition of final overlong syllable
tarm	atram	qabḍ + talm	fuʕu:lun	ʕu:lu	faʕlu	Elision of first short, shortening of final long
talm	atlam	Elision of 1st mutaharrik of xumasī	fuʕu:lun	ʕu:lun	faʕlun	Elision of first short
jabb / xabb or	majbūb or maxbūb	Elision of both asbāb	mafa:ʕi:lun	mafa:	faʕal	Elision of last two longs
jaḥf	majḥūf	rafʕ + batr	fa:ʕila:tun	tun	faʕ	Elision of first three syllables
jadʕ	majdūʕ	Elision of both asbāb and silencing of final mutaharrik	mafʕu:la:tu	la:t	fa:ʕ	Elision of 1st two (long) syllables, elision of final short, lengthening of penultimate long to overlong

jadad v. hadad

*jazl v. xazl

jumum	ajamm	ʕaql + ʕaqb	mufa:ʕalatun	fa:ʕatun	fa:ʕilun	Elision of first and third (short) syllables

Term	Derivation	Foot forms	Result	Description
ḥadad or ḥadd or jadad — aḥadd or majdūd	Elision of watad majmūʕ	mafa:ʕi:lun / mutafa:ʕilun / mustafʕilun / fa:ʕilun	ʕi:lun / mutafa: / mustaf / fa:	Elision of ‿ –
ḥadf — maḥdūf	Elision of final sabab xafīf	mafa:ʕi:lun / fuʕu:lun / fa:ʕila:tun / fa:ʕi:la:tun	fuʕu:lun / faʕal / fa:ʕilun	Elision of final long
xabb v. jabb				
*xabl — maxbūl	xabn + ṭayy	mustafʕilun / mafʕu:la:tu	faʕilatun / faʕila:tu	Shortening of first two longs
*xabn — maxbūn	Elision of 2nd sākin of initial sabab xafīf	mustafʕilun / mustafʕi.lun / mafʕu:la:tu / fa:ʕila:tun / fa:ʕilun	mutafʕilun / mafʕu:la:tu / faʕila:tun / faʕilun	mafa:ʕilun / mafa:ʕi:lu	Shortening of 1st (long) syllable
xarb — axrab	kaff + xarm	mafa:ʕi:lun	fa:ʕi:lu	mafʕu:lu	Elision of first (short) and shortening of final (long)
xarm — axram	Elision of 1st mutaharrik of initial watad majmūʕ of subāʕī (at beginning of verse – cf. ṣalm and taxnīq)	mafa:ʕi:lun	fa:ʕi:lun	mafʕu:lun	Elision of first (short) syllable
*xazl — maxzūl	iḍmār + ṭayy	mutafa:ʕilun	mutfaʕilun	muftaʕilun	Initial two shorts become one long, 3rd (long) becomes short
rabʕ — marbūʕ	ṣalm + xabn	fa:ʕila:tun	falun	faʕal	Elision of first and final (long) syllables

Name	Derived	Component change	Original foot	Intermediate	Resulting foot	Effect	Scansion
*rafʕ	marfūʕ	Elision of first sabab xafīf	mustafʕilun / mafʕu:la:tu	tafʕilun / ʕu:la:tu	fa:ʕilun / mafʕu:lu	Elision of first (long) syllable	
zilal	azall	xarm + hatm	mafa:ʕi:lun	fa:ʕ		Elision of 1st (short), 2nd and 4th (long) syllables, and lengthening of remaining long to overlong	
salx or masx	maslūx or mamsūx	Elision of both asbāb and silencing of final mutaharrik of watad mafrūq	fa:ʕi.la:tun	fa:ʕ		Elision of 2nd (short), and 3rd and 4th (long) syllables and lengthening of remaining long to overlong	
šatr	aštar	qabd + xarm	fuʕu:lun / mafa:ʕi:lun	ʕu:lu / fa:ʕilun	faʕlu	Elision of first (short), shortening of 3rd (long)	
šaʕt v. tašʕit							
*šakl	maškūl	kaff + xabn	fa:ʕila:tun / mustafʕilun / mustafʕi.lun	faʕila:tu / mutafʕilu	mafa:ʕilu	Shortening of first and last syllables	
salm	aslam	Elision of watad mafrūq	fa:ʕi.la:tun / mafʕu:la:tu	la:tun / mafʕu:	faʕlun / faʕlun	Elision of - ꞌ	
		Elision of sabab xafīf and qatʕ of watad majmūʕ	fa:ʕila:tun	fa:ʕil	faʕlun		
tams	matmūs	salm + hadf	fa:ʕila:tun	la:	faʕ	Elision of 1st two (- ꞌ) and final (long) syllables	
*tayy	matwī	Elision of sākin of 2nd sabab xafīf	mustafʕilun / mafʕula:tu	mustafʕilun / mafʕula:tu	muftaʕilun / fa:ʕila:tu	Shortening of 2nd (long) syllable	

*ʿasb	maʿṣūb	Silencing of 2nd mutaḥarrik of sabab taqīl	mufa:ʿalatun	mufa:ʿaltun	mafa:ʿi:lun	Contraction of two shorts to one long	ᴗ — — → — — —
ʿadb	aʿdab	Elision of 1st mutaḥarrik of suba i	mufa:ʿalatun	fa:ʿalatun	mufta ʿilun	Elision of first short	ᴗ — ᴗ — → — ᴗ —
ʿaqs	aʿqas	ʿadb + naqs	mufa:ʿalatun	fa:ʿaltu	mafʿu:lu	Elision of first short, contraction of two shorts to one long, shortening of final long	— — ᴗ → — — ᴗ
*ʿaql	maʿqūl	Elision of 2nd mutaḥarrik of sabab taqīl	mufa:ʿalatun	mufa:ʿatun	mafa:ʿilun	Elision of 4th (short) syllable	ᴗ — ᴗ — → ᴗ — —
*qabd	maqbūḍ	Elision of sakin in 1st sabab xafīf	mafa:ʿi:lun / fuʿu:lun	mafa:ʿilun / fuʿu:lu	Shortening of 3rd (long) syllable	ᴗ — — — → ᴗ — ᴗ —
qasr	maqṣūr	Elision of final sakin and silencing of penultimate mutaḥarrik	mafa:ʿi:lun / fuʿu:lun / fa:ʿi.la:tun / mus.tafʿi.lun	mafa:ʿi:l / fuʿu:l / fa:ʿila:t / mustafʿil	Contraction of final two longs to one overlong; Contraction of final ᴗ— to one long	ᴗ — — — — → ᴗ — — ᴗ — ᴗ ᴗ — — ᴗ — ᴗ —
qasm	aqsam	ʿasb + ʿadb	mufa:ʿalatun	fa:ʿaltun	mafʿu:lun	Elision of initial short, contraction of two shorts to one long	ᴗ — — ᴗ — → — — —
qatʿ	maqtūʿ	Elision of sakin of final watad majmuʿ and silencing of preceding letter	fa:ʿilun / mustafʿil / mutafa:ʿil	faʿlun / mafʿu:lun / fa:ʿila:tun	Elision of final long, lengthening of penultimate short	— ᴗ — → — — ᴗ
qatf	maqtūf	ʿasb + ḥadf	mufa:ʿalatun	mufaʿal / fuʿu:lun	Elision of final long, contraction of two shorts to one long	ᴗ — — ᴗ — → — — ᴗ

Term	Participle	Derivation	Form	Form	Form	Description
kabl	makbūl	xabn + qatʕ			fuʕu:lun	Shortening of initial (long) syllable, elision of penultimate short
kasf or kaṣf	maksūf or makṣūf	Elision of final mutaḥarrik of watad mafrūq	mafʕu:la:tu	mafʕu:la:	mafʕu:lun	Elision of final short
*kaff	makfūf	Elision of final sakin of sabab xafif	mafa:ʕi:lun fa:ʕi.la:tun mus.tafʕi.lun	mafa:ʕi:lu fa:ʕila:tu mustafʕilu		Shortening of final long
masx v. salx						
nahr	manḥūr	Elision of both asbab and final mutaḥarrik	mafʕu:latu	la:	faʕ	Elision of first two longs and final short
*naqṣ	manqūṣ	ʕaṣb + kaff	mufaʕalatun	mufaʕaltu	mafaʕi:lu	Contraction of two shorts to one long, shortening of final long
*waqṣ	mawqūṣ	Elision of 2nd mutaḥarrik of sabab t̲aqil	mutafaʕilun	mufaʕilun	mafaʕilun	Elision of initial short
waqf	mawqūf	Silencing of final mutaḥarrik	mafʕu:la:tu	mafʕu:la:t	mafʕu:la:n	Contraction of final long and short to overlong
hatm or ahtam or hanm	mahtūm	ḥadf + qaṣr	mafaʕi:lun	mafaʕ	fuʕu:l	Elision of last two long syllables, lengthening of remaining long to overlong

TABLE B

aṣl	rukn	zihāf	çilla of addition	çilla of subtr.	Meaning
I. FIRST AṢL					
sabab xafīf	Faʔ(ʕiLuN) Faʔ(ʕiLaʔTuN) MaF(ʕuwLaʔTu)	xabn " } rafʕ		nahr jadʕ	Elision of 2nd letter Elision of whole aṣl Elision of whole aṣl, with other effects – see II, III
sabab taqīl	MuS(TaF.ʕiLuN) MuS(TaFʕi.LuN)	{ xabn rafʕ			
sabab taqīl	MuTa(FaʔʕiLuN)	{ iḍmār waqṣ			Silencing of 2nd letter Elision of 2nd letter
watad majmūʕ	FuʕuW(LuN) MuFaʔ(ʕaLaTuN) MuFaʔ(ʕiYLuN)	} taxnīq		talm ʕaḍb xarm hadad	Elision of 1st letter " = = = " = = = " = = = Elision of whole aṣl
watad mafrūq	Faʔʕi(LaʔTuN)			salm salx	Elision of whole aṣl Silencing of 3rd letter, with other effects – see II, III

II. SECOND ASL

	Pattern	Example	Result	Effect
sabab xafīf	(FuʕuW)LuN	qabḍ		Elision of 2nd letter
	(MaFaʔ)ʕiY(LuN)	"	jabb	Elision of whole asl, with other effects - see III
	(MaF)ʕuW(LaʔTu)	ṭayy		Elision of 2nd letter
	(Faʔʕi)Laʔ(TuN)	–	jadʕ ⎫ nahr ⎬	Elision of whole asl, with other effects - see I, III
	(MuS)TaF(ʕiLuN)	ṭayy		
	(MuTa)Faʔ(ʕiLuN)	–	salx	
sabab taqīl	(MuFaʔ)ʕaLa(TuN)	ʕaṣb		Silencing of 2nd letter
		ʕaql		Elision of 2nd letter
watad majmūʕ	(Faʔ)ʕiLaʔ(TuN)		taṣʕīt	Elision of first letter
	(Faʔ)ʕiLuN		batr	Elision of whole asl
	– see Section III –			
watad mafrūq	(MuS)TaFʕi(LuN)			None

III. THIRD ASL

	Foot				Effect
sabab xafīf	(FuʕuW)LuN)		tasbīq	qaṣr.	Addition of one sākin
				ḥaḏf.	Elision of 2nd silencing of 1st letter
	(Faʔ.ʕiLaʔ)TuN	kaff	tasbīq	qaṣr. ḥaḏf.	Elision of whole aṣl
		kaff			Elision of 2nd letter
	(Faʔʕi.Laʔ)TuN	kaff	tasbīq	qaṣr. ḥaḏf. salx	Elision of whole aṣl, with other effects - see I, II
	(MaFaʔʕiY)LuN	kaff	tasbīq	qaṣr. ḥaḏf. jabb	Elision of whole aṣl, with other effects - see II
	(MuS.TaFʕi)LuN	kaff	tasbīq	qaṣr.	None
	(MuFaʕaLa)TuN	-	-	-	
sabab taqīl	None				
watad majmūʕ	{(MuSTaf)ʕiLuN		idāla	qatʕ	Addition of one sākin
	(MuTaFaʔ)ʕiLuN		tarfīl		Addition of sabab xafīf
	(Faʔ)ʕiLuN}		taṭwil		Addition of watad mafrūq
				ḥadad	Elision of 2nd, Silencing of 3rd, Elision of whole aṣl

watad mafrūq   (MaFՇuW)LaʔTu

	waqf	Silencing of 3rd letter
	jadՇ	Silencing of 3rd letter, with other effects – see I, II
	kasf	Elision of 3rd letter
	naḥr	Elision of 3rd letter, with other effects – see I, II
	salm	Elision of whole aṣl

This table does not include compound ziḥāfāt and Քilal

Effect on Syllables of ziḥāfāt and Քilal

First Syllable

Long	shortened	xabn
	elided	rafՇ
Short	elided	talm, Քaḍb, xarm, waqṣ, taxnīq

Second Syllable

Long	shortened	ṭayy
	elided	tašՇīt, (qatՔ – see below)

First Two Syllables		
Both long	elided	jadʿ⁺, nahr⁺
Both short	one long	iḍmār
Long – short	one overlong	salx⁺
	elided	ṣalm (cf. below)
Short – long	elided	ḥadad
Second and Third Syllables (in Tetrasyllable)		
Short – long	elided	batr
Third and Fourth Syllables (in Pentasyllable)		
Both short	one long	ʿaṣb
Penultimate Syllable		
Long	shortened	qabḍ
Short	elided	ʿaql, qatʿ
Final Syllable		
Long	long + overlong	taṭwīl
	long + long	tarfīl
	one overlong	tasbīḍ, idāla
	shortened	kaff
	elided	ḥadf
Short	elided	kasf, nahr⁺

+ with other effects

Final Two Syllables

Both long	one overlong	qaṣr
	elided	jabb, salx[+]
Long – short	one overlong	waqf, jadʕ[+]
	elided	ṣalm (cf. above)
Short – long	elided	ḥadad

Classification of ziḥāfāt and ʕilal

(a) The following ʕilal affect more than one aṣl:

   batr, jabb, jaḥf, jadʕ, salx, ṣalm, qatʕ, nahr.

(b) The following ʕilal apply to the first foot of the miṣrāʕ:

   ṭarm, talm, jumum, xarb, xarm, šatr, ʕaḍb, ʕaqṣ, qaṣm.

   The following ʕilal apply to the last foot of the miṣrāʕ:

   iḍāla, batr, tarfīl, tasbīġ, tatwīl, ḥadaḍ, ḥaḍf, rabʕ, zilal,
   ṣalm, tams, qaṣr, qatʕ, qaṭf, kabl, kasf, waqf, hatm.

(c) The compound ziḥāfāt are:

   xabn + tayy = xabl   iḍmar + tayy = xazl
   xabn + kaff = šakl   ʕaṣb + kaff = naqṣ

+ with other effects

(d) The following combinations of ziḥāfāt with ꜥilal occur:

qabḍ + talm = tarm   ꜥaql + ꜥaqb = jumum
kaff + xarm = xarb   xabn + qatꜥ = rabꜥ
qabḍ + xarm = šatr   naqs + ꜥaqb = ꜥaqs
ꜥasb + ꜥaqb = qasm   ꜥasb + hadf = qatf
xabn + qatꜥ = kabl   xabn + qatꜥ = taxlīꜥ

All these rank as ꜥilal.

(e) The compound ꜥilal are:

xarm + hatm = zilal   salm + hadf = tams
qasr + hadf = hatm   qatꜥ + hadf = batr
jabb + xarm = batr

TABLE C. The Ten uṣūl with their furūʕ

FĀʕILUN	tarfīl	fa:ʕila:tun	– ⏑ – –
– ⏑ –	id̲āla	fa:ʕila:n	– ⏑ –ᵕ
	xabn + id̲āla	faʕila:n	⏑ ⏑ –ᵕ
	*xabn	faʕilun	⏑ ⏑ –
	qaṭʕ	faʕlun	– –
	taxlīʕ	faʕal	⏑ –
	ḥad̲ad̲	faʕ	–
FUʕŪLUN	tasbīq̇	fuʕu:la:n	⏑ – –ᵕ
⏑ – –	*qabḍ	fuʕu:lu	⏑ – ⏑
	t̲alm	faʕlun	– –
	qaṣr	fuʕu:l	⏑ –ᵕ
	ḥad̲f	faʕal	⏑ –
	t̲arm	faʕlu	– ⏑
	šatr	faʕlu	– ⏑
	batr	faʕ	–
MAFĀʕĪLUN	tasbīq̇	mafa:ʕi:la:n	⏑ – – –ᵕ
⏑ – – –	*qabḍ	mafa:ʕilun	⏑ – ⏑ –
	*kaff	mafa:ʕi:lu	⏑ – – ⏑
	xarm	mafʕu:lun	– – –
	taxnīq	mafʕu:lun	– – –
	qaṣr	fuʕu:la:n	⏑ – –ᵕ
	ḥad̲f	fuʕu:lun	⏑ – –
	šatr	fa:ʕilun	– ⏑ –
	xarb	mafʕu:lu	– – ⏑
	ḥad̲ad̲	faʕlun	– –
	hatm	fuʕu:l	⏑ –ᵕ
	jabb	faʕal	⏑ –
	zilal	fa:ʕ	–⏑
	batr	faʕ	–

MUSTAFʕILUN	tatwīl	mustafʕila:ta:n	– – ∪ – –⌣
– – ∪ –	tarfīl	mustafʕila:tun	– – ∪ – –
	xabn + tarfīl	mafa:ʕila:tun	∪ – ∪ – –
	ṭayy + tarfīl	muftaʕila:tun	– ∪ ∪ – –
	idāla	mustafʕila:n	– – ∪ –⌣
	xabn + idāla	mafa:ʕila:n	∪ – ∪ –⌣
	ṭayy + idāla	muftaʕila:n	– ∪ ∪ –⌣
	*xabn	mafa:ʕilun	∪ – ∪ –
	*ṭayy	muftaʕilun	– ∪ ∪ –
	*kaff	mustafʕilu	– – ∪ ∪
	xabl + idāla	faʕilata:n	∪ ∪ ∪ –⌣
	*xabl	faʕilatun	∪ ∪ ∪ –
	*šakl	mafa:ʕilu	∪ – ∪ ∪
	qaṭʕ + idāla	mafʕu:la:n	– – –⌣
	qaṭʕ	mafʕu:lun	– – –
	kabl	fuʕu:lun	∪ – –
	taxlīʕ	fuʕu:lun	∪ – –
	rafʕ	fa:ʕilun	– ∪ –
	ḥadad	faʕlun	– –

MUFĀʕALATUN	*ʕaṣb	mafa:ʕi:lun	∪ – – –
∪ – ∪ ∪ –	*ʕaql	mafa:ʕilun	∪ – ∪ –
	*naqṣ	mafa:ʕi:lu	∪ – – ∪
	ʕaḍb	muftaʕilun	– ∪ ∪ –
	qaṣm	mafʕu:lun	– – –
	qaṭf	fuʕu:lun	∪ – –
	jumum	fa:ʕilun	– ∪ –
	ʕaqṣ	mafʕu:lu	– – ∪

MUTAFĀʕILUN	tarfīl	mutafa:ʕila:tun	∪ ∪ – ∪ – –
∪ ∪ – ∪ –	iḍmār + tarfīl	mustafʕila:tun	– – ∪ – –
	waqṣ + tarfīl	mafa:ʕila:tun	∪ – ∪ – –
	xazl + tarfīl	muftaʕila:tun	– ∪ ∪ – –
	idāla	mutafa:ʕila:n	∪ ∪ – ∪ –⌣
	iḍmār + idāla	mustafʕila:n	– – ∪ –⌣
	*iḍmār	mustafʕilun	– – ∪ –

waqṣ + idāla	mafa:ʕila:n	∪ − ∪ ∿
xazl + idāla	muftaʕila:n	− ∪ ∪ ∿
qaṭʕ	faʕila:tun	∪ ∪ − −
*waqṣ	mafa:ʕilun	∪ − ∪ −
*xazl	muftaʕilun	− ∪ ∪ −
qaṭʕ + idmār	mafʕu:lun	− − −
ḥadad	faʕilun	∪ ∪ −
ḥadad + idmār	faʕlun	− −

FĀʕILĀTUN	tasbīḍ	fa:ʕila:ta:n	− ∪ − ∿
− ∪ − −	xabn + tasbīḍ	faʕili:ya:n	∪ ∪ − ∿
	*xabn	faʕila:tun	∪ ∪ − −
	*kaff	fa:ʕila:tu	− ∪ − ∪
	*šakl	faʕila:tu	∪ ∪ − ∪
	tašʕīt	mafʕu:lun	− − −
	qaṣr	fa:ʕila:n	− ∪ − ∪
	ḥadf .	fa:ʕilun	− ∪ −
	xabn + qaṣr	faʕila:n	∪ ∪ − ∿
	xabn + ḥadf	faʕilun	∪ ∪ −
	ṣalm + tasbīḍ	faʕla:n	− − ∿
	ṣalm	faʕlun	− −
	batr	faʕlun	− −
	rabʕ	faʕal	∪ −
	jaḥf + tasbīḍ	fa:ʕ	− ∿
	jaḥf	faʕ	−

MAFʕŪLĀTU	*xabn	mafa:ʕi:lu	∪ − − ∪
− − − ∪	*ṭayy	fa:ʕila:tu	− ∪ − ∪
	*xabl	faʕila:tu	∪ ∪ − ∪
	waqf	mafʕu:la:n	− − − ∿
	kasf	mafʕu:lun	− − −
	xabn + waqf	fuʕu:la:n	∪ − − ∿
	ṭayy + waqf	fa:ʕila:n	− ∪ − ∿
	xabn + kasf	fuʕu:lun	∪ − −
	ṭayy + kasf	fa:ʕilun	− ∪ −
	rafʕ	mafʕu:lu	− − ∪

	xabl + kasf	faʕilun	∪ ∪ −
	ṣalm	faʕlun	− −
	jadʕ	fa:ʕ	⌣
	naḥr	faʕ	−

FĀʕI.LĀTUN	tasbīḍ	fa:ʕi.la:ta:n	− ∪ − ⌣
− ∪ − −	*kaff	fa:ʕila:tu	− ∪ − ∪
	qaṣr	fa:ʕi.la:n	− ∪ ⌣
	haḏf	fa:ʕi.lun	− ∪ −
	ṣalm	faʕlun	− −
	salx	fa:ʕ	⌣
	ṭams	faʕ	−

MUS.TAFʕI.LUN	tasbīḍ	mus.tafʕi.la:n	− − ∪ ⌣
− − ∪ −	*xabn	ma.fa:ʕi.lun	∪ − ∪ −
	*kaff	mus.tafʕi.lu	− − ∪ ∪
	*šakl	ma.fa:ʕi.lu	∪ − ∪ ∪
	qaṣr	maf.ʕu:lu.n	− − −
	xabn + qaṣr	fu.ʕu:lu.n	∪ − −

TABLE D. The furūʕ, showing how they are derived from the uṣūl

No. of Syllables	farʕ		zihāf/ʕilla	aṣl
6	mutafa:ʕila:tun	˘ ˘ – –	tarfīl	mutafa:ʕilun
5	mustafʕila:ta:n	– – ˘ –	taṭwīl	mustafʕilun
	mustafʕila:tun	– – ˘ –	tarfīl	mustafʕilun
			idmār + tarfīl	mutafa:ʕilun
	mafa:ʕila:tun	˘ – ˘ –	waqṣ + tarfīl	mutafa:ʕilun
			xabn + tarfīl	mustafʕilun
	mutafaʕila:n	˘ ˘ ˘ –	idāla	mutafa:ʕilun
	muftaʕila:tun	– ˘ ˘ –	xazl + tarfīl	mutafa:ʕilun
			ṭayy + tarfīl	mustafʕilun
	mutafa:ʕilun	˘ ˘ – ˘	sālim	mutafa:ʕilun
	mufa:ʕalatun	˘ – ˘ ˘	sālim	mufa:ʕalatun
4	mafa:ʕi:la:n	˘ – – –	tasbīġ	mafa:ʕi:lun
	fa:ʕila:ta:n	– ˘ – –	tasbīġ	fa:.ʕila:.tun
			idāla	fa:.ʕi.la:.tun
	mustafʕila:n	– – ˘ –	idmār + idāla	mustafʕilun
				mutafa:ʕilun
	mafa:ʕi:lun	˘ – – ˘	sālim	mafa:ʕi:lun
			ʕaṣb	mufa:ʕalatun
	fa:.ʕila:..tun	– ˘ – ˘	sālim	fa:.ʕila:..tun
			tarfīl	fa:ʕilun
	fa:ʕi.la:..tun	– ˘ ˘ –	sālim	fa:ʕi.la:..tun

mus.tafSilun		‒ ‿	sālim	mus.taf.Silun
mus.tafSi.lun		‒ ‒	idmār	mutafa:Silun
mafSu:la:tu		‒ ‒ ‿	sālim	mus.tafSi.lun
faSili:ya:n		‒ ‒ ‿	sālim	mafSu:la:tu
mafa:Sila:n		‿ ‒ ‿	xabn + tasbīq	fa:Sila:tun
		? ‒ ‿	waqs̩ + idāla	mutafa:Silun
		? ‿ ‿	xabn + idāla	mustafSilun
muftaSila:n		? ‿ ‒	t̩ayy + idāla	mustafSilun
		? ‒ ‿	xazl + idāla	mutafa:Silun
faSila:tun		‒ ‿ ‿	xabn	fa:Sila:tun
		‒ ‿ ‿	qatS	mutafa:Silun
mafa:Silun		‒ ‿ ‿	qabd̩	mafa:Si:lun
			xabn	mustafSilun
				mus.tafSi.lun
		‿	Saql	mufa:Salatun
		‒ ‒	waqs̩	mutafa:Silun
mafa:Si:lu		‿ ‿	kaff	mafa:Si:lun
			naqs̩	mufa:Salatun
			xabn	mafSu:la:tu
muftaSilun		‒ ‿ ‿	t̩ayy	mustafSilun
		‒ ‒	Sad̩b	mufa:Salatun
fa:Sila:tu		‿ ‒	kaff	fa:.Sila:.tun
				fa:Si.la:.tun
			t̩ayy	mafSu:la:tu

3

				mus.taf.ⁿilun
mustafⁿilu	˘	kaff	–	mus.tafⁿi.lun
				mustafⁿilun
faⁿilata:n	˘ ˘	xabl + idāla	–	mustafⁿilun
faⁿilatun	˘ ˘	xabl	˘	fa:ⁿila:tun
faⁿila:tu	– ˘	śakl		mafⁿu:la:tu
		xabl		mus.taf.ⁿilun
mafa:ⁿilu	˘	śakl	˘	mus.tafⁿi.lun
				mustafⁿilun
mafⁿu:la:n	˘	qatˤ + idāla	–	mafⁿu:la:tu
		waqf	–	mafa:ⁿi:lun
mafⁿu:lun		xarm		mafa:ⁿilun
		taxnīq		mafa:ⁿilun
		qatˤ		mus.taf.ⁿilun
				mus.tafⁿi.lun
		qasm		mufa:ⁿalatun
		idˤmar + qatˤ		mutafa:ⁿilun
		taśⁿīt		fa:ⁿila:tun
		kasf	˘	mafⁿu:la:tu
fuⁿu:la:n		tasbīq	–	fuⁿu:lun
		qasr		mafa:ⁿi:lun
		xabn + waqf		mafⁿu:la:tu

base		modification	result
fa:ʕila:n	⏑ / —	idāla	fa:ʕilun
		qasr	fa:.ʕila:tun
			fa:ʕi.la:.tun
fuʕu:lun	— / ⏑	ṭayy + waqf	mafʕu:la:tu
		sālim	fuʕu:lun
		haḏf	mafaʕi:lun
		kabl	mustafʕilun
		taxlīʕ	mustafʕilun
		qaṣr + xabn	mus.tafʕi.lun
		qaṭf	mufa:ʕalatun
		xabn + kasf	mufaʕu:la:tu
fa:ʕilun	— / ⏑	sālim	fa:ʕilun
		šatr	mafaʕi:lun
		rafʕ	mustafʕilun
		jumum	mufa:ʕalatun
		haḏf	fa:ʕila:tun
mafʕu:lu	⏑ / —	ṭayy + kasf	fa:ʕi.la:tun
		xarb	mafʕu:la:tu
		ʕaqṣ	mafaʕi:lun
		rafʕ	mufa:ʕalatun
faʕila:n	⏑ / —	xabn + qaṣr	mafʕu:la:tu
		xabn + idāla	fa:ʕila:tun
			fa:ʕilun

faʕilun	xabn		fa:ʕilun
	hadad		mutafa:ʕilun
	xabn + hadf		fa:ʕila:tun
	xabl + kasf		mafʕu:la:tu
	qabd		fuʕu:lun
fuʕu:lu	salm + tasbi:ʕ		fa:ʕila:tun
	qatʕ		fa:ʕilun
faʕla:n	talm		fuʕu:lun
faʕlun	hadad		mafa:ʕi:lun
	idmar + hadad		mutafa:ʕilun
	batr		fa:ʕila:tun
	salm		mafʕu:la:tu
	salm		fa:ʕila:tun
			fa:ʕi.la:tun
fuʕu:l	qasr		fuʕu:lun
	hatm		mafa:ʕi:lun
faʕal	hadf		fuʕu:lun
	jabb		mafa:ʕi:lun
	taxli:ʕ		fa:ʕilun
	rabʕ		fa:ʕila:tun
faʕlu	tarm		fuʕu:lun
	šatr		fuʕu:lun

2

fa:ʕ	zilal	mafa:ʕi:lun
	jaḥf + tasbīġ	fa:ʕila:tun
	salx	fa:ʕi.la:tun
	jadʕ	mafʕu:la:tu
faʕ	batr	fuʕu:lun
	batr	mafa:ʕi:lun
	jaḥf	fa:ʕila:tun
	nahr	mafʕu:la:tu
	tams	fa:ʕi.la:tun
1	hadad	fa:ʕilun

The following terms are used to distinguish the various
types of "sound" foot:

sālim: a foot in which there is no zihāf.

ṣahih: a foot in which there is no ʕilla of
subtraction (where such is possible).

muʕarrā: a foot in which there is no ʕilla of addition.

mawfūr: a foot which is immune from xarm.

mujarrad: a foot which is immune from xazm (the prefixing of a letter or letters before the first foot of a bayt
- a practice found in some Arabic verses, but rarely in
Persian).

barīʔ: a foot which is immune from muʕāqaba (see
below).

An important distinction needs to be noted between Arabic
and Persian verse.   In the former, "sub-metres" within each
"standard" metre (baḥr) are distinguished only by the ʕilal,
whereas in Persian, contrary to the practice envisaged by
al-Xalīl, the zihāfāt have to be pressed into this service.
This is because the number of distinct metres that may not
be combined in the same poem is much larger in Persian (over
two hundred) than in Arabic (about 67), though the variations
permissible within each metre are correspondingly fewer.
Persian does not use five of the Arabic buḥūr, though three
of its own are added (see below).

As has been indicated, an Arabic or Persian poem is
composed of couplets of verses (bayt, pl. abyāt) each
composed of two hemistichs (miṣrāʕ, also misraʕ), each of

which is composed of from two to four (rarely one) arkān.
Each rukn is named according to its position in the bayt, as
follows:

First miṣrāʕ: ṣadr - ḥašw (maximum of two) - ʕarūḍ.

Second miṣrāʕ: ibtidāʔ (also maṭlaʕ) - ḥašw - ḍarb
                 (also ʕajz).

The metres are made up of arkān in various combinations.
At the base lie the "standard" metres, of which there are
generally reckoned to be nineteen, including three said to
have been introduced for Persian poetry only.   They are of
two kinds, munfarid (all feet the same) and murakkab (feet
of two kinds).

The "standard" miṣrāʕ consists of four feet in ten of
the metres, and three in the other nine.   Since the whole
bayt is taken into account, the first group are known as
mutamman (eightfold) and the second as musaddas (sixfold).

The standard metres (baḥr, pl. buḥūr) are as follows:

(a) munfarid

1. hazaj (trilling):   mafāʕīlun   mafāʕīlun
                               mafāʕīlun   mafāʕīlun

2. rajaz (trembling):   mustafʕilun   mustafʕilun
                               mustafʕilun   mustafʕilun

3. ramal (trotting):   fāʕilātun   fāʕilātun
                               fāʕilātun   fāʕilātun

4. mutaqārib (nearing):   fuʕūlun   fuʕūlun
                               fuʕūlun   fuʕūlun

5. mutadārik (overtaking):   fāʕilun   fāʕilun
                               fāʕilun   fāʕilun

6. kāmil (complete):   mutafāʕilun   mutafāʕilun
                              mutafāʕilun   mutafāʕilun

7. wāfir (abundant):   mufāʕalatun   mufāʕalatun
                              mufāʕalatun   mufāʕalatun

(b) murakkab (i) mutamman

8. ṭawīl (long):   fuʕūlun   mafāʕīlun
                              fuʕūlun   mafāʕīlun

9. madīd (protracted):   fāʕilātun   fāʕilūn
                              fāʕilātun   fāʕilun

10. basīṭ (spread out):   mustafʕilun   fāʕilun
                              mustafʕilun   fāʕilun

(ii) musaddas

11. mujtatt (cut off):   mustafʕilun   fāʕilātun
                              fāʕilātun

12. muḍāriʕ (similar):   mafāʕīlun   fāʕilātun
                              mafāʕīlun

13. munsariḥ (quick-paced):   mustafʕilun   mafʕūlātu
                              mustafʕilun

14. muqtaḍab (untrained):   mafʕūlātu   mustafʕilun
                              mustafʕilun

15. sarīʕ (swift):   mustafʕilun   mustafʕilun
                              mafʕūlātu

16. xafīf (light):   fāʕilātun   mustafʕilun
                              fāʕilātun

17. qarīb (near):   mafāʕīlun   mafāʕīlun
                              fāʕilātun

18. ḍarīb (strange)
    jadīd (new)   : fāʕilātun   fāʕilātun   mafāʕīlun

19. mušākil (resembling):fāʕilātun   mafāʕīlun   mafāʕīlun

Nos. 1-4 and 6-16 are said to have been laid down by al-
Xalīl, and indeed he is credited with having "invented" Nos.
11, 12 and 14.   No. 5 is attributed to al-Axfaš. Nos. 6-10
are found only in Arabic verse (though it should be added
that few of the others are found in Persian in their
unmodified form).   Nos. 17-19 are regarded as Persian metres,
and are said to have been laid down by Moulana Yusef in the
fourth/tenth century;   they are in fact of rare occurrence,
though examples of qarīb are attributed to Faralavi (fl. 300/
900), Šahid Balxi (fl. 300/900), and Daqiqi (330/942-370/981).

The metres actually used by the poets (wazn, awzān al-
šiʕr), as opposed to the theoretical buḥūr, are derived
from these by the various modifications already described,
and also by reducing the number of feet (it has been pointed
out that these terms are possibly derived from Greek: baḥr,
"sea" = rhuthmos, "flowing";   wazn, "weight" = metron,
"measure").[3]   A metre that follows the standard pattern is
called sālim;   if it is modified in some way, it is ɣayr
sālim or muzāḥif.   A musaddas metre derived from an original
mutamman is described as majzūʔ;   a murabbaʕ from a musaddas
is murabbaʕ majzūʔ; a mutallat (three-foot) from a musaddas
is maštūr; a mutannā (two-foot) is manḥūk, and a muwaḥḥad
(one-foot) is maštūr manḥūk.   muxammas (five-foot) verses
are rarely found, musabbaʕ (seven-foot) never.   Certain
metres with a caesura or break in the middle of each miṣrāʕ
are recognised as consisting of two repeated halves, and are
known as mukarrar or (in Persian) dū-pāra.

A ḍarb with a different modification to the ˤarūḍ is
called a ḏāya; an ˤarūḍ with a different modification to
the ḍarb is known as a faṣl.

Two further terms (which are often confused) are employed
to account for certain alternations of modification within a
foot or line.   These are muˤāqaba and murāqaba.

(a) Both terms are used to describe the alternation of
two letters within a foot, e.g. in the metre muḍāriˤ the
foot mafāˤīlun (◡ - - -) may become either mafāˤilun (◡ - ◡ -)
by qabḍ or mafāˤīlu (◡ - - ◡) by kaff, but never a combination
of both; or, in other words, the last two syllables of the
foot can never both be short.   This is known as muˤāqaba
(or murāqaba) between Y and N.

(b) The term murāqaba is applied to a similar rule for
the foot mutafāˤilun; if the fourth letter is elided (by
ṭayy), then the second letter must be silenced (by iḍmār):
thus MuTaFaʔˤiLuN becomes MuFTaˤiLuN (the combined ziḥāf
known as xazl).   In Western notation this means that, in
the foot ◡ ◡ - ◡ -, if the third syllable is shortened, the
first two shorts must be contracted to one long (- ◡ ◡ -).

(c) A similar alternation takes place between two con-
secutive feet, this being known as muˤāqaba in respect to
what precedes or what follows.   This applies principally to
the foot fāˤilātun (in the metre ramal), where two sabab
xafīf are juxtaposed, at the end of one foot and the beginning of the next.   If the sākin letter of one of these is
dropped, the other must be retained.   Thus fāˤilātun/

fāᶜilātun (the sālim form) may become either fāᶜilātun/
faᶜilātun (- ᴗ - -/ᴗ ᴗ - -) or fāᶜilātu/fāᶜilātun (- ᴗ - ᴗ /- ᴗ - -),
or to put it another way, the final syllable of the first
foot and the initial syllable of the second foot cannot both
be short.   We may also get muᶜāqaba ṭarafayn (in respect to
both sides): fāᶜilātun/faᶜilātu/fāᶜilātun (- ᴗ - -/ᴗ ᴗ - ᴗ /
- ᴗ - -).   These three figures are also known as ᶜajz, ṣadr,
and ṭarafān respectively.

The general effect of the rules in paragraphs (a), (b)
and (c) is to underline that three short syllables do not
occur in succession.   This in fact happens in Arabic in the
primitive rajaz metre (rarely in others), but never in·
Persian.

(d) The term murāqaba is also used to describe the
alternation of two ziḥāfāt in a metre.   Thus, in the
muqtaḍab mutamman metre, in which the two feet mafᶜūlātu
and mustafᶜilun alternate (unlike the sound musaddas form),
the third foot (mafᶜūlātu) may in common with the two
mustafᶜilun feet be maṭwī, while the first foot is maxbūn:

   mafāᶜīlu   muftaᶜilun   fāᶜilātun   muftaᶜilun
   ᴗ ‾ ‾ ᴗ   ‾ ᴗ ᴗ ‾   ‾ ᴗ ‾ ‾   ‾ ᴗ ᴗ ‾

A favourite device of prosodists is to compose verses
that may be scanned in more than one metre (mutalawwin,
mulawwan).   This is comparatively rare in Arabic, but is
common in Persian, where the possibility of reading certain
vowels (e.g. the iḍāfa) as either long or short makes this
figure quite easy to achieve.

The first of the following examples may be scanned either:

faʕilātun faʕilātun faʕilun (ramal musaddas maḥdūf aw maqṣūr)

or muftaʕilun muftaʕilun faʕilun (sarīʕ maṭwī maksūf aw

mawqūf).

ʔei šode: dar xɑ:ne-ye: jɑ:n manzelat
    šode   ye
xɑ:ne-ye: jɑ:n yɑ:fte: z-ɑ:n manzelat
    ye   yɑ:fte
ʔei šode: mohr-e: rox-e: to: zein-e carx
    šode   -e
carx ʔaz ʔɑ:n ɑ:made: dar ʕein-e carx
         ɑ:n ɑ:made
               (Ahli Širazi, d.942/1535-6)

The second example may be scanned in three ways:

mafāʕīlun mafāʕīlun mafāʕīlun mafāʕīlun (hazaj mutamman sālim)

or faʕilātun faʕilātun faʕilātun faʕilātun (ramal mutamman

maxbūn) or mafāʕilun faʕilātun mafāʕilun faʕilātun (mujtatt

mutamman maxbūn).

lab-e: to: ḥɑ:mi-ye: loʔloʔ xaṭ-e: to: markaz-e: lɑ:le:
 -e to   -ye   -e to   -e
šab-e: to: ḥɑ:mel-e: koukab mah-e: to: bɑ: xaṭ-e: hɑ:le:
 -e to   -e   -e to   -e

               (Salmɑn Saveji, c.700/1300-777/1375)

It will be observed that the characteristic of the zihāf is that (except in the case of mutafāʕilun and mufāʕalatun) it alters the quantitative, but not the syllabic, length of the foot. It follows from this that each hemistich of an Arabic poem in a given metre (with the exceptions noted above, and in certain metres that allow the second

hemistich to be shortened or lengthened by a syllable)
contains the same number of syllables, though the total
quantitative length may vary quite considerably.   For
example, the following two miṣrāʕ from the same poem each
contain twelve syllables, but the first adds up to 18 morae
(◡) and the second to 21.

...wa šǎʕiṯat   baʕda-d-diha: ni jummati:

◡ ◡ ◡ ─   ─ ─ ◡ ─   ◡ ─ ◡ ─

... ʔin lam ʔuna: jizha: fa-juz zu:limmati:

─ ─ ◡ ─ ─ ─ ◡ ─   ─ ─ ◡ ─

(Jaḥdar b. Ḍubayʕa)

As we shall see, the reverse is true of Persian metres,
in which the quantitative length of each hemistich remains
virtually constant, while there may be a wide range in the
number of syllables.

In theory all of the ziḥāfāt and ʕilal applicable to a
given rukn may occur in any baḥr in which that rukn is found.
In practice this is probably not the case, though in the
absence of a statistical analysis of Arabic poetry no firm
statement can be made.   The following table of Arabic metres
is based on the views of the prosodists and of scholars like
Wright and Noeldeke.[4]   The "western" scansion is given for
the hemistich;   allowance must be made in practice for slight
differences between the first and second hemistichs of a bayt.

HAZAJ   aṣl: mafa:ʕi:lun (murabbaʕ)

ziḥāfāt: kaff: mafa:ʕi:lu
ʕilal: haḏf   fuʕu:lun

◡ ─ ─ ̌─   ◡ ─ ─ ─
◡ ─ ─ ̌─   ◡ ─ ─

RAJAZ

aṣl:		mustafʕilun (musaddas or murabbaʕ)
zihāfāt:	ṭayy:	muftaʕilun
	xabn:	mafa:ʕilun
	xabl:	faʕilatun
ʕilal:	taxlīʕ, kabl:	fuʕu:lun
	qaṭʕ:	mafʕu:lun

```
⏑⏑⏑⏑⏑⏑ - ⏑⏑⏑⏑⏑ - ⏑⏑⏑⏑ -
⏑⏑⏑⏑⏑⏑ - ⏑⏑⏑⏑⏑ - ⏑⏑ - -

⏑⏑⏑⏑ ⏑ - - - ⏑ -
⏑⏑⏑⏑ ⏑ - ⏑ - -
```

RAMAL

aṣl:		fa:ʕila:tun (musaddas or murabbaʕ)
zihāfāt:	xabn:	faʕila:tun
	kaff:	fa:ʕila:tu
	šakl:	faʕila:tu
ʕilal:	ḥaḏf:	fa:ʕilun
	xabn + ḥaḏf:	faʕilun

```
- ⏑ - -   - ⏑ - -   - ⏑ - -   - ⏑ -
- ⏑ - -   - ⏑ - -   - ⏑ - -
- ⏑ - -   - ⏑ - -   - ⏑ -
- ⏑ - -   - ⏑ - -
- ⏑ - -   - ⏑ -
```

MUTAQĀRIB

aṣl:		fuʕu:lun (mutamman)
zihāfāt:	qabḍ:	fuʕu:lu
ʕilal:	ḥaḏf:	faʕal
	batr:	faʕ

```
◡ ⁻ ⁻   ◡ ⁻ ⁻   ◡ ⁻ ⁻   ◡ ⁻ ⁻
       ◡          ◡          ◡          ◡
◡ ⁻ ⁻   ◡ ⁻ ⁻   ◡ ⁻ ⁻   ◡ ⁻
   ◡       ◡        ◡
◡ ⁻ ⁻   ◡ ⁻ ⁻   ◡ ⁻ ⁻   ⁻
   ◡       ◡
```

MUTADĀRIK

<u>a</u><u>s</u>l:		fa:ˤilun (mutamman or musaddas)
zi<u>h</u>āfāt:	xabn:	faˤilun
ˤilal:	qa<u>t</u>ˤ:	faˤlun
	tarfīl:	fa:ˤila:tun (only in musaddas)

```
⁻ ◡ ⁻   ⁻ ◡ ⁻   ⁻ ◡ ⁻   ⁻ ◡ ⁻
◡        ◡        ◡        ◡

⁻ ◡ ⁻   ⁻ ◡ ⁻   ⁻ ◡ ⁻ ⁻
◡        ◡        ◡

⁻ ◡ ⁻   ⁻ ◡ ⁻   ⁻ ◡ ⁻
◡        ◡        ◡
```

KĀMIL

<u>a</u><u>s</u>l:		mutafa:ˤilun (musaddas or murabbaˤ)
zi<u>h</u>āfāt:	i<u>d</u>mār:	mustafˤilun
ˤilal:	qa<u>t</u>ˤ:	faˤila:tun
	qa<u>t</u>ˤ + i<u>d</u>mār:	mafˤu:lun
	<u>h</u>a<u>d</u>a<u>d</u>:	faˤilun
	<u>h</u>a<u>d</u>a<u>d</u> + i<u>d</u>mār:	faˤlun
	tarfīl:	mutafa:ˤila:tun (only in murabbaˤ)
	tarfīl + i<u>d</u>mār:	mustafˤila:tun (only in murabbaˤ)

```
◡ ◡ ⁻ ◡ ⁻   ◡ ◡ ⁻ ◡ ⁻   ◡ ◡ ⁻ ◡ ⁻

◡ ◡ ⁻ ◡ ⁻   ◡ ◡ ⁻ ◡ ⁻   ◡ ◡ ⁻ ⁻

◡ ◡ ⁻ ◡ ⁻   ◡ ◡ ⁻ ◡ ⁻   ⁻ ⁻

◡ ◡ ⁻ ◡ ⁻   ◡ ◡ ⁻ ◡ ⁻ ⁻

◡ ◡ ⁻ ◡ ⁻   ◡ ◡ ⁻ ◡ ⁻

◡ ◡ ⁻ ◡ ⁻   ◡ ◡ ⁻ ⁻
```

WĀFIR

aṣl: mufa:ʕalatun (musaddas)

ziḥāfāt: ʕaṣb: mafa:ʕi:lun

ʕilal: qaṭf: fuʕu:lun

∪ ‾ ͜∪∪ ‾   ∪ ‾ ͜∪∪ ‾   ∪ ‾ ‾

∪ ‾ ͜∪∪ ‾   ∪ ‾ ͜∪∪ ‾

ṬAWĪL

aṣl: fuʕu:lun   mafa:ʕi:lun (muṯamman)

ziḥāfāt: qabḍ: fuʕu:lu   mafa:ʕilun

ʕilal: ṯalm: faʕlun (at beginning of **bayt** only)
           ṯalm + qabḍ: faʕlu (at beginning of **bayt** only)
           ḥaḏf: fuʕu:lun

∪ ‾ ‾   ∪ ‾ ‾ ‾   ∪ ‾ ‾   ∪ ‾ ‾ ‾
    ∪   ∪   ∪   ∪

∪ ‾ ‾   ∪ ‾ ‾ ‾   ∪ ‾ ∪   ∪ ‾ ‾
    ∪   ∪

MADĪD

aṣl: fa:ʕila:tun   fa:ʕilun (muṯamman or
                                                       musaddas)

ziḥāfāt: xabn: faʕila:tun   faʕilun

ʕilal: ḥaḏf: fa: ilun (in musaddas only)
           xabn + ḥaḏf: faʕilun (in musaddas only)
           ṣalm, batr: faʕlun (in musaddas only)

‾ ∪ ‾ ‾   ‾ ∪ ‾   ‾ ∪ ‾ ‾   ‾ ∪ ‾
  ∪   ∪   ∪   ∪

‾ ∪ ‾ ‾   ‾ ∪ ‾   ‾ ∪ ‾ ‾
  ∪   ∪   ∪

‾ ∪ ‾ ‾   ‾ ∪ ‾   ‾ ∪ ‾
  ∪   ∪   ∪

‾ ∪ ‾ ‾   ‾ ∪ ‾   ‾ ‾
  ∪   ∪

BASĪṬ

aṣl: mustafʕilun   fa:ʕilun (muṯamman or
                                                     musaddas)

zihāfāt: xabn: mafa:ʕilun   faʕilun
            ṭayy: muftaʕilun
            xabl: faʕilatun

ʕilal: qaṭʕ: faʕlun (in muṯamman only)
            taxlīʕ, kabl: fuʕu:lun (in musaddas only)

```
- - ᴜ -    - ᴜ -    - - ᴜ -    ᴜ ᴜ -
  ᴜ ᴜ        ᴜ        ᴜ          ‿‿
ᴜ ᴜ ᴜ -    - ᴜ -    - - ᴜ -
  ᴜ ᴜ        ᴜ        ᴜ
- - ᴜ -    - ᴜ -    ᴜ - -
  ᴜ ᴜ
```

MUJTAṮṮ

asl: mustafʕilun   fa:ʕila:tun   (murabbaʕ)

zihāfāt: xabn: mafa:ʕilun   faʕila:tun

ʕilal: taš ʕīṯ: mafʕu:lun

```
- - ᴜ -    - ᴜ - -
  ᴜ          ‿
```

MUḌĀRIʕ

asl: mafa:ʕi:lun   fa:ʕila:tun (murabbaʕ)

zihāfāt: qabḍ: mafa:ʕilun
         kaff: mafa:ʕi:lu

```
ᴜ - - -    - ᴜ - -
    ᴜ ᴜ
```

MUNSARIḤ

asl: mustafʕilun   mafʕu:la:tu (musaddas)

zihāfāt: xabn: mafa:ʕilun
         ṭayy: muftaʕilun   fa: ila:tu
         xabl: faʕilatun

```
- - ᴜ -    - - - ᴜ    - ᴜ ᴜ -
  ᴜ ᴜ          ᴜ
```

MUQTAḌAB

asl: mafʕu:la:tu   mustafʕilun   (murabbaʕ)

zihāfāt: ṭayy: fa:ʕila:tu   muftaʕilun

    xabn: mafaːʕiːlu
    xabl: faʕilaːtu

‾ ‾ ‾ ◡   ‾ ◡ ◡ ‾
◡ ◡

SARĪʕ

asl: mustafʕilun   mustafʕilun   mafʕuːlaːtu
                                             (musaddas)
zihāfāt: ṭayy: muftaʕilun
         xabn: mafaːʕilun
         xabl: faʕilatun

ʕilal: ṭayy + kasf: faːʕilun
        xabl + kasf: faʕilun
        ṣalm: faʕlun

‾ ‾ ◡ ‾   ‾ ‾ ◡ ‾   ‾ ◡ ‾
◡ ◡   ◡ ◡   ◡
                 ‾ ‾

‾ ‾ ◡ ‾   ‾ ‾ ◡ ‾
◡ ◡   ◡ ◡

XAFĪF

asl: faːʕilaːtun   mustafʕilun (musaddas
                                        or murabbaʕ)

zihāfāt: xabn: faʕilaːtun   mafaːʕilun

ʕilal: kabl: fuʕuːlun (murabbaʕ only)
        ḥad̲f: faːʕilun (in musaddas only)
        tašʕīt̲:   mafʕuːlun (in musaddas only)
        xabn + ḥad̲f: faʕilun (in musaddas only)
        batr: faʕlun (in musaddas only)

‾ ◡ ‾ ‾   ‾ ‾ ◡ ‾   ‾ ◡ ‾ ‾
◡   ◡   ◡
‾ ◡ ‾ ‾   ‾ ‾ ◡ ‾   ‾ ◡ ‾
◡   ◡   ◡
‾ ◡ ‾ ‾   ◡ ‾ ◡ ‾
◡
‾ ◡ ‾ ‾   ◡ ‾ ‾
◡

The Persian metres are dealt with fully in the next two
chapters, and so will not be listed here.

The normal order of the terminology in the description
of a particular metre is as follows:

(a) the name of the baḥr

(b) the number of feet

(c) the ʿilal affecting the ṣadr and the ibtidāʾ

(d) the ziḥāfāt

(e) the ʿilal affecting the ʿarūḍ and the ḍarb.

To illustrate the method of scansion (taqṭīʿ), there
follow some examples of Arabic and Persian verse in a variety
of metres:

ARABIC

1. <u>rajaz musaddas maṭwī maxbūl maxbūn</u>

qad yatimat binti: wa ʔa:mat kannati:

$-\ \smile\ \smile\ -\ |\ -\ -\ \smile\ -\ |\ -\ -\ \smile\ -$

  maṭwī   sālim   sālim

         wa šaʿiṯat baʿda d-diha:ni jummati:

        $\smile\ \smile\ \smile\ -\ |\ -\ -\ \smile\ -\ |\ \smile\ -\ \smile\ -$

         maxbūl   sālim   maxbūn

                   (Jaḥdar b. Ḍubayʿa)

2. <u>hazaj murabbaʿ makfūf</u>

ʔaya: ṭaʿnata ma: šayxin   kabi:rin yafanin ba:li:

$\smile\ -\ \ -\ \smile|\smile\ -\ \ -\ -\ \ |\ \ \smile\ -\ \ -\ \smile|\smile\ -\ \ -\ -$

  makfūf   sālim   makfūf   sālim

               (al-Find al-Zamānī)

3. <u>ramal musaddas maxbūn maḥḏūf</u>

ṭa:la layli: wa taʿanna:ni: ṭ-ṭarab

$-\ \smile\ -\ -\ |\ \smile\ \smile\ -\ -\ |\ -\ \ \smile\ -$

  sālim   maxbūn   maḥḏūf

> wa-Ꜥtara:ni: ṭu:lu hammin wa wasab
> − ᵕ − − | − ᵕ − − | ᵕ ᵕ −
> sālim   sālim   maxbūn mahḏūf
>   (Ꜥumar b. Abī RabīꜤa)

4. kāmil murabbaꜤ muḍmar muraffal

ya: badru wa l-ʔamta:lu yaḍ...
− − ᵕ − | − − − ᵕ −
   muḍmar   muḍmar

> ...ribuha: li-di: l-lubbi l-ḥaki:mu
> ᵕ ᵕ − ᵕ − | − − ᵕ − −
> sālim   muḍmar muraffal
>   (Yazīd b. al-Ḥakam al-Ṯaqafī)

5. wāfir musaddas maꜥṣūb maqṭūf

fa-ʔinni: law tuxa:lifuni: šima:li:
ᵕ − − − | ᵕ − − ᵕ ᵕ − | ᵕ − −
  maꜥṣūb   sālim   maqṭūf

> bi-naṣrin lam tuṣa:hib-ha: yami:ni:
> ᵕ − − − | ᵕ − − − | ᵕ − −
> maꜥṣūb   maꜥṣūb   maqṭūf
>   (al-MuṯaqqibꜤ al-Ꜥabdī)

6. ṭawīl muṯamman aṯlam maqbūḍ

law ʔanna layla: l-ʔaxyali:yata sallamat
− − | ᵕ − − − | ᵕ − ᵕ | ᵕ − ᵕ −
aṯlam   sālim   maqbūḍ   maqbūḍ

> Ꜥalayya wa du:ni: turbatun wa ṣafa:ʔihu
> ᵕ − ᵕ | ᵕ − − − | ᵕ − ᵕ | ᵕ − ᵕ −
> maqbūḍ   sālim   maqbūḍ   maqbūḍ
>   (Tawba b. Ḥumayyir al-Ꜥuqaylī)

7. basīṭ muṯamman maxbūn maqṭūꜤ al-ḍarb

turi:du ʔamran fa-ma: tadri: ʔa Ꜥa:jiluhu:
ᵕ − ᵕ − | − − ᵕ − | − − ᵕ − | ᵕ ᵕ −
  maxbūn   sālim   sālim   maxbūn

> xayrun li-nafsika ʔamma: fi:hi taʔxi:ru:
> − − ᵕ − | ᵕ ᵕ − | − − ᵕ − | − − −
> sālim   maxbūn   sālim   maqṭūꜤ
>   (Jabala b. Ḥurayṯ al-Ꜥudrī)

8. sarī⁥ musaddas maṭwī maxbūn maksūf

raʔatki ⁥ayni: fa-da⁥a:ni: l-hawa:
ᵕ − ᵕ − | −   ᵕ ᵕ − | −   ᵕ −
   maxbūn   maṭwī   maṭwī maksūf

       ʔilayki li-l-hayni wa lam ʔa⁥lami:
      ᵕ − ᵕ − | −   ᵕ   ᵕ   − | −   ᵕ −
        maxbūn   maṭwī   maṭwī maksūf
              (⁥umar b. Abī Rabī⁥a)

9. xafīf musaddas maxbūn

la: buhayrun ʔaq̇na: qati:lan wa la: rah...
−   ᵕ − − | −   −   ᵕ − | −   ᵕ −   −
  sālim   sālim   sālim

      ...ṭu kulaybin taza:jaru: ⁥an ḍala:li
      ᵕ   ᵕ − − | ᵕ −   ᵕ − | −   ᵕ −   −
        maxbūn   maxbūn   sālim
          (al-Ḥāriṯ b. ⁥ubād)

PERSIAN

1. hazaj musaddas maḥdūf aw maqṣūr

ʔagar ʔi:n-ast možgɑ:n-e: tar-e: man
ᵕ − − ╀ − − − − | ᵕ − −
  sālim   sālim   maḥdūf

      naxɑ:had ʔɑᵢ:ftɑ:b-e: maḥšaram su:xt
      ᵕ − − ╀ − − − − | ᵕ −   ⸯ
        sālim   sālim   maqṣūr
            (Farḥat)

2. hazaj mutamman axrab makfūf maḥdūf

žolm-ast ke bi:ru:n koniy-am ʔaz qafas aknu:n
−   ⸯ | ᵕ − −   − ᵕ| ᵕ − −   − ᵕ| ᵕ − −
axrab   makfūf   makfūf   maḥdūf

    k-az ju:r-e to ʔam ri:xte šod ba:l o par ɑ:njɑ:
    −   −   ᵕ | ᵕ −   ⸯ | ᵕ −   −   ᵕ | ᵕ − −
      axrab   makfūf   makfūf   maḥdūf
         (Majid Ṭaleqɑni)

3. <u>hazaj muṯamman axrab maqbūḍ makfūf ahtam abtar</u>

ʔabr ɑ:mad o bɑ:z bar sar-e: sabze geri:st

– – ᴗ | ᴗ ¬ – | ᴗ – – ᴗ | ᴗ ¬

axrab maqbūḍ makfūf ahtam

bi: bɑ:de-ye golrang nami:bɑ:yad zi:st

– – ᴗ | ᴗ – ¬ | ᴗ – – – | ¬

axrab makfūf sālim abtar

(ʕomar Xayyɑm)

4. <u>rajaz muṯamman maṭwī maxbūn</u>

bɑ: to padi:d mi:konam ḥɑ:l-e tabɑh-e xi:š-rɑ:

– ᴗ ᴗ + – ᴗ – | – ᴗ ᴗ – | ᴗ ¬ –

maṭwī maxbūn maṭwī maxbūn

tɑ: to naṣi:ḥati: koni: cašm-e siyɑ:h-e xi:š-rɑ:

– ᴗ ᴗ – | ᴗ – ᴗ – | – ᴗ ᴗ – | ᴗ ¬ –

maṭwī maxbūn maṭwī maxbūn

(Neżɑmi)

5. <u>ramal muṯamman maškūl sālim al-ʕarūḍ wa-l-ḍarb</u>

sar-e zolf-e to: na mošk ast o be mošk-nɑ:b mɑ:nad

ᴗ ᴗ – ᴗ | – ᴗ – – | ᴗ ᴗ – + – –

maškūl sālim maškūl sālim

rox-e roušan-e: to ʔei du:st be-ʔɑ:ftɑ:b mɑ:nad

ᴗ ᴗ – ᴗ | – ᴗ – + ᴗ ¬ | ¬ – –

maškūl sālim maškūl sālim

(Farroxi)

6. <u>mujtaṯṯ muṯamman maxbūn maḥḏūf aṣlam musabbaq̇</u>

nešɑ:n-e mehr o vafɑ: ni:st dar tabassom-e gol

ᴗ – ᴗ – | ᴗ ᴗ – + – ᴗ – | ᴗ ᴗ –

maxbūn maxbūn maxbūn maxbūn maḥḏūf

be-nɑ:l-e bolbol-e bi:-del ke jɑ:y-e feryɑ:d ast

ᴗ – ᴗ – | ᴗ ᴗ – – | ᴗ – ᴗ – | – ¬

maxbūn maxbūn maxbūn aṣlam musabbaq̇

(Ḥɑfeż)

7. muḏāriς muṯamman axrab makfūf maḥḏūf aw maqṣūr

besyɑ:r zolf-e por-šekan u: dar ham u:ftɑ:d

    - ⌣ | - ⌣ - ⌣| ⌣ -   -   ⌣ ⌒ ⌒
  axrab   makfūf   makfūf | maqṣūr

    ?ammɑ: be-del-robɑ:?i-ye zolfat kam u:ftɑ:d

    - - ⌣| - ⌣ - ⌣| ⌣ -   -   ⌣| -⌣ ⌒
  axrab   makfūf   makfūf   maqṣūr
                    (Veṣɑl-e Širɑzi)

8. sarīς musaddas maṭwī maksūf aw mawqūf

?ɑ:teš-e su:zɑ:n nakonad bɑ: sepand

    - ⌣ ⌣ -| -   ⌣ ⌣ -| -   ⌣ -
  maṭwī   maṭwī   maṭwī mawqūf

    ?ɑnce konad du:d-e del-e: mostmand

    - ⌣ ⌣ -| -   ⌣ ⌣ -| ⌒   ⌒
    maṭwī   maṭwī   maṭwī mawqūf
                    (Saςdi)

9. xafīf musaddas maxbūn maḥḏūf aw maqṣūr aw aṣlam musabbaḋ

ςɑ:ṣiyɑ:n az gonɑ:h toube konand

    - ⌣ -   - | ⌣ ⌒   - | ⌣   ⌣ -
  sālim   maxbūn   maqṣūr

    ςɑ:refɑ:n az ςebɑ:dat esteḋfɑ:r

    - ⌣ -   - | ⌄ -   ⌣ -| -   ⌒
    sālim   maxbūn   aṣlam musabbaḋ
                    (Saςdi)

II. Critique of Xalīl's system as applied to Persian metres

Xalīl's system of ʿarūḍ may be said to have two distinct merits. It offers (as we shall see shortly) a convincing, though hitherto hardly understood, account of the Arabic metres; and it has been equipped with such a complexity of ·ingenious modifications that it can, by the use of a certain latitude, be applied to the analysis of virtually any metrical system that is based on quantity (indeed, some modern theorists have even tried to apply it to English and French verse). It was adapted at a very early stage to Persian verse (an aspect of the intense respect that medieval Islam had for the Arabic language and its concomitant sciences); but from the first the Persian grammarians seem to have found it a task of some difficulty. As has already been pointed out, the ziḥāfāt, which in the Arabic system represent minor deviations in one and the same metre, when applied to Persian verse have to be used to distinguish one metre from another. As a result metres in what are clearly quite different patterns are arbitrarily grouped under one head, because their "feet" can be most conveniently described as different muzāḥif forms of certain basic feet belonging to a particular sālim Arabic metre.

This may best be seen if we examine the traditional

analysis of a number of the commonest Persian metres. We
shall find not only that the standard Persian form often
differs markedly from its Arabic "original" (and even when it
is similar is not permitted the variations that are normal in
Arabic), but also that metres of completely different
patterns are taken to be derived from one and the same
original.

Firstly, let us take two metres both classified as hazaj
mutamman:

(a) hazaj mutamman sālim

gah ɑːn ɑːrɑːsteː zolfaš zareː gardad gahiː canbar (ʕonṣori)

ᵛ - - -ᑊ- - - - | ᵛ - - - - | ᵛ - - -

mafaːʕiːlun mafaːʕiːlun mafaːʕiːlun mafaːʕiːlun

Apart from the fact that this metre is mutamman, whereas
the Arabic "parent" is normally murabbaʕ, it is permissible
to regard them as the same (though it should be noted that in
Persian the shortening of the final syllable of each foot
(kaff) is not allowed - or rather, if it occurs, it converts
the pattern into another metre).

(b) hazaj mutamman axrab maqbūd abtar

cuːn ast ke ʕešq ʔavval az tan xiːzad   (Abolfaraj Runi)

- ᵛ | ᵛ ᵛ -| ᵛ - - - -| -

mafʕuːlu ᴍafaːʕilun mafaːʕiːlun   faʕ

(For the moment we are leaving out of consideration overlong
syllables, since these are ignored in the Xalīl system, and
are equivalent in every case to - ᵛ).

The plethora of technical terms warns us that we have
gone some way from the original hazaj. In fact, by

ingenious allocation of the foot divisions, it is possible
to isolate one sālim foot (the third), but the other three
require much more explanation.   Reference to our tables
shows that mafʕu:lu is derived from mafa:ʕi:lun by xarb,
mafa:ʕilun by qabḍ, and faʕ by batr.   This metre is in fact
the distinctive and popular metre used for the rubāʕī or
quatrain so characteristic of Persian poetry, and to account
for all the variants of it that may be found in conjunction
another seven technical terms would have to be added to
those already given.   The prosodists in desperation
devised two "trees", each containing 12 variants and distinguished by the ʕilla, either xarb or xarm, applied to the
first foot.   As the diagram shows, many of the variants have
to be described by using ʕilla terms such as axrab or aštar
for the internal feet, or by devising special terms like
taxnīq to indicate an internal xarm.

In fact the rubāʕī metre is by no means as complex as
these diagrams would suggest.   As long ago as 1867
Blochmann[5] demonstrated that it was in fact basically the
following:

$$\overline{}\ \overline{}\ \underset{\rule{1.2em}{0.4pt}}{\smile\ \smile} \Bigg|\ \overline{}\ \overline{}\ \underset{\rule{1.2em}{0.4pt}}{\smile\ \smile} \Bigg|\ \overline{}\ \overline{}\ \smile\ \smile \Bigg|\ \overline{\underset{\smile}{}}$$
$$\overline{}\ \smile\ \overline{}\ \smile$$

When we take into account the fact that in Persian verse
throughout (as will be shown in the following chapter) any
pair of short syllables (except at the beginning of a line)
may be replaced by one long, while any final syllable may be
long or overlong, without affecting the metre, we shall see

The rubā:ʕī Trees

A. "axrab"

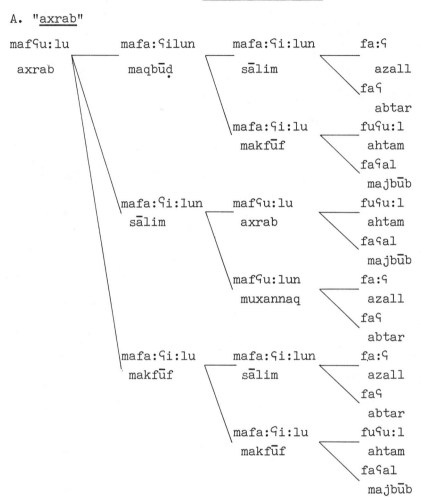

that the only variant in the above metre not common to all
metres is the alternation of - ᴗ - ᴗ with - - ᴗ ᴗ as the
second foot.   This would be a much more important distinction on which to divide this rubā:ʕī metre into two categories
than the almost meaningless axrab/axram difference.

B. "axram"

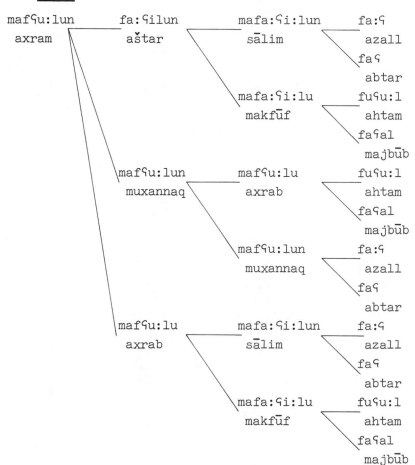

We may carry this argument a little further by looking at three Persian metres that are so widely used as to justify their being regarded as "standard", and are also (as we shall see more clearly in the following chapter) in identical metrical patterns.   Yet under the Xalīl system they have to be derived - at some distance - from three different bases.

The first (including permitted variations) is as follows:

⏑ – ⏑ – ⏑⏑ – – ⏑ – ⏑ – ⏑⏑ –̮

This is regarded by the prosodists as being a derivation of the mujtaṯṯ metre (which does not occur in Persian in its "sound" form). This conclusion is arrived at as follows:

The sālim form is the following:

– – ⏑ – | – ⏑ – – | – – ⏑ – | – ⏑ – –

By applying xabn to all four feet we get:

⏑ – ⏑ – | ⏑ ⏑ – – | ⏑ – ⏑ – | ⏑ ⏑ – –

which gives us the "standard" Persian pattern. The shortening of the last foot is arrived at by applying the ʕilla ḥadf.

⏑ – ⏑ – | ⏑ ⏑ – – | ⏑ – ⏑ – | ⏑ ⏑ –

So far the process is fairly simple; but when we try to account for the variations referred to above, we run into difficulties. The contraction of the first pair of shorts (in the second foot) into one long has to be explained by dropping xabn in the case of this foot only, and applying instead the ʕilla (!) tašʕīṯ. This gives us a foot – – – instead of – ⏑ – –. The last foot is even more complex. The possible variants are: ⏑ ⏑ –̮, – –, and – –̮. ⏑⏑–⏑, though for practical purposes the same as ⏑ ⏑ –, is given a different name - qaṣr. – – may be arrived at in two ways: either by ṣalm, the elision of the watad mafrūq (fa:ʕi, – ⏑) from the foot fa:ʕi:la:tun, leaving la:tun = faʕlun; or by qaṭʕ, the elision of the final sabab xafīf (tun) by ḥaḏf, plus the elision of the sākin of the watad majmūʕ (la:) and the "silencing" of the preceding mutaḥarrik - leaving us with fa:ʕil = faʕlun. To explain the form – –̮, the term tasbīq̇ is used for the "over-lengthening" of the final syllable.

The result of all this is:

∪ — ∪ —   ∪ ∪ — —   ∪ — ∪ —   ∪ ∪ —
maxbūn   maxbūn   maxbūn   maxbūn maḥdūf

— — —   ∪ ∪ —∪
mušaՙՙat   maxbūn maqsūr

                                    — —
                                    maqṭūՙ aw aṣlam

                                    — ⌣
                                    maqṭuՙ aw aṣlam musabbaɗ

Thus a full description of this common Persian metre
would have to be: mujtatt mutamman maxbūn mušaՙՙat maḥdūf
aw maqsūr aw maqṭūՙ (aw aṣlam) musabbaɗ.

The second metre is:

— — ∪ — ∪ — ∪ ∪ — — ∪ —.∪ —
                ‾‾‾‾‾   ⌣

This is considered to be a farՙ of the metre muḍāriՙ:

∪ — — —| — ∪ — —| ∪ — — —| — ∪ — —

To obtain the "standard" Persian form we first apply kaff
to all four feet:

∪ — — ∪| — ∪ — ∪| ∪ — — ∪| — ∪ — ∪

The first foot must also lose its initial short syllable,
which is achieved by applying the ՙilla xarm. The combination of kaff and xarm is known as xarb. We also have the
usual terms for the catalexis in the final foot - ḥadf and
qaṣr. To explain the substitution of one long for the two
shorts, since these occur in two different feet, it has to
be assumed that in that case only the second foot is sālim
instead of makfūf, and that the third foot is axrab (although

once again this is a misuse of an ʿilla).

```
  ‾ ‾ ⌣      ‾ ⌣ ‾ ⌣      ⌣ ‾ ‾ ⌣      ‾ ⌣ ‾
 axrab      makfūf       makfūf       mahḏūf
```

```
  ‾ ⌣ ‾ ‾      ‾ ‾ ⌣      ‾ ⌣ ⸯ
   sālim        axrab     maqṣūr
```

The metre is thus known as: muḍāriʿ muṯamman axrab
makfūf mahḏūf aw maqṣūr.

Our third example follows much the same pattern:

```
  ⌣
  ‾ ⌣ ‾ ‾ ⌣ ‾ ⌣ ‾ ⌣ ⌣ ‾
                   ‾‾ ⸯ
```

This is regarded as a derivation of xafīf, the sālim form of
which is:

```
 ‾ ⌣ ‾ ‾ |  ‾ ‾ ⌣ ‾ |  ‾ ⌣ ‾ ‾
```

The general ziḥāf is xabn, though to account for the
alternation of the first syllable the first foot may be sālim
as well. The last foot is treated as the last foot of our
first example, that is, by the application of haḏf, qaṣr,
qaṭʿ, ṣalm, or tasbīġ.

```
  ⌣ ⌣ ‾ ‾      ⌣ ‾ ⌣ ‾      ⌣ ⌣ ‾
 maxbūn       maxbūn       maxbūn mahḏūf
```

```
  ‾ ⌣ ‾ ‾                   ⌣ ⌣ ⸯ
  sālim                    maxbūn maqṣūr
```

```
                            ‾ ‾
                           aṣlam (aw maqṭūʿ)
```

```
                            ‾ ⸯ
                           aṣlam (aw maqṭūʿ) musabbaġ
```

The metre is therefore known as: xafīf musaddas maxbūn
mahḏūf aw maqṣūr aw aṣlam (aw maqṭūʿ) musabbaġ.

It may be of interest if we anticipate at this point the

theme of the next chapter, and set out these three metres (in
their simple form) so as to emphasise their identity of
pattern:

    ᴗ – ᴗ – ᴗ ᴗ – – ᴗ – ᴗ – ᴗ ᴗ –   (mujta<u>tt</u>)

    – – ᴗ – ᴗ – ᴗ ᴗ – – ᴗ – ᴗ –   (mudāriˁ)

    ᴗ ᴗ – – ᴗ – ᴗ – ᴗ ᴗ –   (xafīf)

The above facts suggest that there is an <u>a priori</u> case
against the general supposition that the Persian metres are
copied from Arabic.   At the very least it is clear that the
traditional system (the use of which is the only thing that
has given rise to this supposition) does not depict, in the
light of modern phonetic knowledge, a process of development
and change in metres that could actually have taken place.
Moreover it is inconceivable that, if some such "derivation"
of Persian from Arabic metres had taken place by some as yet
unidentified method, the highly modified forms which are now
the most common in use should so completely have supplanted
the "originals" in the course of two centuries as to have
left no trace of them whatever.

   There are various other differences that serve to point
the marked dissimilarity between the two systems.   Arabic
abyāt to a large extent ignore the break between the two
miṣrāˁ, even to the extent of permitting it to fall in the
middle of a word;   in Persian there is always a marked break
in the sense as well as in the words.   In an Arabic miṣrāˁ
the total of morae (ᴗ) may vary considerably;   for instance,
in the basīṭ metre there may be as many as 24 and as few as

18 morae in a hemistich of 14 syllables.   In Persian however
the quantitative length of a hemistich may vary only by the
lengthening of the final syllable (and in certain cases of
the initial) by one mora, a maximum variation of two morae no
matter what the length of the line.   On the other hand the
number of syllables (which in Arabic metres, except for the
kāmil and the wāfir, is roughly constant) varies considerably
in Persian verses, and in some metres may range as widely as
from ten to fifteen to the hemistich.

It is already apparent that the gulf between the two
metrical systems is widening, and this fact seems to have
been recognised even by the early prosodists who sought to
press both into the same mold.   They pointed out that the
ṭawīl, basīṭ, madīd, kāmil and wāfir were "Arabic" metres,
whereas at the other end of the scale the qarīb, ḍarīb
(jadīd), and mušākil were "Persian" metres "invented" by
Moulana Yusef in the fourth/tenth century (the idea that
prosodists "invent" viable metres is of course an absurd one;
prosodists follow poets, not poets prosodists).   That the
metres mujtatt, muḍāriʕ and muqtaḍab were both different in
character and later in time is confirmed by the tradition
that they were invented by al-Xalīl,[6] as well as by the fact
that they are rare in early Arabic poetry.   It is outside
the scope of this study to attempt a full statistical survey
of the metres of Arabic verse, and the following figures are
based merely on two samples, one the collection compiled by
Noeldeke, which covers a period from pre-Islamic times up to

the Umayyads, and the dīwān of ʿalī b. al-Jahm, an Arab from
Xorasan who died in 249/863, and was therefore subject to the
full pressure of Persian culture and literary tradition. In
the first collection, 134 poems are composed in the purely
Arabic metres kāmil, wāfir, basīṭ and ṭawīl (the latter
accounting for 80), whereas only 21 are in the metres
(regarded as common to both languages) xafīf, ramal, sarīʿ,
hazaj, rajaz, and mutaqārib.   Other metres do not figure at
all.

There is a marked change in the proportions used by the
Xorasani poet, though the first group still predominates with
96, as against 68 shared by the second group, which now
includes mujtatt and munsariḥ.

An examination of the extent to which individual hemistichs would by scansion fit into a Persian poem is also
revealing.   Out of 264 hemistichs examined in the 21 poems
in the Noeldeke collection composed in metres admissible in
Persian, only 62 could be so fitted, and of these only 23
were in scansions in general use in the latter language.   In
the dīwān of ʿalī b. al-Jahm the figures are 589, 115, and 48
respectively – roughly the same proportion.   It seems a
reasonable conclusion that the natural patterns of Arabic
verse do not suit Persian, and that any resemblance between
metres in the two language is largely coincidental; indeed
it occurs mainly in metres introduced into Arabic verse in
Umayyad and ʿabbāsid times.   The influence may then have
been the other way, and these new metres were originally
Persian metres copied and adapted into the Arabic system.

Metre	Noeldeke No. of poems	Noeldeke No. of hemistichs	Noeldeke No. of "Persian"	ʿalī b. al-Jahm No. of poems	ʿalī b. al-Jahm No. of hemistichs	ʿalī b. al-Jahm No. of "Persian"
kāmil	16			32	80*	32 (4.5.12)
wāfir	23			14	68	16 (3.1.08)
basīṭ	15			22	10	2 (3.1.11)
ṭawīl	80			28	80*	3 (3.4.11)
	134			96		
xafīf	8	82	26 (4.5.12)+	18		1 (2.3.11) 6 (3.4.08) 1 (5.2.08)≠ 7 (5.6.08)≠
ramal (short)	1	16	3 (3.1.08)	6		
ramal (long)	2	30	2 (3.1.11)	2		
sarīʕ	2	30	2 (3.4.11)	16		
hazaj	2	36	10 (3.2.07)	—	—	—
rajaz	4	32	0	3	59	
mutaqārib	2	38	12 (1.1.12) 7 (1.1.11)	9	98*	13 (1.1.12) 19 (1.1.11)
munsariḥ (short)	—	—	—	4	20	3 (5.3.15)
munsariḥ (long)	—	—	—	8	66	11 (5.3.16)
mujtatt	—	—	—	2	8	1 (4.5.16)
	21	264	62	68	489*	115

+ The bracketed numbers in the "Persian" column refer to the metre code numbers given in the table in Chapter III.

* A part only of the poems in these groups was analysed.

≠ In Persian this metre is found only in the "doubled" form.

Other evidence of the sharp distinction felt between the
two systems may be seen in the rarity with which Persian
poets use the "Arabic" metres even when they are translating
from Arabic verse. For instance, seven examples chosen at
random from the Tarjomanol-balāḍe show ṭawīl translated in
munsariḥ, kāmil in muḍāriʕ, munsariḥ in muḍāriʕ, mutaqārib
in mujtatt, basīṭ in sarīʕ, and again in mujtatt, and wāfir
in hazaj. This is not simply a question of using fresh
metres where the originals are in metres unknown to Persian
verse (though it is hard to see why, if the Persian poets
copied their metres from the Arabs, they should have completely ignored those that are most common in Arabic). As will
be seen, two of the above Arabic buḥūr - mutaqārib and
munsariḥ - are common to Persian too, though not in the form
found in the Arabic verse; yet they were not chosen for the
Persian translation. It is clear that in the mind of the
prosodist Raduyani the two systems, in spite of their
nomenclature, were quite distinct, and not to be confused.

Arabic metres are occasionally used by Persian poets,
but that this is a conscious trick is evident from the
qaṣīda composed by Amir Moʕezzi (d. 542/1147-8) in a form of
basīṭ, the last two couplets of which are:

goftam seta:yeš-e to: bar vazn-e šeʕr-e ʕarab
taqti:ʕ -e ʔu: be-ʕaru:z ellα coni:n nakoni
mustafʕilun faʕilun mustafʕilun faʕilun
ʔabla: l-hawa: ʔasafan yawma n-nawa: badani:

I have spoken your praise in the metre of Arabic poetry,
You may only scan it in ʕarūḍ in this way:

<u>mustafʕilun</u> <u>faʕilun</u> <u>mustafʕilun</u> <u>faʕilun</u>
"Passion has worn out my body in grief on the day of
                              separation."

The final Arabic hemistich is a quotation from al-Mutanabbī
(d. 354/965).   Curiously, this qaṣīda is cited by Daudpota
as evidence for his view that the Persian metres are copied
from Arabic.[7]   The very fact that Amir Moʕezzi draws
attention so elaborately to his use of this Arabic metre, and
employs it nowhere else in his dīwān, is clear proof that it
was unfamiliar to his Persian readers.

   One other example is a macaronic verse by Šahīd Balxi
(3rd/9th century) in alternate lines of Arabic and Persian,
composed in munsariḥ musaddas maqtūʕ maxbūn maṭwī:

yara: miḥnati: ṯumma yaxfiḍu l-baṣara:
 ◡ ‒   ‒   ◡ ‒   ‒   ◡ ‒ ◡ ‒   ◡ ‒

         fadat-hu nafsi: tara:hu qad safara:
          ◡ ‒ ◡ ‒   ‒   ◡ ‒ ◡ ‒   ◡ ◡ ‒

da:nad k-az vey be-man hami: ce rasad
 ‒ ‒   ‒   ‒   ◡ ‒   ◡ ‒   ◡ ◡ ‒

         di:gar ba:re: ze ešq bi: xabara:
          ‒ ‒   ‒   ‒   ◡   ◡̆ ‒   ◡ ◡ ‒

ʔa ma: tara: wajnatayya min ḍamazih
 ◡ ‒ ◡ ‒   ‒   ◡ ‒ ◡ ‒   ◡ ◡ ‒

         wa sa:ʔilan ka l-juma:ni mubtadira:
          ◡ ‒ ◡ ‒   ‒   ◡ ‒ ◡ ‒   ◡ ◡ ‒

co sadd-e yaʔju:j ba:yadi: del-e man
 ◡ ‒   ◡ ‒   ◡̆   ‒ ◡ ‒   ◡̆ ◡̆ . ‒

         ke ba:šadi: ḍamzaga:nš-ra: separa:
          ◡ ‒ ◡ ‒   ‒ ◡ ◡̆   ‒   ◡ ◡ ‒
                                     etc.

   There is an extra syllable at the beginning of the first
bayt, but otherwise the pattern is regular and identical in

both Arabic and Persian (more regular, in fact, than is
usual in Arabic verses in this metre).   It is significant
that no other example of Persian verse in this metre has
been found, either contemporary with Šahid or later.   The
broken rhythm is, as we shall see, quite alien to Persian.

The most penetrating examination of the Arabic metrical
system is that made by Gotthold Weil, and if his conclusions
are sound (as they seem to be), they complete the severance
of the two systems.   For while there can be no doubt that
Persian verse is primarily quantitative, with accent - if it
comes into it at all - playing a secondary and even con-
flicting role - Weil has shown very cogently that the basis
of the Arabic metres is stress, with quantity in a subordin-
ate position.   He draws this conclusion logically from al-
Xalīl's "Circles" (<u>dawāʔir</u>), the prosodist's device for
grouping together metres with common characteristics.   For
long it was not clear why this system of grouping was
adopted by al-Xalīl (and indeed the secret must have been
lost at a very early date).   Weil's view is that Arabic
metres are formed round a series of stressed "nuclei" (Kern),
which are in fact the awtād (whether majmūʕ or mafrūq), and
unlike the other syllables in the line are not subject to
modification by the ziḥāfāt.   The purpose of the Circles is
to pin-point the position of the watad in any given metre.
As the following table shows, these invariable "nuclei" are
to be found in a regular sequence, separated by anything from
one to three variable syllables that may be either long or

short (in other words, whose quantitative length is of no
significance).

In the following tables, to save space, the Circles are
represented by straight lines broken at an arbitrary point.
The order of the Circles and the metres has also been
modified from those used by al-Xalīl and Weil respectively,
in order to harmonise them.   The alternative Circle names
are those suggested by later prosodists.

AL-XALĪL'S FIVE CIRCLES

(a) al-dāʔiratu l-muttafiqa (aw al-munfarida aw al-muštabiha)

mutaqārib

FuʕuW LuN FuʕuW LuN FuʕuW LuN FuʕuW LuN

⎸mutadārik
ʕiLuN⎸Faʔ ʕiLuN Faʔ ʕiLuN Faʔ ʕiLuN Faʔ

(b) al-dāʔiratu l-mujtaliba (aw al-muʔtalifa)

hazaj

MaFaʔ ʕiY LuN MaFaʔ ʕiY LuN MaFaʔ ʕiY LuN MaFaʔ ʕiY LuN

⎸rajaz
ʕiLuN⎸MuS TaF ʕiLuN MuS TaF ʕiLuN MuS TaF ʕiLuN MuS TaF

⎸ramal
ʕiLaʔ TuN⎸Faʔ ʕiLaʔ TuN Faʔ ʕiLaʔ TuN Faʔ ʕiLaʔ TuN Faʔ

(c) al-dāʔiratu l-muʔtalifa

kāmil

MuTa Faʔ ʕiLuN MuTa Faʔ ʕiLuN MuTa Faʔ ʕiLuN MuTa Faʔ ʕiLuN

⎸wāfir
ʕaLa TuN⎸MuFaʔ ʕaLa TuN MuFaʔ ʕaLa TuN MuFaʔ ʕaLa TuN MuFaʔ

(d) al-dāʔiratu l-muxtalifa

ṭawīl

FuʕuW LuN MaFaʔ ʕiY LuN FuʕuW LuN MaFaʔ ʕiY LuN

      |madīd
ʕiLuN|Faʔ ʕiLaʔ TuN Faʔ ʕiLuN Faʔ ʕiLaʔ TuN Faʔ

             |basīṭ
ʕiLuN Faʔ ʕiLuN|MuS TaF ʕiLuN Faʔ ʕiLuN MuS TaF

(e) al-dā?iratu l-muštabiha

muḍāriʕ
MaFaʔ ʕiY LuN Faʔʕi Laʔ TuN MaFaʔ ʕiY LuN

      |muqtadab
ʕiLuN|MaF ʕuW LaʔTu MuS TaF ʕiLuN MuS TaF

        |mujtatt
ʕiLaʔ TuN|MuS TaFʕi LuN Faʔ ʕiLaʔ TuN Faʔ

             |sarīʕ
ʕiLuN MaF ʕuW LaʔTu|MuS TaF ʕiLuN MuS TaF

                 |munsariḥ
ʕiLuN MaF ʕuW LaʔTu MuS TaF ʕiLuN|MuS TaF

                    |xafīf
ʕiLaʔ TuN MuS TaFʕi LuN Faʔ ʕiLaʔ TuN|Faʔ

Weil's interpretation of the Circles

		w.mj.	w.mj.	w.mj.	w.mj.	w.mj.
A.	mutaqārib	ᵕ - x	ᵕ - x	ᵕ - x	ᵕ - x	
	mutadārik	x	ᵕ - x	ᵕ - x	ᵕ - x	ᵕ -
B.	hazaj	ᵕ - x x	ᵕ - x x	ᵕ - x x	ᵕ - x x	
	rajaz	x x	ᵕ - x x	ᵕ - x x	ᵕ - x x	ᵕ -
	ramal		x ᵕ - x x	ᵕ - x x	ᵕ - x x	ᵕ - x
C.	wāfir	ᵕ - x͜x͟x	ᵕ - x͜x͟x	ᵕ - x͜x͟x	ᵕ - x͜x͟x	
	kāmil	x͜x͟x	ᵕ - x͜x͟x	ᵕ - x͜x͟x	ᵕ - x͜x͟x	ᵕ -
D.	ṭawīl	ᵕ - x	ᵕ - x x	ᵕ - x	ᵕ - x x	
	madīd	x	ᵕ - x x	ᵕ - x	ᵕ - x x	ᵕ -
	basīṭ		x x ᵕ - x	ᵕ - x x	ᵕ - x ᵕ -	

```
            w.mj.   w.mf.   w.mj.   w.mj.   w.mf.   w.mj.
E. mudāriᶜ   - x x -  ◡ x x ◡ - x x
   muqtadab  x x -  ◡ x x ◡ - x x ◡ -
   mujtatt     x -  ◡ x x ◡ - x x ◡ - x
   sarīᶜ         x x ◡ - x x ◡ - x x -  ◡
   munsariḥ        x x ◡ - x x -  ◡ x x ◡ -
   xafīf           x ◡ - x x -  ◡ x x ◡ - x
```

Examination of al-Xalīl's circle (e) will now explain the difference between the feet mus.taf.ᶜilun and mus.tafᶜi.lun, and between fa:.ᶜila:.tun and fa:ᶜi.la:.tun; the second of each of these pairs, containing the watad mafrūq, is used only in mujtatt and xafīf, and in mudāriᶜ respectively. The "weak" watad mafrūq in fact only occurs in the six later metres, and even in these only once in a hemistich, as against twice for the watad majmūᶜ; in general it appears that these metres account for not more than 5% of all the metres actually used by Arab poets. It suggests that this form of "Kern" did not come easily to the natural rhythm of Arabic verse, and it is tempting to think that its introduction might have owed its origin to an attempt to imitate the alternating patterns of Persian verse. Weil points out (though he draws a different conclusion) that, out of seventy-one Wine-songs composed by Abū Nuwās (d. 196/810), no fewer than 22 are in the group of metres that employ the watad mafrūq - that is to say, 30% as against the normal 5%.[8] He suggests that the weakened rhythm may have been felt to be particularly suited to the drinking song; but it might equally well have arisen under Persian influence, which is evident in many other aspects of Abū Nuwās' verse.

When we turn to the Persian metres, we find that the watad (whether majmūʕ or mafrūq) plays no such significant role. This can be most easily seen when we compare the ostensibly similar Arabic and Persian hazaj metres. Whereas the Arabic version is built round the inviolable watad majmūʕ:

$$\smile \; \acute{-} \; x \; x \; \Big| \; \smile \; \acute{-} \; x \; x \; \Big| \; \smile \; \acute{-} \; x \; x \; \ldots\ldots$$

the Persian metre of the same name may, as a variant on the form

$$\smile \; - \; - \; \smile \; \Big| \; \smile \; - \; - \; \smile \; \Big| \; \smile \; - \; -$$

assume the shape

$$\smile \; - \; - \; - \; \Big| \quad - \; - \; \smile \; \Big| \; \smile \; - \; -$$

in which the second watad has disappeared. Persian metres, unlike the Arabic, follow an undulating, carefully balanced sequence of long and short syllables (with the overlong syllable playing an important role). It is probable that the question of stress does not arise at all; as Xɑnlari has pointed out, the natural stress in Persian speech tends to occur at two- or three-syllable intervals, and cannot be fitted into the quantitative pattern.

By the time that the Arabic science of prosody came to be applied to Persian verse, the significance of al-Xalīl's circles had been entirely forgotten. Had this not been so, it is unlikely that the attempt would even have been made, for its irrelevance would have been obvious. As it was, the prosodists found considerable difficulty in making the

transition.   At a fairly early stage they seem to have put
al-Xalīl's "circles" technique to a new use, by grouping
together muzāhif forms of the metres in order to draw
attention to common metrical patterns of long and short
syllables.   Thus in the Qabus-name (written in 475/1082-3)
we find references to circles, one of which includes the
following:

hazaj makfūf mafa:ʕi:lu mafa:ʕi:lu mafa:ʕi:lu mafa:ʕi:lu

hazaj axrab   mafʕu:lu mafa:ʕi:lu mafa:ʕi:lu mafa:ʕi:lu

rajaz maṭwī   muftaʕilun muftaʕilun muftaʕilun muftaʕilun

ramal maxbūn   faʕila:tun faʕila:tun faʕila:tun faʕila:
                                                              tun

The most original writer on this subject, Naṣiroddin Ṭusi,
set out in his Meʕyarol-ašʕar (written in 649/1251-2) what
was probably the furthest extent of thinking along these
lines - his three new circles, the basic patterns of which
were:

1. ᴗ - - ᴗ ᴗ - - ᴗ ᴗ - - ᴗ ᴗ - - ...

2.   - ᴗ ᴗ - - ᴗ ᴗ - - ᴗ - ᴗ...

3.   - ᴗ ᴗ - - ᴗ - ᴗ - ᴗ ᴗ - - ᴗ - ᴗ ...

ṬUSI'S CIRCLES

1. al-dāʔiratu l-mujtalibatu l-zāʔidatu l-zāḥifa

hazaj makfūf

MaFaʔ ʕiY Lu MaFaʔ ʕiY Lu MaFaʔ ʕiY Lu MaFaʔ ʕiY Lu

       | rajaz maṭwī
ʕiLuN | MuF Ta ʕiLuN MuF Ta ʕiLuN MuF Ta ʕiLuN MuF Ta

              | ramal maxbūn
ʕiLaʔ TuN | Fa ʕiLaʔ TuN Fa ʕiLaʔ TuN Fa ʕiLaʔ TuN Fa

2. al-dā ?iratu l-muštabihatu l-muzāḥifa

sarī˅ maṭwī

MuF Ta ˅iLuN MuF Ta ˅iLuN Fa? ˅i La? Tu

<u>qarīb makfūf</u>
La? Tu|MaFa? ˅iY Lu MaFa? ˅iY Lu Fa? ˅i

<u>munsariḥ maṭwī</u>
MuF Ta ˅iLuN|MuF Ta ˅iLuN Fa? ˅i La? Tu

<u>xafīf maxbūn</u>
LuN Fa ˅iLa? TuN|Fa ˅iLa? TuN Ma Fa? ˅i

<u>muqtaḍab maṭwī</u>
MuF Ta ˅iLuN MuF Ta ˅iLuN|Fa? ˅i La? Tu

<u>mujtatt maxbūn</u>
LuN Fa ˅iLa? TuN Fa ˅iLa? TuN|Ma Fa? ˅i

3. al-dā ?iratu l-muštabihatu l-zā?ida

munsariḥ maṭwī

MuF Ta ˅iLuN Fa? ˅i La? Tu MuF Ta ˅iLuN Fa? ˅i La? Tu

<u>mudāri˅ makfūf</u>
La? Tu|MaFa?˅iY Lu Fa? ˅i La? Tu MaFa? ˅iY Lu Fa? ˅i

<u>muqtaḍab maṭwī</u>
MuF Ta ˅iLuN|Fa? ˅i La? Tu MuF Ta ˅iLuN Fa? ˅i La? Tu

<u>mujtatt maxbūn</u>
LuN Fa ˅iLa? TuN|Ma Fa? ˅i LuN Fa ˅iLa? TuN Ma Fa? ˅i

<u>muhmal</u>
La? Tu MaFa? ˅iY Lu|Fa? ˅i La? Tu MaFa? ˅iY Lu Fa? ˅i

However already in his <u>al-Mo˅jam fi ma˅ayire aš˅are-l-</u>

<u>˅ajam</u>, written in 614/1217-8, Šams-e Qeis had protested

against this proliferation of circles, and particularly

against the inclusion in different circles of the sālim and

muzāḥif forms of the same baḥr.   The force of the Xalīl

tradition was too strong, and although Šams-e Qeis himself

was prepared to allow circles (to which he gave fresh names)
that in fact differed from Ṭusi's only in the omission of
buḥūr that were already listed elsewhere in a different form,
he seems like Ṭusi to have been unable to think of a metre
as a section of a continuous pattern rather than a collection
of formulae.

ŠAMS-E QEIS'S CIRCLES

1. al-dāʔiratu l-muʔtalifa (= al-Xalīl's al-mujtaliba)
hazaj sālim, rajaz sālim, ramal sālim

2. al-dāʔiratu l-muxtalifa
munsariḥ maṭwī
MuF Ta ʕiLuN Faʔ ʕi Laʔ Tu MuF Ta ʕiLuN Faʔ ʕi Laʔ Tu

     |mudāriʕ makfūf
Laʔ Tu |MaFaʔ ʕiY Lu Faʔ ʕi Laʔ Tu MaFaʔ ʕiY Lu Faʔ ʕi

     |muqtaḍab maṭwī
MuF Ta ʕiLuN|Faʔ ʕi Laʔ Tu MuF Ta ʕiLuN Faʔ ʕi Laʔ Tu

     |mujtatt maxbūn
LuN Fa ʕiLaʔ TuN |Ma Faʔ ʕi LuN Fa ʕiLaʔ TuN Ma Faʔ ʕi

3. al-dāʔiratu l-mutanazzaʕa
sarīʕ maṭwī
MuF Ta ʕiLuN MuF Ta ʕiLuN Faʔ ʕi Laʔ Tu

    |ḡarīb maxbūn
LuN |Fa ʕiLaʔ TuN Fa ʕiLaʔ TuN Ma Faʔ ʕi

    |ḡarīb makfūf
Laʔ Tu |MaFaʔ ʕiY Lu MaFaʔ ʕiY Lu Faʔ ʕi

     |xafīf maxbūn
LuN Fa ʕiLaʔ TuN |Fa ʕiLaʔ TuN Ma Faʔ ʕi

      |mušākil makfūf
Laʔ Tu MaFaʔ ʕiY Lu MaFaʔ ʕiY Lu |Faʔ ʕi

4. al-dāʔiratu l-muttafiqa (= al-Xalīl's al-muttafiqa)
mutaqārib sālim, mutadārik sālim

It is noticeable that in both these sets of new circles
the role of the watad has almost completely disappeared.

Another contribution by Naṣiroddin Ṭusi to the science of
prosody was the use of the general term taskīn to indicate
the silencing of the second of two mutaḥarrik letters - or as
we should say, the substitution of one long for two short
syllables. He was not, however, prepared to admit this as a
general rule; it could only occur within a foot - in fact,
within the following: faⱿila:tun (becomes mafⱿu:lun),
faⱿila:tu (becomes mafⱿu:lu), faⱿilun (becomes faⱿlun),
faⱿila:n (becomes faⱿla:n), and muftaⱿilun (becomes
mafⱿu:lun). Moreover it could not occur when the effect
would be to produce a different baḥr (the example he gives
is faⱿila:tu fa:Ɀila:tun - ramal maškūl sālim al-Ɀarūḍ wa l-
ḍarb - which may not be alternated by taskīn with mafⱿu:lu
fa:Ɀila:tun, as that would be muḍāriⱿ axrab makfūf). Once
again we see the great weight of the traditional buḥūr and
the traditional feet. The first scholar to point out that a
similar process was at any rate theoretically possible whenever two short syllables came together was Blochmann's Indian
colleague, Moulavi ɑqɑ Aḥmad ⱿAli, in his Resɑle-e tarɑne.
It was on the basis of this discovery that Blochmann in his
section of the same work offered his simple statement of the
rubāⱿī metre already referred to, in place of the "Trees" of
the prosodists. Unfortunately the suggestive ideas put

forward in this treatise were never followed up either by
the authors themselves or by any other scholar.

An interesting treatise on the rubāʕī metre was published
in 1942 by Masʕud Farzad.   Farzad arrives at the same
conclusion as Blochmann regarding the essential nature of
this metre, though he does not seem to know of Blochmann's
work and arrives at his result by a different route.
According to him, the basic formula is:

$$- \mid - \cup \cup - \parallel - \cup \cup - \mid - \cup \cup -$$
$$\cup - \cup -$$

Perhaps the most important point made by Farzad is that a
metre need not necessarily be regarded as starting with a
complete foot.   It is this assumption that has misled so
many prosodists into classifying separately metres that
differ only in the point of the common pattern at which they
start.   On the other hand he perhaps attaches too much
importance to foot divisions, which are only significant if
one assumes them to indicate the position of an accent (and
as he himself says, "neither the meaning nor the accent of a
Persian word is of any significance in scansion.").   He
appears at one point to recognise the relationship between
such patterns as

$$- - \cup \cup - - \cup \cup - - \cup \cup -$$
and $$\cup \cup - - \cup \cup - - \cup \cup - - \cup \cup -$$

But in his final classification of Persian metres as a whole
he brings in an element of confusion by re-introducing his
concept of foot divisions and relating all metres to one or
other of the following basic feet or "prosodic words":

⏑ – – –, – ⏑ – –, – – ⏑ –, all of which he derives from a common ancestor – – – –. Farzad has developed his views in a number of thoughtful works; but his determination to use the "prosodic word" as his unit has prevented him from seeing through to all the possibilities.

Parviz Natel Xanlari's analysis, first published in 1948 and again in a revised form in 1958, offers another fundamental approach to the problem. He appears to have come the closest of anyone to recognising the basic similarity of the patterns of Persian verse, though by restricting himself too rigidly to the limits imposed by "circles" he has been obliged to introduce no fewer than fourteen of these to account for all the known metres of Persian verse (admittedly he includes two metres - in one circle - that are not Persian, kāmil and wāfir, and indeed others that exist only theoretically). But a more fundamental flaw in his approach is his division of the verses into dissyllabic, or occasionally trisyllabic, feet. Although this is based on his perfectly correct view that the natural accent in Persian occurs at approximately such intervals, he is probably mistaken in thinking that metre and accent must go hand in hand. By failing to separate them, he tends to obscure the basic quantitative patterns. The same criticism has to be made of the ideas of two other workers in the field, ʕali Naqi Vaziri (1938) and Mahdi Ḥamidi (1963), who also categorise their metres according to feet of varying length and shape; Ḥamidi posits nine, ranging from one to five syllables, while Vaziri

has discovered no fewer than fourteen (though it must be
said that some at least of these, e.g. ◡ ◡ ◡ ◡ -, are never
found in Persian verse).

There is not space here to discuss in the detail they
deserve the theories of Amir Faridun Moʿtamed (1962-3),
though since his main interest is to evolve a theory that can
be applied with equal success to the verse of any language,
it is inevitable that his ideas move a long way from the
practical problems of identifying the metres actually in use
among Persian poets.   He is at any rate right to insist on
the necessity of imbalance as a concomitant of balance, and
to stress that rhythm only exists when there is inequality -
a view which would seem to deal the death-blow to the concept
of syllabic verse.   That some such system of balance lies at
the bottom of the Persian metres is certain, and in the next
chapter it will be suggested that it is to be found in the
quantitative patterns, and most easily seen when these are
stripped of their artificial covering of foot-divisions.

III. The Persian metres

We have now seen that the "circles" devised by al-Xalīl for
the Arabic metres, so far from being purely decorative,
enable us to draw very definite conclusions as to the
structure of these metres.   Since we are concerned here
primarily with the Persian metres, we do not need to pursue
this line of enquiry any further.   We are however entitled
to conclude that the rhythm of a repeated "Kern" separated
by a variable number of indeterminate syllables must bear a
close relation to the rhythms of spoken Arabic verse and
spoken Arabic in general.   If this is the case, it clearly
cannot bear any such relation to Persian verse and speech.
We cannot therefore look to the theories of the classical
prosodists for any light on the structure of the Persian
metres, and must instead return to the source and base our
conclusions on direct analysis of the abundant material
available to us in the dīwāns and anthologies of the poets,
both classical and modern.

The analysis of the Persian metres that follows is based
entirely on the classical literary form, including later
simulation of the classical tradition.   In Chapter V some
reference will be made to Persian verse in its spoken forms,
the part played by natural accent and stress in verse-rhythm,

the relationship between classical verse-metres and those
of popular verse, songs and recitation, and the links with
pre-Islamic verse and Indo-European verse generally. At the
moment however we are in the happy position of being able to
investigate as a distinct unit the system of metres already
in use at the time that Persian verse re-emerged into the
light of written record in the third/ninth century, and
which has remained virtually unchanged (apart from modern
experiment) since that date in the composition of written
verse.

The unit of any quantitative verse must be the syllable.
Whereas in many languages, for example English, the precise
delimitation of the syllable is at times open to question,
in Persian the rule is very simple. All syllables begin
with one consonant, and one only. Thus where consonant
clusters occur (and they rarely exceed three in Persian),
all but the last must be regarded as belonging to the
previous syllable. This rule has a basis in the phonetic
structure of Persian, which does not (in the standard
language) permit of a word beginning with more than one
consonant. We are thus not faced in Persian with the
difficulty presented in English by the fact that words such
as eat, teat, treat, street are all monosyllabic and therefore of the same quantitative length.

For prosodic purposes, syllables in Persian are
reckoned to be of three kinds:

.(a) short: consonant – short vowel (a, e, o)   ba ⌣

(b) <u>long</u>:   consonant - short vowel - consonant   bad -

consonant - long vowel (<u>a</u>, <u>i</u>, <u>u</u>)   ba: -

(c) <u>overlong</u>: consonant - short vowel - two (or

more) consonants   badr ⌣

consonant - long vowel - one (or

more) consonants   ba:d ⌣

ba:ft ⌣

Diphthongs (<u>ei</u>, <u>ou</u>) are regarded as short vowel +
consonant, as they are in fact written (<u>ay</u>, <u>aw</u>).

The theoretical ratio of these three types of syllable is
1:2:3, and the whole quantitative basis of the metrical
system rests on these ratios.   With the exception of the
optional addition of a single mora (⌣) to the length of a
final long syllable or of an initial short syllable, all
lines of a poem are of exactly the same quantitative length.
Any change in the quantitative length of any other syllable
must be balanced by a corresponding reduction or increase in
the total number of syllables in the line, so as to maintain
the total quantity.

After considering the syllable, it is usual to define
next the feet, and then to group these into metres. This
method is not however very profitable in the present case,
and may even be misleading.   In a purely quantitative metre,
into which accent does not enter as a rhythmical element,
the division of a line into "feet" cannot be more than a
convenience, a mnemonic device.   The important feature is
the pattern of the syllables, and it is proposed now to

introduce those that are characteristic of Persian verse.
For this purpose the "standard" pattern to be that which is
most fully "disintegrated", and thus contains the largest
possible number of syllables. In point of fact the "overlong" syllable never occurs in a standard pattern, since it
is analysable into two syllables; the same is sometimes
true of the long syllables. In considering the patterns,
therefore, it is to be assumed that in all cases the
following optional changes may take place:

(a) two short syllables ($\smile\,\smile$) may be replaced by one long
(-), except at the beginning of a line.

(b) a long syllable followed by a short ($-\,\smile$) may be replaced by one overlong ($\frown$).

(c) the first of two short syllables at the beginning of
a line ($\smile\,\smile$) may be replaced by one long ($-\,\smile$).

(d) the final syllable (never short) may be either long
or overlong.

(a) and (b) are known to the prosodists as <u>sakta</u>. A
<u>sakta-yi malih</u> is one in which the quantitative length
remains unchanged; a <u>sakta-yi qabīh</u> is one in which an
overlong syllable is used where the pattern requires only a
long syllable.

There are five main patterns in Persian verse,
accounting for 85% of all known metres, and all but 0.1% of
the metres actually used by poets. In addition there are a
further nine "irregular" patterns.

		1.	2.	3.	4.	5.	6.	7.	8.	
Regular	1.	˘	—	—	˘	—	—			....
	2.	˘	—	—	—	˘	—	—	—	....
	3.	˘	˘	—	—	˘	˘	—	—	....
	4.	˘	—	˘	—	˘	˘	—	—	....
	5.	—	—	˘	˘	—	˘	—	˘	....
Irregular	6.	˘	—	˘	—	˘	—	˘	—	....
	7.	˘	—	˘	—	—				....
	8.	˘	—	˘	—	—	—			....
	9.	˘	—	—	˘	—	—	˘	—	....
	10.	˘	—	—	—	˘	—	—		....
	11.	˘	—	—	—	—	˘	—	—	....
	12.	˘	—	—	˘	—	˘	˘	—	....
	13.	—	—	˘	˘	—	—	—	˘	....
	14.	˘	—	—	—	˘	—	˘	˘	—	....

It will be seen that Pattern 1 is a repeating sequence of three syllables, Patterns 2 and 3 of four syllables, and Patterns 4 and 5 of eight syllables.   Even the other nine irregular patterns, with the exception of one, can be fitted into repeating sequences of not more than eight syllables.

If we think of these patterns as "tapes" or "ribbons" of indefinite length, we shall see how individual metres are arrived at by cutting off specific lengths (ranging in practice from five to sixteen syllables), differentiated by the point at which the initial cut is made.

For the purpose of easy identification, a code number has been allotted to each metre, in which the first figure indicates the pattern, the second figure the initial syllable (as numbered in the table above), and the remaining two figures the number of syllables.   It is to be assumed that

the final syllable of a line will always be long (or overlong), no matter which type of syllable comes at that point
in the pattern.

Two special categories of metre are to be noted here:

(a) <u>Doubled Metres</u>: A short section of the pattern
(rarely more than eight syllables or less than five) is
repeated, making a line of up to sixteen syllables. In the
case of eight-syllable halves the result is indistinguishable
from the normal sixteen-syllable version, except for a marked
break in the words at the half-way point, sometimes further
emphasised by a rhyme. Some metres of this type are found
only in the "doubled" form, others are equally common in
either and may be found mixed in the same poem. Seven-
syllable halves may also sometimes be fitted into the
fourteen-syllable pattern by the use of an overlong syllable
at the end of the first half. These metres are coded by
giving the syllable length of the half-hemistich followed
by (2), e.g. 1.1.05(2).

(b) <u>Broken Metres</u>: Certain metres of Patterns 4 and 5
are formed by the omission of a four-syllable section of
the pattern, with the effect that the preceding four-
syllable section is repeated before the rest of the pattern
is completed. This is indicated in the coding by showing
separately the number of syllables before and after the
"break" in the pattern, e.g. 4.1.04/08.

The following table gives a complete list of all recognised Persian metres, including some that are cited only in

the prosody books.   They are classified under patterns,
and within each pattern according to syllabic length, starting with the shortest.   Each entry gives the code number,
the "standard" form of the metre, the traditional Arabic
designation, and an example from a Persian poet or failing
that a prosodist.   A certain number have also been included
on the authority of modern writers on prosody, such as
Xanlari and Jhaveri, even when these are unsupported by
examples.   Metres that are explicitly or obviously copied
from Arabic are omitted, as also are those that are clear
fabrications of the prosodists.   The Arabic terminology is
that appropriate to the "standard" form.   For the various
optional modifications substitute terms such as maqṣūr for
maḥd̲ūf, makfūf for maškūl, etc., or additional terms such as
musabbaǧ, mudā̲l, etc., will have to be used.   On the other
hand the example verses quoted are not necessarily in the
"standard" form.

   * attested by poet's example.

   + attested by prosodist's example.

   o listed by prosodist without example.

+ 1.1.08   ᴗ − − ᴗ − − ᴗ −   mutaqārib musaddas maḥdūf
                nega:ra: koja:ʔi: bey-a:y ::
                        be-ǧorbat ʔaz i:n bas mapa:y
                                    (al-Moᵓjam)

* 1.1.09   ᴗ − − ᴗ − − ᴗ − −   mutaqārib musaddas sālim
                ʔala: ʔei siyah zolf-ba:ram ::
                        pari:ša:ntar az ru:zga:ram
                                    (Laᵓli)

+ 1.1.10   ᵕ — — ᵕ — — ᵕ — — —   <u>mutaqārib mutamman abtar</u>

maraː baː negaːram soxan baːšad ::
   nehaːniː soxanhᵅ:-ye cuːn šakkar
                    (al-Moˁjam)

o 1.1.05(2)   ᵕ — — ᵕ —|ᵕ — — ᵕ —   <u>mutaqārib murabbaˁ mahdūf</u>

* 1.1.11   ᵕ ⌐ — ᵕ — — ᵕ — — ᵕ —   <u>mutaqārib mutamman mahdūf</u>

pay-eː mahd-e ʔaṭfaːl-e jaːhat sazad ::
   ke ˁeqd-eː ṣorayyaː šavad baːz-piːc
                    (Šahid Balxi)

* 1.1.12   ᵕ — — ᵕ — — ᵕ — — ᵕ — — <u>mutaqārib mutamman sālim</u>

magar ḍeib o ˁeib-ast k-iːzad nadaːdat ::
   degar har ce baːyest daːniːyo daːriː
                    (Firuz Mašreqi)

* 1.1.06(2)   ᵕ — — ᵕ — —| ᵕ — — ᵕ — — <u>mutaqārib mutamman sālim</u>

co maːh az namuːdan . co xuːr az šanuːdan ::
   be-gaːh-eː rabuːdan . co šaːhiːn o baːziː
                    (Moṣˁabi)

* 1.1.07(2)   ᵕ — — ᵕ — — —| ᵕ — — ᵕ — — — <u>mutaqārib musaddas abtar</u>
                      (or <u>tawīl mutamman sālim</u>)

man az maːdariː zaːdam . ke paːram pedarʔuː
                                        buːd ::
   šodam xaːk-e ʔaːn paːʔiː . kaz iːn piːš-sar
                                        ʔuː buːd
                    (Ouḥadi)

o 1.1.08(2)   ᵕ — — ᵕ — — ᵕ—| ᵕ — — ᵕ — — ᵕ —

+ 1.2.07   — — ᵕ — — ᵕ —   <u>munsariḥ murabbaˁ muxtalif al-
                                      ajzāʔ</u>

ʔaːn ruːy-e ʔaːn tork biːn ::
   guːʔiː ke maːh-eː samaːst
                    (al-Moˁjam)

* 1.2.08   - - ⌄ - - ⌄ - -   <u>mutaqārib musaddas atlam</u>

solṭa:n-e seir-e: solu:kam ::
    farma:n-rava:y-e: molu:kam
      (Ṣafa Eṣfahani)

+ 1.2.10   - - ⌄ - - ⌄ - - ⌄ -   <u>mutaqārib mutamman atlam</u>
                                   <u>maḥdūf</u>

ya:r-e: saman-bar delam-ra: bebord ::
    bas dar ʕena: vu: neda:mat separd
      (al-Moʕjam)

* 1.2.05(2) - - ⌄ - - | - - ⌄ - -   <u>mutaqārib mutamman atlam</u>
                   (or <u>rajaz murabbaʕ muraffal</u>)

ʔei haft darya: . gouhar ʕaṭa: kon ::
    v-i:n mass-e ma:ra: . cu:n ki:miya: kon
      (Šams-e Tabriz)

o 1.2.11   - - ⌄ - - ⌄ - - ⌄ - -   <u>mutaqārib mutamman atram</u>

o 1.2.07(2) - - ⌄ - - ⌄ - | - - ⌄ - - - ⌄ -
                               <u>munsariḥ sālim al-</u>
         <u>ṣadrayn maṭwī maksuf al-ḍarbayn</u>

* 1.2.08(2) - - ⌄ - - ⌄ - - | - - ⌄ - - ⌄ - -

del bordiy az man be-yaq̇ma: . ʔei tork-e
                    q̇a:ratgar-e: man ::
    di:di: ce ʔa:vardiy a:xer . ʔaz dast-e
                del be:-sar-e: man
      (Ṣafa Eṣfahani)

o 1.3.09   - ⌄ - - ⌄ - - ⌄ -   <u>mutadārik musaddas sālim</u>

* 1.3.10   - ⌄ - - ⌄ - - ⌄ - -   <u>mutadārik mutamman aḥadd</u>

takye bar zandaga:ni rava: ni:st ::
    carx-ra: rasm-e mehr o vafa: ni:st
      (Pur Daʔud)

* 1.3.12   - ⌄ - - ⌄ - - ⌄ - - ⌄ -   <u>mutadārik mutamman sālim</u>
                 (or <u>muḥdat</u>, according to Adib
         Ṣaber & Rašid Vaṭvaṭ)

ʔei ṣabɑ: ṣobḥ-dam cu:n rasi: su:-ye ʔu: ::
ḥa:l-e man ʕarže deh bɑ: sag-e: ku:ye ʔu:
(Moštɑq)

* 1.3.07(2)   - ◡ - - ◡ - - | - ◡ - - ◡ - -

du:š mi:goft jɑ:nam . k-ei sepehr-e: moʕažžam
:: bas moʕallaq zanɑ:ni: . šoʕle-hɑ:
ʔandar aškam
(Šams-e Tabriz)

+ 2.1.07   ◡ - - - ◡ - -   hazaj murabbaʕ maḥdūf

beyɑ: jɑ:nɑ: kojɑ:ʔi: ::   cerɑ: zi: mɑ: nayɑ:ʔi:
(al-Moʕjam)

* 2.1.08   ◡ - - - ◡ - - -   hazaj murabbaʕ sālim

ce ʕešq-ast i:n ke dar del šod   ::
k-az u: pɑ:yam dar i:n gel šod
(Ouḥadi)

* 2.1.11   ◡ - - - ◡ - - - ◡ - -   hazaj musaddas maḥdūf

negɑ:ri:nɑ: be-naqd-e: jɑ:nt nadham   ::
gerɑ:ni: dar bahɑ: ʔarzɑ:nt nadham
(Maḥmud Varrɑq)

*2.1.12   ◡ - - - ◡ - - - ◡ - - -   hazaj musaddas sālim

agar bɑ: man degar kɑ:vi: xori: nɑ:gah   ::
be-sar bar ti:q̇ o bar pahlu:y šangi:ne:
(Farɑlɑvi)

* 2.1.14   ◡ - - - ◡ - - - ◡ - - - ◡ -   hazaj muṯamman majbūb

delam cu:n mɑ:r mi:pi:cad ze mehram sar mapi:c
:: roxat cu:n mɑ:h mi:tɑ:bad ze xɑ:ju: rox
matɑ:b
(Xɑju)

o 2.1.07(2)   ◡ - - - ◡ - - | ◡ - - - ◡ - -   hazaj murabbaʕ maḥdūf

+ 2.1.15   ◡ - - - ◡ - - - ◡ - - - ◡ - -   hazaj muṯamman maḥdūf

negɑ:ri:nɑ: ʔagar bɑ: man nadɑ:ri: dar del ɑ:zɑ:r

```
              :: be-qoul-e: došmanɑ:n az man ce gardi: xi:re
                                        bi:zɑ:r
                   (al-MoSjam)
```

* 2.1.16   ◡ - - - ◡ - - - ◡ - - - ◡ - - -   hazaj mu<u>t</u>amman salim

  2.1.08(2) yaki: ʔaz jɑ:y bar jestam . conɑ:n ši:r-e:
                biyɑ:bɑ:ni: ::   va ɖi:vi: bar zadam cu:n
                ši:r bar ru:bɑ:h-e darɖɑ:ni:
                   (Rabenjani)

+ 2.2.15   - - - ◡ - - - ◡ - - - ◡ - - -   hazaj mu<u>t</u>amman axram
                                                         al-ṣadr

            bar ferdous-e reẓvɑ:n gar na roxsɑ:rat dali:lasti:
            :: mardom-rɑ: suy-e: nɑ:-di:de di:dan kei
                                        sabi:lasti:
                   (al-MoSjam)

o 2.3.07   - - ◡ - - - -   rajaz murabbaS a<u>ḥadd</u> al-Saru<u>ḏ</u> wa l-
                                                         ḍarb

* 2.3.08   - - ◡ - - - ◡ -   <u>rajaz murabbaS salim</u>

            di:šab nafahmi:dam cerɑ: ::
                ranji:d ʔaz man yɑ:r-e man
                   (Sarmad)

+ 2.3.09   - - ◡ - - - ◡ - -   <u>rajaz murabbaS muraffal</u>

            bi: to: marɑ: zande: nabi:nand   ::   man <u>z</u>arre ʔam
                                to: ʔɑ:ftɑ:bi
                   (MeSyar)

+ 2.3.11   - - ◡ - - - ◡ - - - -   <u>rajaz musaddas maqtuS</u>

            Sɑ:šeq šodam bar delbari: Sayyɑ:ri   ::
                šokr-e: labi: si:mi:n-bari: xu:nxɑ:ri:
                   (al-MoSjam)

* 2.3.12   - - ◡ - - - ◡ - - - ◡ -   <u>rajaz musaddas salim</u>

            pi:š ɑ:r sɑ:qi: ʔɑ:n mey-e: cu:n zang-rɑ: ::
                tɑ: mɑ: bar andɑ:zi:m nɑ:m u: nang-rɑ:
                   (Ouḥadi)

* 2.3.04(3) -- ◡-| -- -- ◡-| -- -◡-   <u>rajaz musaddas sālim</u>

    šou bar go<u>z</u>ar . v-andar negar . yɑ: dar safar

    :: yɑ: dar ḥaẓar . di:di: pesar . z-u:

                                  xu:btar

              (Badiʕ Balxi)

* 2.3.13   -- -◡-- -- ◡-- -◡--   <u>rajaz musaddas muraffal</u>

    raḥm ei xodɑ:y-e: dɑ:dgar kardi: nakardi: ::

    ʔebqɑ: be-farzand-e: bašar kardi: nakardi:

              (ʕɑref)

*2.3.14   -- ◡-- -- ◡-- ◡---

    ʔakbar co di:d u: bi:kasi:-ye: šah-e baḥr u: bar

    gašte: ḍari:b u: bi:navɑ: ʔa:n vɑ:re<u>s</u>-e: ḥeidar

            (Šakeri)

*2.3.07(2)   -- ◡-- -- | -- ◡-- --   <u>hazaj murabbaʕ aštar</u>

                                <u>maḥdūf</u>

    su:d u: ziyɑ:n dar qalb-e: . bɑ:zɑ:riyɑ:n jɑ:

                            karde: ::

    parvɑ:y-e jɑ:n kei dɑ:ran⌣d i:n mardom-e:

                            souda:ʔi:

            (Reẓazɑde Šafaq)

\+ 2.3.15   -- ◡-- -- ◡-- ◡---   <u>rajaz mutamman maqtūʕ</u>

    tɑ: kei koni: mɑ:hɑ: setam . bar ʕɑ:šeq-e:

                        bi:cɑ:re: ::

    ru:zi: bovad k-az ju:r-e to: . gardad ze

                        šahr ɑ:vɑ:re:

            (Meʕyar)

* 2.3.08(2) -- ◡-- -◡-| -- ◡-- -◡-   <u>rajaz mutamman sālim</u>

  2.3.16   xu:šɑ: nabi:<u>d</u>-e: ḍɑ:reji: . bɑ: du:stɑ:n-e:

                           yak-dele: ::

    gi:ti: be-ʔɑ:rɑ:m andaru:n . majles be-bang

                        u: velvele:

        (Abu Salik Gorgani, or Šaker

          Boxɑri, or Rudagi)

* 2.3.09(2) -- ᴗ --- ᴗ -- │ -- ᴗ --- ᴗ -- <u>rajaz murabbaʕ</u>
<u>muraffal</u>

Ɂei ru:yat az ferdous bɑ:bi: . vaz sonbolat bar
gol neqɑ:bi: ::
har lahže-Ɂi: zɑ:n pic-tɑ:bi: . dar halq-e
jɑ:n-e: man tanɑ:bi:
(Xɑju)

+ 2.4.07   - ᴗ --- ᴗ -   <u>ramal murabbaʕ mahdūf</u>

bɑ:de bar gi:r ei sanam :: ru:d bar dɑ:r u: be-zan
(Meʕyar)

+ 2.4.08   - ᴗ --- ᴗ --   <u>ramal murabbaʕ sālim</u>

man hami:še: mostmandam :: v-az ɖam-e: ʕešqat
nežandam
(Meʕyar)

+ 2.4.09   - ᴗ --- ᴗ ---   <u>ramal musaddas mahdūf</u>

man torɑ: Ɂei bot xari:dɑ:ram ::
gar to mɑ:-rɑ: nɑ:-xari:dɑ:ri:
(al-Moʕjam)

* 2.4.05(2) - ᴗ --- │ - ᴗ ---

bešnav ei farzand . tɑ: Ɂaz i:n daftar ::
xɑ:namat Ɂaz bar . rɑ:z-e teimu:ri:
(Adibolmamɑlek)

* 2.4.11   - ᴗ --- ᴗ --- ᴗ -   <u>ramal musaddas mahdūf</u>

xu:n-e xod-rɑ: gar be-ri:zi: bar zami:n ::
beh ke Ɂɑ:b-e: ru:y ri:zi: dar kenɑ:r
(Abu Salik Gorgɑni)

* 2.4.12   - ᴗ --│- ᴗ --│- ᴗ --   <u>ramal musaddas sālim</u>

hargezat ʕɑ:dat na-bu:d i:n bi:-vafɑɁi: ::
ɖeir az i:ɳ noubat ke dar peivand-e mɑ:Ɂi:
(Ouhadi)

* 2.4.13   - ᴗ --│- ᴗ --│- ᴗ --│-   <u>ramal mutamman majhūf</u>

mɑ:h-e kɑ:nu:n ast žɑ:žak nɑ:-tavɑ:ni: bastan ::

ham ʔaz iːn kuːmak bar-eː xošk uː hamiː band
　　　　　　　　　　αːn-rαː
(Rabenjani)

* 2.4.15　　─ ᵕ ─ ─|─ ᵕ ─ ─|─ ᵕ ─ ─|─ ᵕ ─　　ramal mu<u>t</u>amman ma<u>ḫ</u>duf

ʔabr-e ʔaːzaːriː caman-hαː-rαː por az ḥourαː
　　　　　　　　　　konad ::
　　ba:d̨ por golbon konad golbon por az diːbαː
　　　　　　　　　　konad
(Manucehri)

* 2.4.16　　─ ᵕ ─ ─ ─ ᵕ ─ ─ ─ ᵕ ─ ─ ─ ᵕ ─ ─　　ramal mu<u>t</u>amman salim

sahmgiːn αːbiː ke mor d̨αːbiː dar uː ʔeiman na-buːdiː
:: kamtariːn mouj αːsyαː-sang az kenαːraš dar
　　　　　　　　　　rabuːdiː
(Saʕdi)

* 2.4.08(2)　　─ ᵕ ─ ─ ─ ᵕ ─ ─ | ─ ᵕ ─ ─ ─ ᵕ ─ ─　　ramal mu<u>t</u>amman salim

kαːr kαːr-eː ʕešq-e moškel . bαːr-eː hajr o
　　　　　　　　　　sangiːn ::
　　kαːr o bαːram dαːnad αːnku . dαːrad iːnsαːn
　　　　　　　　　　kαːr o bαːriː
(Ḥabib Yad̨maʔi)

+ 3.1.08　　ᵕ ᵕ ─ ─ ᵕ ᵕ ─ ─　　ramal murabbaʕ maxbun

delam αːvαːre to kardiː :: xeradam pαːk to bordiː
(al-Moʕjam)

* 3.1.11　　ᵕ ᵕ ─ ─ ᵕ ᵕ ─ ─ ᵕ ᵕ ─　　ramal musaddas maxbun ma<u>ḫ</u>duf

ruːzam az dardaš cuːn niːm-šab-ast ::
　　šabam az yαːdaš cuːn šαːvd̨arαː
(Rabenjani)

* 3.1.12　　ᵕ ᵕ ─ ─ ᵕ ᵕ ─ ─ ᵕ ᵕ ─ ─　　ramal musaddas maxbun

šakar-eː tang-e to tang-eː šakar αːmad ::
　　ḥoqqe-yeː laʕl-e to darj-eː gohar αːmad
(Xαju)

* 3.1.13 ‿ ‿ − − ‿ ‿ − − ‿ ‿ − − − <u>ramal mutamman maxbūn majhūf</u>

zeh-e dɑ:nɑ:-rɑ: gu:yand ke dɑ:nad goft   ::
    hi:c nɑ:dɑ:n-rɑ: dɑ:nande na-gu:yad zeh
        (Rudagi)

* 3.1.14 ‿ ‿ − − ‿ ‿ − − ‿ ‿ − − ‿ − <u>ramal mutamman maxbūn marbūʕ</u>

bot-e man gar be-sazɑ: hormat-e man dɑ:nadi: ::
    na marɑ: gah konadi: xɑ:r o gahi: rɑ:nadi:
        (al-Moʕjam)

* 3.1.07(2) ‿ ‿ − − ‿ ‿ − | ‿ ‿ − − ‿ ‿ − <u>madīd mutamman maxbūn</u>

yɑ:raki: hast marɑ: . be-leṭɑ:fat malaku: ::
    be-ḥalɑ:vat šakaru: . be-malɑ:ḥat namaku:
        (Qaʔɑni)

* 3.1.15 ‿ ‿ − − ‿ ‿ − − ‿ ‿ − − ‿ ‿ − <u>ramal mutamman maxbūn</u>
                                            <u>maḥdūf</u>

ʔei ʔami:ri: ke ʔami:rɑ:n-e jahɑ:n xɑ:ṣe va ʕa:m
    :: bande vu: cɑ:ker o moulɑ:t va sagband o
                                            ḍolɑ:m
        (Moḥammad b. Vaṣif)

* 3.1.16 ‿ ‿ − − ‿ ‿ − − ‿ ‿ − − ‿ ‿ − − <u>ramal mutamman maxbūn</u>

ʔei xodɑ:ʔi: ke be-joz to: malek-ol-ʕarš nadɑ:nam
    :: be-joz az nɑ:m-e to nɑ:mi: na bar ɑ:yad
                                            be-zabɑ:nam
        (Sanaʔi)

+ 3.2.07 ‿ − − ‿ ‿ − − <u>hazaj murabbaʕ makfūf maḥdūf</u>

cerɑ: bɑ:z nayɑ:ʔi: :: ʕazɑ:bam ce namɑ:ʔi:
        (al-Moʕjam)

+ 3.2.11 ‿ − − ‿ ‿ − − ‿ ‿ − − <u>hazaj musaddas makfūf maḥdūf</u>

siyah cašm o siyah zolf ḍolɑ:mi: ::
    tabah kard delam-rɑ: be-salɑ:mi:
        (al-Moʕjam)

* .2.07(2) ‿ − − ‿ ‿ − − | ‿ − − ‿ ‿ − − <u>hazaj mutamman makfūf</u>
                                            <u>maḥdūf</u>

ʔa lɑ: vaqt-e ṣabu:ḥast . na garm ast o na sard
                                             ast ::
    na ʔabr ast o na xorši:d . na bɑ:d ast o na
                           gard ast
                    (Manucehri)

* 3.2.15   ˅ - - ˅ ˅ - - ˅ ˅ - - ˅ ˅ - - hazaj mu<u>t</u>amman mak<u>fū</u>f
                                              ma<u>ḥdū</u>f

jahɑ:n-e: šode fartu:t co pɑ:ɖande sar u: gi:s ::
  konu:n gašt siyah mu:y o be-di:de: šod jammɑ:s
                    (Abu Šoʕeib)

* 3.3.06   - - ˅ ˅ - -   hazaj murabbaʕ axrab <u>makfūf</u> ma<u>ḥdū</u>f

man bi: to coni:n zɑ:r ::
    [to ʔaz du:r hami: xand]

             (al-Moʕjam)

o 3.3.07   - - ˅ ˅ - - -

+ 3.3.09   - - ˅ ˅ - - ˅ ˅ -   hazaj musaddas axrab <u>makfū</u>f
                                              <u>majbū</u>b

[jɑ:n az ṭarab u: del az neša:ṭ] ::
    tɑ: betvɑ:ni: bɑ:z madɑ:r
             (al-Moʕjam)

* 3.3.10   - - ˅ ˅ - - ˅ ˅ - -   hazaj musaddas axrab <u>makfū</u>f
                                              ma<u>ḥdū</u>f

tɑ: kei davam az gerd-e dar-e: to: ::
    k-andar to nami:bi:nam carbu:
             (Šahid Balxi)

* 3.3.05(2) - - ˅ ˅ - | - ˅ ˅ -   mutadārik maxbūn maqṭūʕ

talxi: nakonad . ši:ri:n <u>z</u>aqanam ::
    xɑ:li: nakonad . ʔaz mei dahanam
= 5.1.05(2)   (Šams-e Tabriz)

* 3.3.11   - - ˅ ˅ - - ˅ ˅ - - -   hazaj musaddas axrab <u>makfū</u>f
                                        <u>sā</u>lim al-ʕarū<u>ḍ</u> wa l-<u>ḍ</u>arb

sɑ:qi: bedeh ɑ:n golgu:n qarqaf-rɑ: ::
na:-ya:fte ʔaz ʔa:teš-e gaztaf-rɑ:
(Loukari)

* 3.3.06(2) -- ᵕ ᵕ -- | -- ᵕ ᵕ --

zɑ:n nafxe ke šod joft . bɑ: torbat-e ʔa:dam ::
ʔaz xɑ:k bar ɑ:mad . bar carx-e moˤaẓẓam
(Šams-e Tabriz)

* 3.3.13   -- ᵕ ᵕ -- ᵕ ᵕ -- ᵕ ᵕ - hazaj muṯamman axrab maqbūḏ
makfūf majbūb

jɑ:ʔi: ke gozargɑ:h-e del-e: maḥzu:nast ::
[ʔa:njɑ: do hazɑ:r ti:re bɑ:lɑ: xu:nast]
(Rudagi)
rubāˤī metre, cf. 5.1.13

* 3.3.14   -- ᵕ ᵕ -- ᵕ ᵕ -- ᵕ ᵕ -- hazaj muṯamman axrab makfūf
maḥdūf

ʔei ʔaz rox-e to: tɑ:fte zi:bɑ:ʔiy o ʔourang ::
ʔafru:xte ʔaz ṭalˤat-e to: masnad o ʔourang
(Šahid Balxi)

* 3.3.07(2) -- ᵕ ᵕ --- | -- ᵕ ᵕ --- hazaj axrab al-ṣadrayn
sālim al-ḍarbayn

tɑ: kei konad u: xɑ:ram . tɑ: kei zanad u:
sangam ::
farsu:de šavam ʔa:xer . gar ʔa:han o gar
sangam
(Abu Šakur)

* 3.3.15   -- ᵕ ᵕ -- ᵕ ᵕ -- ᵕ ᵕ --- hazaj muṯamman axrab
makfūf sālim al-ˤarūḍ wa l-ḍarb

tɑ: man pay-e ʔa:n zolf-e sar-afkande hami: dɑ:ram
:: cu:n šamˤ gahi: gerye va gah xande hami:
dɑ:ram
(Xɑqɑni)

+ 3.4.08   - ᵕ ᵕ -- ᵕ ᵕ - rajaz murabbaˤ maṭwī

```
              ǧa:liye zolfi: va be-rox  ::
              sorxtar az golna:ri:
                     (al-Moⁱjam)
```

o 3.4.09   - ᴜ - - - ᴜ - - -

+ 3.4.10   - ᴜ ᴜ - - ᴜ ᴜ - - -   sarīⁱ musaddas maṭwī aslam

```
              cand xoram ?az to bota: ẓarbat  ::
              cand zani: bar del-e man ḥarbat
                     (al-Moⁱjam)
```

* 3.4.05(2)   - ᴜ ᴜ - - | - ᴜ ᴜ - -

```
              ja:n-e man ast u:  .  hei ma-bari:daš  ::
              ?a:n-e man ast u:  .  hei ma-koši:daš
                     (Moulavi)
```

*3.4.11   - ᴜ ᴜ - - ᴜ ᴜ - - ᴜ -   sarīⁱ musaddas maṭwī maksūf

```
              ku:šeš-e bande: sabab az baxšeš ast  ::
              ka:r-e qaẓa: bu:d o tora: ⁱeib ni:st
                     (Moḥammad b. Vaṣif)
```

* 3.4.12   - ᴜ ᴜ - - ᴜ ᴜ - - ᴜ ᴜ -   rajaz musaddas maṭwī

```
              na:m-e labat cu:n be-zaba:n mi:ya:yad  ::
              ?a:b-e ḥaya:tam be-daha:n mi:ya:yad
                     (Jami)
```

* 3.4.06(2)   - ᴜ ᴜ - - - | - ᴜ ᴜ - - -   sarīⁱ murabbaⁱ maṭwī aslam

```
              ba:z co dalla:ka:n  .  ni:štari: da:ri:  ::
              bahr-e del azordan  .  šu:r o šari: da:ri:
                     (Šehab Toršizi)
```

* 3.4.13   - ᴜ ᴜ - - ᴜ ᴜ - - ᴜ ᴜ - -   sarīⁱ mutamman maṭwī manhūr

```
              xosrav-e ?anjom be-gah-e: ba:m bar a:mad  ::
              ya: mah-e xallox be-lab-e: ba:m bar a:mad
                     (Xaju)
```

+ 3.4.14   - ᴜ ᴜ - - ᴜ ᴜ - - ᴜˇᴜ - - -   rajaz mutamman maṭwī aḥadd

```
              sarv ast a:n ya: ba:la:  .  ma:h ast a:n ya: ru:y
              :: zolf ast a:n ya: couga:n  .  xa:l ast a:n
                                                  ya: ku:y
```

(al-Moⁿjam)

* 3.4.16   - ᵕ ᵕ - - ᵕ ᵕ - - ᵕ ᵕ - - ᵕ ᵕ -   rajaz mu_tamman matwī

  3.4.08(2) ⁿešq-e to ba-rbu:d ze man . mɑ:ye-ye mɑ:ʔi:y o
                                           mani: ::
              xod nabovad ⁿešq-e torɑ: . cɑ:re ze
                                            bi:-xi:štani:
              (Sanɑ?i)

+ 4.1.08   ᵕ - ᵕ - ᵕ ᵕ -   mujtatt murabbaⁿ maxbūn

              jafɑ: makon ke naša:yad ::
              rahi: ma-koš ke na-bɑ:yad
              (al-Moⁿjam)

* 4.1.05(2) ᵕ - ᵕ - - | ᵕ - ᵕ - -   mutaqārib mu_tamman maqbūd
                                                          a_tlam

              gol-e: bahɑ:ri: . bot-e: tata:ri: ::
                nabi:d dɑ:ri: . cerɑ: nayɑ:ri:
              (Rudagi)

+ 4.1.11   ᵕ - ᵕ - ᵕ ᵕ - - ᵕ - -   mujtatt musaddas maxbūn makbūl

              morɑ:d-e rɑ:y-e yaki: yɑ:r dɑ:ram :: ....
              (Tarjomɑnol-Balɑɖe)

* 4.1.12   ᵕ - ᵕ - ᵕ ᵕ - - ᵕ - ᵕ - mujtatt musaddas maxbūn

              [conɑ:n tɑ:fte tar gaštam az nahi:b] ::
                ke gaštam az ɖam o ʔandi:še nɑ:šaki:b
              cf. 4.6.03/08 (ⁿamɑre Marvazi)

+ 4.1.04/08 ᵕ - ᵕ - ....ᵕ - ᵕ - ᵕ ᵕ - -   qarīb musaddas maqbūd

              negɑ:r-e man sevɑ:r-e man be-safar šod ::
              hami: ravad co sarkašɑ:n be-jahɑ:n dar
              (al-Moⁿjam)

* 4.1.13   ᵕ - ᵕ - ᵕ ᵕ - - ᵕ - ᵕ - -   mujtatt maxbūn majhūf

              boti: ke ɖamzaš sandɑ:n konad go_zɑ:re: ::
              delam be-možgɑ:n kardast pɑ:re pɑ:re:

(Daqiqi)

* 4.1.15   ◡ - ◡ - ◡ ◡ - - ◡ - ◡ - ◡ ◡ -   mujtatt mutamman maxbūn
                                                          maḥdūf

mara: be-ja:n-e to sougand o ṣaʕb sougandi: ::
ke hargez az to na-gardam na bešnavam pandi:
(Šahid Balxi)

* 4.1.16   ◡ - ◡ - ◡ ◡ - - ◡ - ◡ - ◡ ◡ - -   mujtatt mutamman maxbūn

hame: niyu:še-ye xa:je: be-ni:kuʔi:y o be-ṣolḥ
                                                      ast ::
hame: niyu:še-ye na:da:n be-jang o fetne va
                                   ḍouḍa:st
(Rudagi)

* 4.1.05(4) ◡ - ◡ - - | ◡ - ◡ - - | ◡ - ◡ - - | ◡ - ◡ - -

na-xa:nd ṭefl-e: . jonu:n-meza:jam . xaṭi: ze
                    past u:. boland-e hasti: ::
      šavam fela:ṭu: . n-e molk-e da:neš . agar
                šena:sam . sar az kaf-e: pa:
(Bidel)

+ 4.2.07   - ◡ - ◡ ◡ - -   mušākil murabbaʕ maḥdūf

ru:zga:r-e xaza:n ast :: ba:d-e sard vaza:n ast
(al-Moʕjam)

o 4.2.11   - ◡ - ◡ ◡ - - ◡ - ◡ -

+4.2.07/04 - ◡ - ◡ ◡ - -,. . . . . ◡ ◡ - -   mušākil musaddas
                                                          makfūf maḥdūf

ʔei nega:r-e siyah-cašm-e siyah-mu:y ::
      sarv-e qadd-e neku:-ru:y-e neku:-gu:y
(al-Moʕjam)

* 4.2.14   - ◡ - ◡ ◡ - - ◡ - ◡ - ◡ ◡ -   mujtatt mutamman maxbūn
                                                          marfūʕ

bar sax a:vat-e ʔu: ni:l-ra: baxi:l šoma:r ::
bar šoja:ʕat-e ʔu: pi:l-ra: zali:l anga:r
(Manṭeqi Razi)

o 4.2.07(2) - ⌣ - ⌣ ⌣ - - | - ⌣ - ⌣ ⌣ - - mušākil mutamman mahdūf

+ 4.2.15 - ⌣ - ⌣ ⌣ - - ⌣ - ⌣ - ⌣ ⌣ - - mušākil mutamman makfūf
mahdūf

ka:r-e ja:n ze ǧam-e: ʕešqat ei nega:r be-sa:ma:n
:: hast cu:n sar-e zolfein-e del-roba:t
pari:ša:n
(al-Moʕjam)

* 4.4.07 - ⌣ ⌣ - - ⌣ - munsarih murabbaʕ matwī maksūf

molk-e malek ʔa:rsla:n :: sa:ken-e rouzol-jena:n
(Masʕud Saʕd Salman)

o 4.4.08 - ⌣ ⌣ - - ⌣ - - munsarih murabbaʕ matwī

* 4.4.10 - ⌣ ⌣ - - ⌣ - ⌣ - - munsarih musaddas matwī maxbūn
ahadd

ʔei be-to bar pa:y-e šahrya:ri: ::
v-ei be-to bar ja:y-e pa:dša:hi:
(Masʕud Saʕd Salman)

* 4.4.12 - ⌣ ⌣ - - ⌣ - ⌣ - ⌣ ⌣ - munsarih musaddas matwī

herze va mefla:k bi: niya:z az to: ::
ba: to bara:bar ke ra:z bogša:yad
(Abu Šakur Balxi)

* 4.4.05/07 - ⌣ ⌣ - - ....⌣ ⌣ - - - ⌣ - -

del havas-e: sabze va sahra: nada:rad ::
meil be-golgašt o tama:ša: nada:rad
(ʕaref)

* 4.4.13 - ⌣ ⌣ - - ⌣ - ⌣ - ⌣ ⌣ - - munsarih mutamman matwī
manhūr (or munsarih musaddas
matwī muraffal)

hi:zom xa:ham hami: do ʔamne ze ju:dat ::
cu:n do jari:b u: do xomm-e si:ki: cu:n xu:n
(Rabenjani)

* 4.4.05/08 - ⌣ ⌣ - - ....⌣ ⌣ - - ⌣ -⌣ -

del be-jaha:n bastanat ei ja:n-e man xaṭa:st ::
za:n ke jaha:n xa:ne-ye ʔandu:h o ʔebtela:st
(Adib Ṭusi)

* 4.4.07(2)   - ᴗ ᴗ - - ᴗ - | - ᴗ ᴗ - - ᴗ -   munsariḥ muṯamman maṭwī
                                                           maksūf

qand joda: kon ʔaz u:y . du:r šav az zahr-e
                                         dand ::
harce be-ʔa:xer beh-ast . ja:n-e tora:
                                ʔa:n pasand
(Rudagi)

o 4.4.15   - ᴗ ᴗ - - ᴗ - ᴗ - ᴗ ᴗ - - ᴗ-   munsariḥ muṯamman maṯwī
                                                           maksūf
cf. 4.4.07(2)

+ 4.5.08   ᴗ ᴗ - - ᴗ - ᴗ -   ḋarīb murabbaʕ maxbūn (or xafīf
                                        murabbaʕ maxbūn)

del-e man mi: cera: bari: ::
cu:n ḋam-e: man na-mi:xori:
(al-Moʕjam)

+ 4.5.09   ᴗ ᴗ - - ᴗ - ᴗ - -   xafīf musaddas maxbūn majḥūf

rox-e cu:n a:yene: ze xorši:d ::
zade bar ru:y-e naqš-e ʔa:za:r
(al-Moʕjam)

* 4.5.11   ᴗ ᴗ - - ᴗ - ᴗ - ᴗ ᴗ -   xafīf musaddas maxbūn maḥḏūf

mehtari: gar be-ka:m-e ši:r dar ast ::
šou xaṭar-kon ze ka:m-e ši:r be-ju:y
(Ḥanżale Baḋḋisi)

* 4.5.12   ᴗ ᴗ - - ᴗ - ᴗ - ᴗ ᴗ - -   xafīf musaddas maxbūn

sabze-ha: nou dami:d o ya:r naya:rad ::
sare šod ba:ḋ o ʔa:n baha:r nayᵅ:mad
(Amir Xosrou)

* 4.5.04/08 ᴗ ᴗ - - .... ᴗ ᴗ - - ᴗ - ᴗ -   ḋarīb (jadīd)
                                                   musaddas maxbūn

ʔajal ar ʔaz gel-e man gol bar ɑ:varad   ::
  gol-e man bɑ:d-e havɑ:yat be-parvarad
        (Salmɑn Saveji)

* 4.5.04/11 ᴗ ᴗ − − . . . . ᴗ ᴗ − −ᴗ − ᴗ − ᴗ ᴗ −

  tɑ: padi:d ɑ:madat emsɑ:l xaṭṭ-e ḍɑ:liye-bɑ:r   ::
  ḍɑ:liye: ti:r šod u: bu:y-e xu:nš ʕanbar
                                    xɑ:r
        (Abu Manṣur Marvazi)

* 4.5.16   ᴗ ᴗ − − ᴗ − ᴗ − ᴗ ᴗ − − ᴗ − ᴗ − xafīf muṭamman maxbūn

  4.5.08(2) gar konad yɑ:riy-e: marɑ: be-ḍam-e: ʕešq-e ʔɑ:n
                                                 sanam   ::
             be-tavɑ:nad zadu:d z-i:n del-e ḍamxɑ:re
                                  zang-e ḍam
        (Rudagi)

+ 4.6.07   ᴗ − − ᴗ − ᴗ − muḍāriʕ murabbaʕ makfūf maḥḍūf

  marɑ: košt bi: ḥadi:d   ::
     siyah cašm-e bu: saʕi:d
        (al-Moʕjam)

+ 4.6.09   ᴗ − − ᴗ − ᴗ − ᴗ − muḍāriʕ musaddas makfūf matmūs

  del az yɑ:r-e bi:-vafɑ: be-kaš   ::
     bovad yɑ:r-e bi:-vafɑ: naxoš
        (al-Moʕjam)

* 4.6.10   ᴗ − − ᴗ − ᴗ − ᴗ ᴗ −

  be-rɑ:di:š rɑ:d mɑ:nd be-zeft   ::
     be-mardi:š mard mɑ:nd be-zan
        (Šɑker)

o 4.6.11   ᴗ − − ᴗ − ᴗ − ᴗ ᴗ − − muḍāriʕ musaddas makfūf mahdūf

* 4.6.03/08 ᴗ − − . . . . ᴗ ᴗ − − ᴗ − ᴗ − garīb musaddas makfūf
                                                            mahḍūf

     na hamcu:n rox-e xu:bat gol-e: bahɑ:r   ::
        na cu:n to: be-neku:ʔi: bot-e: bahɑ:r
             (Farɑlavi)

o 4.6.03/09 ◡ − − .... ◡ ◡ − − ◡ − ◡ − − <u>qarīb musaddas makfūf</u>

* 4.6.07(2) ◡ − − ◡ − ◡ −   ◡ − − ◡ − ◡ −

        bed-i:n xorrami: jahɑ:n . bed-i:n tɑ:zagi:
                                  bahɑ:r ::
           bed-i:n roušani: šarɑ:b . bed-i:n ni:kuʔi:
                                  negɑ:r
           (Farroxi)

* 4.6.15   ◡ − − ◡ − ◡ − ◡ ◡ − − ◡ − ◡ − <u>muḍāriʕ muṯamman makfūf</u>
                                              <u>maḥdūf</u>

        jahɑ:n-ra: ʔagarce hast farɑ:vɑ:n kade: rasad ::
        ham az bandagɑ:nš har kadeʔi:-ra: kadi:vari:
           (ʕonṣori)

o 4.6.08(2) ◡ − − ◡ − ◡ − − │ ◡ − − ◡ − ◡ − −

* 4.7.06   − − ◡ − ◡ − <u>muḍāriʕ murabbaʕ axrab maḥdūf</u>
        di:šab ke bastaram :: bar bɑ:m-e xɑ:ne bu:d
           (Sarmad)

+ 4.7.07   − − ◡ − ◡ − − <u>munsariḥ murabbaʕ maxbūn maksūf</u>
        ḥalqe: šodast poštam :: hamcu: do zolfakɑ:nat
           (al-Moʕjam)

o 4.7.08   − − ◡ − ◡ − ◡ −

* 4.7.10   − − ◡ − ◡ − ◡ ◡ − − <u>muḍāriʕ musaddas axrab makfūf</u>
                                             <u>maḥdūf</u>

        ʔemru:z hi:c xalq co man ni:st ::
        joz ranj az i:n nahi:f badan ni:st
           (Masʕud Saʕd Salmɑn)

* 4.7.02/08 − − .... ◡ ◡ − − ◡ − ◡ − <u>qarīb musaddas axrab</u>
                                              <u>makfūf maḥdūf</u>

        ʔei man rahiy ɑ:n ru:y-e cu:n qamar ::
        v-ɑ:n zolf-e šabe:-rang por ze mɑ:z
           (Šahid Balxi)

* 4.7.11   − − ◡ − ◡ − ◡ ◡ − − − <u>muḍāriʕ musaddas axrab makfūf</u>
                                        <u>sālim al ʕarūḍ wa l-ḍarb</u>

gar dangal ɑ:madast pesar tɑ: kei ::
    bar bandiyaš be-ʔɑ:xor-e har mehtar
    (Rabenjani)

* 4.7.02/09 - - .... ᴗ ᴗ - - ᴗ - ᴗ - -   <u>qarīb musaddas axrab</u>
                                           <u>makfūf</u>

bar xɑ:n-e vey andar miyɑ:n-e xɑ:ne: ::
    ham nɑ:n-e tanok bu:d o ham venɑ:ne:
    (Daqiqi)

* 4.7.12   - - ᴗ - ᴗ - ᴗ ᴗ - - ᴗ -   <u>muḍāriʕ mutamman axrab makfūf</u>
                                             <u>maṭmūs</u>

ʔei zi:nahɑ:r-e xɑ:r bed-i:n ru:zgɑ:r ::
    ʔaz yɑ:r-e xi:štan ke xorad zi:nahɑ:r
    (Farroxi)

* 4.7.06(2) - - ᴗ - ᴗ - | - - ᴗ - ᴗ -

ʔei karde mɑ:h-rɑ: . ʔaz ti:re šab neqɑ:b ::
    dar šab fekande ci:n . bar mah fekande
                                       tɑ:b
    (Xɑju)

* 4.7.02/11 - - .... ᴗ ᴗ - - ᴗ - ᴗ - ᴗ ᴗ -

ʔaḥmaq ʔagar az toxme-e: keyɑ:n bɑ:šad ::
    bi:-qadr-tar az toxm-e mɑ:kiyɑ:n bɑ:šad
    (Qɑʔani)

* 4.7.14   - - ᴗ - ᴗ - ᴗ ᴗ - - ᴗ - ᴗ -   <u>muḍāriʕ mutamman axrab</u>
                                           <u>makfūf maḥdūf</u>

yɑ:ram sepand agarce bar ɑ:teš hami: fegand ::
    ʔaz bahr-e cašm tɑ: narasad mar verɑ: gazand
    (Ḥanẓale Bɑḍǧisi)

* 4.7.07(2) - - ᴗ - ᴗ - - | - - ᴗ - ᴗ - -   <u>muḍāriʕ mutamman axrab</u>
                                           <u>al-ṣadrayn</u>

raftam be-mɑ:h-e rouze: . bɑ:zɑ:r-e marsmande:
    :: tɑ: gu:sfand ʔɑ:ram . farbeh konam
                                      be-rande:
              (Rabenjani)

* 4.7.15   − − ∪ − ∪ − ∪ ∪ − − ∪ − ∪ − −   <u>mudāriʕ</u> <u>mutamman</u> axrab
makfūf sālim al-ʕarūḍ wa l-ḍarb

di:di: ke hi:c-gu:ne mora: ʕa:t-e man na-kardi: ::
dar ka:r-e man qadam na-neha:di: be-pa:ymardi:
(Xaqani)

o 4.7.08(2)   − − ∪ − ∪ − ∪ − | − − ∪ − ∪ − ∪ −   ramal <u>mutamman</u> <u>sālim</u>
<u>wa maxbūn</u>

+ 4.8.08   − ∪ − ∪ − ∪ ∪ −   <u>muqtaḍab murabbaʕ maṭwī</u>

tork-e xu:b-ru:y-e mara: ::
gu: cera: na xoš-maneši:
(al-Moʕjam)

* 4.8.05(2)   − ∪ − ∪ − | − ∪ − ∪ −

xaṭṭ-e ʕanbari:n . bar šakar ma-kaš ::
ṭouq-e mošk-ci:n . gerd-e xor ma-kaš
(Jami)

+ 4.8.11   − ∪ − ∪ − ∪ ∪ − − ∪ −   <u>muqtaḍab musaddas maṭwī marfūʕ</u>

ʔa:n bozorgva:r malek faẓl kard ::
dar gozašt har ce ze man di:de bu:d
(al-Moʕjam)

+ 4.8.16   − ∪ − ∪ − ∪ ∪ − − ∪ − ∪ − ∪ ∪ −   <u>muqtaḍab mutamman maṭwī</u>

ʔei nešaste ḍa:fel o bar kaf neha:de raṭl-e zari:
:: hi:c ʔandoh u: ḍam-e ʔa:n ru:z ba:z pas
na-xori:
(al-Moʕjam)

* 4.8.08(2)   − ∪ − ∪ − ∪ ∪ − | − ∪ − ∪ − ∪ ∪ −   <u>muqtaḍab mutamman</u>
<u>maṭwī</u>

dar baha:r o mousem-e gol . zandagi:st bas
del-xa:h ::
vi:že ʔar nega:r va mei . hast hamdam u:
ham-ra:h
cf. 5.5.07(2)
(Pur DaʔudE)

* 4.8.05(4) - ᵕ - ᵕ - | - ᵕ - ᵕ - | - ᵕ - ᵕ - | - ᵕ - ᵕ - <u>ramal</u>
                            mu<u>t</u>amman makfū̱f maj<u>ḫ</u>ū̱f

    yɑ:raki: mɑrɑ:st . rend o ba<u>z</u>le-gu: . šu:x o
                          del-robɑ: . xu:b o xoš-serest
    :: <u>t</u>orre-ʔaš ʕabi:r . peikaraš ḥari:r .
        ʕɑ:reẓaš baha:r . <u>t</u>alʕataš behešt
        (QɑʔɑnI)

+ 5.1.08   - - ᵕ ᵕ - ᵕ - -   <u>qarīb musaddas ma<u>t</u>mū̱s</u>

    dɑ:rande-e mɑ: xodɑ:yast ::
      ru:zi:-deh-e mɑ: be-jɑ:yast
      (al-Moʕjam)

+ 5.1.09   - - ᵕ ᵕ - ᵕ - ᵕ -   <u>hazaj musaddas axrab makfū̱f</u>
                                              <u>majbū̱b</u>

    jɑ:n az <u>t</u>arab u: del az nešɑ:<u>t</u> ::
      [tɑ: betvɑ:ni: bɑ:z madɑ:r]
    cf. 3.3.09
                          (al-Moʕjam)

* 5.1.10   - - ᵕ ᵕ - ᵕ - ᵕ - -   <u>hazaj musaddas axrab al-ṣadrayn</u>
                <u>maqbū̱<u>d</u> al-ḥašawayn mah<u>d</u>ū̱f al-ḍarbayn</u>

    dar janb-e ʕolu:v-e hemmatat carx ::
      mɑ:nande-ye vošm pi:š-e carǧ ast
      (Abu Salik Gorgɑni)

* 5.1.05(2)   - - ᵕ ᵕ - | - - ᵕ ᵕ -   <u>mutadārik mu<u>t</u>amman maxbū̱n</u>
                                                   <u>maq<u>t</u>ū̱ʕ</u>

    talxi: nakonad . ši:ri:n <u>z</u>aqanam ::
      xɑ:li: nakonad . ʔaz mei dahanam
    = 3.3.05(2)   (Šams-e Tabriz)

* 5.1.11   - - ᵕ ᵕ - ᵕ - ᵕ - - -   <u>hazaj musaddas axrab al-ṣadrayn</u>
                <u>maqbū̱<u>d</u> al-ḥašawayn sālim al-ḍarbayn</u>

    morǧi:st xadang ʔei ʕajab di:di: ::
      morǧi: ke hame: šekɑ:r-e ʔu: jɑ:nɑ:

(Firuz Mašreqi)

* 5.1.13   ‒ ‒ ⏑ ⏑ ‒ ⏑ ‒ ⏑ ‒ ‒ ⏑ ⏑ ‒   hazaj mu<u>t</u>amman axrab maqbū<u>d</u>
makfūf majbūb

ʔei qɑːmat-e toː be-ṣuːrat-eː kɑːvanjak ::
hasti: to be-cašm-e har kasi: bolkanjak
(Šahid Balxi)

+ 5.1.15   ‒ ‒ ⏑ ⏑ ‒ ⏑ ‒ ⏑ ‒ ‒ ⏑ ⏑ ‒ ‒ ‒   hazaj mu<u>t</u>amman axrab
5.1.09/6   maqbū<u>d</u> makfūf ṣaḥīḥ al-ʕarū<u>d</u> wa l-ḍarb

ʔɑːn sarv-e sahiː ke bɑːr-e xoršiːd ravɑːn dɑːrad
 :: [hamvɑːre setɑːre ʔaz do cašm-e man ravɑːn
dɑːrad]
(al-Moʕjam)

+ 5.2.07   ‒ ⏑ ⏑ ‒ ⏑ ‒ ‒   munsariḥ murabbaʕ maxbūn maksūf

delbar-e man kojɑː raft :: v-az bar-e man
cerɑː raft
(al-Moʕjam)

* 5.2.11   ‒ ⏑ ⏑ ‒ ⏑ ‒ ⏑ ‒ ‒ ⏑ ‒

tɑː del-e man ze dast-e man nastadiː ::
sar be-sar ei negɑːr diːgar šodiː
(Farroxi)

o 5.2.12   ‒ ⏑ ⏑ ‒ ⏑ ‒ ⏑ ‒ ‒ ⏑ ⏑ ‒   rajaz musaddas ma<u>t</u>wī maxbun

+ 5.2.08/04   ‒ ⏑ ⏑ ‒ ⏑ ‒ ⏑ ‒ .... ⏑ ‒ ⏑ ‒   rajaz musaddas
ma<u>t</u>wī maxbūn

bar man-e xaste-jɑːn makon coniːn setam ::
k-iːn delam az pay-eː to šod coniːn be-ḍam
(al-Moʕjam)

* 5.2.08(2)   ‒ ⏑ ⏑ ‒|⏑ ‒ ⏑ ‒|‒ ⏑ ⏑ ‒|⏑ ‒ ⏑ ‒   rajaz mu<u>t</u>amman ma<u>t</u>wī
maxbūn

5.2.16   bɑː to padiːd́ miːkonam . ḥɑːlːe tabɑːh-e
xiːš-rɑː ::
tɑː to naṣiːḥati: koni: . cašm-e siyɑːh-e
xiːš-rɑː

(Nežami)

+ 5.2.12/04 - ◡ ◡ - ◡ - ◡ - - ◡ ◡ - .... - ◡ ◡ - rajaz muṯamman
+ 5.2.08/08 - ◡ ◡ - ◡ - ◡ - .... ◡ - ◡ - - ◡ ◡ - maṯwī maxbūn

    bas co toʔi: negɑ:r-e man v-az do jahɑ:n
                    bi:zɑ:ram ::
    kon nažari: be-kɑ:r-e man v-agar na del
                    bar dɑ:ram
    (al-Moʕjam)

* 5.2.04/12 - ◡ ◡ - .... - ◡ ◡ - ◡ - ◡ - - ◡ ◡ - rajaz juzʔ
                āxir al-ḥašw maxbūn wa l-bāqī maṯwī

    dast-e kasi: bar narasad be-šɑ:x-e hovvi:yat-e to:
    :: ta: rag-e ʔanni:yat-e ʔu: ze bi:x o bon
                bar nakani:
    (Sanɑʔi)

* 5.3.06(2) ◡ ◡ - ◡ - - | ◡ ◡ - ◡ - -

    del-e man ke bɑ:šad . ke torɑ: nabɑ:šad ::
      tan-e man ke bɑ:šad . ke fenɑ: nabɑ:sad
      (Šams-e Tabriz)

+ 5.3.03/09 ◡ ◡ - .... - ◡ ◡ - ◡ - ◡ - - ramal musaddas
                          maškūl

    ʔei ṣanam ni:z zamɑ:naki: vafɑ: dɑ:r ::
      magozar ti:z coni:n bar asb-e rahvɑ:r
      (al-MoʕjaM)

* 5.3.14 ◡ ◡ - ◡ - ◡ - - ◡ ◡ - ◡ - -

    ce konam ḥadi:s̱-e šakkar co labat gazi:dam ::
      ce konam nabɑ:t-e meṣri: co šakar mazi:dam
      (Xɑju)

* 5.3.15 ◡ ◡ - ◡ - ◡ - - ◡ ◡ - ◡ - ◡ -

    ze delat ce dɑ:d xɑ:ham ke na dɑ:var-e: mani: ::
      ze ḍamat ce šɑ:d bɑ:sam ke na ḍam-xor-e:
                    mani:
    (Xɑqɑni)

* 5.3.16   ◡◡ − ◡ − ◡ − − ◡◡ − ◡ − ◡ − −   <u>ramal mutamman maškūl</u>
                              <u>sālim al-ʕarūḏ wa l-ḍarb</u>

         sar-e zolf-rɑ: matɑ:bɑ:n . sar-e zolf-rɑ: ce
                                                   tɑ:bi: ::
         ke dar ɑ:n do zolf nɑ:-tɑ:ftagi: be-tɑ:b
                                                   mɑ:nad
         cf. 6.2.08(2)
                         (Farroxi)

+ 5.4.12   ◡ − ◡ − ◡ − − ◡◡ − ◡ −

         cerɑ: hami: negɑ:rɑ: to jafɑ: koni: ::
              vafɑ: kon ar na yɑ:ri: to jafɑ: makon
                         (al-Moʕjam)

o 5.4.13   ◡ − ◡ − ◡ − − ◡◡ − ◡ − −

+ 5.4.07(2)   ◡ − ◡ − ◡ − − | ◡ − ◡ − ◡ − −   <u>hazaj mutamman maqbūḏ</u>
                                    <u>maḥḏūf al-ḥašw wa l-ḍarb</u>

         marɑ: ḍam-e: to ʔei du:st . ze xɑ:n o mɑ:n bar
                                                   ɑ:vard ::
              marɑ: ferɑ:qat ei mɑ:h . ze mɑ:l o jɑ:n
                                                   bar ɑ:vard
         cf. 6.1.07(2)
                         (al-Moʕjam)

o 5.4.15   ◡ − ◡ − ◡ − − ◡◡ − ◡ − ◡ − −   <u>hazaj mutamman maqbūḏ</u>
                                    <u>makfūf maḥḏūf</u>

o 5.4.16   ◡ − ◡ − ◡ − − ◡◡ − ◡ − ◡ − − −

+ 5.4.08(2)   ◡ − ◡ − ◡ − − − | ◡ − ◡ − ◡ − − −   <u>hazaj mutamman maqbūḏ</u>
                                      <u>al-ṣadr</u>

         cerɑ: hami: negɑ:ri:nam . hami:še nazd-e man
                                                   nɑ:yad ::
              [tɑ: marɑ: nabɑ:yad zɑ:r . nɑ:li:dan
                                   be-dard-e del]
                         (al-Moʕjam)

+ 5.5.08   − ◡ − ◡ − − ◡ −   <u>muqtaḍab murabbaʕ maṭwī sālim al-</u>
                                    <u>ʕarūḏ wa l-ḍarb</u>

```
                    dast bɑ:z dɑ:r az delam  ::
                    v-ar na jɑ:n ze tan bogselam
                           (al-MoꞶjam)
```

* 5.5.07(2) - ᴗ - ᴗ - - - | - ᴗ - ᴗ - - -   hazaj mut̲amman aštar
                                                            al-ṣadr

```
         vaqt-rɑ: ḍani:mat dɑ:n  .  ?ɑ:n-qadar ke betvɑ:ni:
         ::  ḥa:ṣel az ḥayɑ:t ei jɑ:n  .  ?i:n dam ast
                                                    nɑ:dɑ:ni:
                           (Ḥɑfeż)
```

o 5.5.08(2) - ᴗ - ᴗ - - ᴗ - | - ᴗ - ᴗ - - ᴗ -

+ 5.6.07   ᴗ - ᴗ - - ᴗ -   mujtat̲t̲ murabbaꞶ maxbūn maḥdūf

```
         delam be-to: hast šɑ:d  ::  torɑ: ze man ni:st
                                               yɑ:d
                           (al-MoꞶjam)
```

+ 5.6.04/07 ᴗ - ᴗ - .... ᴗ - ᴗ - - ᴗ -   sarīꞶ musaddas maxbūn
                                                           mat̲wī maksūf

```
         do ḍamze cu:n do nɑ:jex-e: laškari:  ::
             hami: koni: be-har do ?ɑ:n delbari:
                           (al-MoꞶjam)
```

+ 5.6.12   ᴗ - ᴗ - - ᴗ ᴗ - ᴗ - ᴗ -   rajaz musaddas maxbūn mud̲āl
                                                         al-Ꞷarūd̲

```
         zami:n mobaꞶꞶad nabovad ?az ɑ:smɑ:n  ::
             conɑ:nke baxl-e: to ze to: mobaꞶꞶad :
                           (al-MoꞶjam)
```

+ (variant) - - ᴗ - - ᴗ ᴗ - ᴗ - ᴗ -   rajaz musaddas sālim al-ṣadrayn
                                             mat̲wī al-ḥašawayn maxbūn al-ḍarbayn

```
         har cand bar man ze ḍamat qiyɑ:mat ast  ::
             Ꞷɑ:šeq šodan joz be-to bar ḍorɑ:mat ast
                           (al-MoꞶjam)
```

* 5.6.07(2) ᴗ - ᴗ - - ᴗ- | ᴗ - ᴗ - - ᴗ -   munsariḥ mut̲amman maxbūn
                                                      mat̲wī maksūf

```
         jahɑ:n-e fartu:t bɑ:z  .  javɑ:niy az sar gereft
```

```
          ::  be-sar ze yɑ:qu:t-e sorx  .  šaqɑ:yeq afsar
                                               gereft
                    (QɑʔɑnI)
```

* 5.6.08(2) ᴗ - ᴗ - - ᴗ ᴗ - | ᴗ - ᴗ - - ᴗ ᴗ - rajaz mu̱tamman maxbūn
                                                              ma̱twī

5.6.16   feɖɑ:n konɑ:n har sa̤hari: . be-ku:y-e to:
                                               mi:go̱zaram ::
              co ni:st rah su:y-e to ʔam . be-su:y-e to:
                                               mi:go̱zaram
           cf. 5.2.12/04
                    (Jɑmi)

* 6.1.12   ᴗ - ᴗ - ᴗ - ᴗ - ᴗ - hazaj musaddas maqbū̱d (or
                                    rajaz musaddas maxbūn)

           feɖɑ:n az i:n ɖorɑ:b bi:n o vɑ:y-e ʔu: ::
              ke dar navɑ: fekandam ɑ:n navɑ:-ye ʔu:
                    (Manucehri)

* 6.1.08(2) ᴗ - ᴗ - ᴗ - ᴗ - | ᴗ - ᴗ - ᴗ - ᴗ - hazaj mu̱tamman maqbū̱d
                                    (or rajaz mu̱tamman maxbūn)

           ce karde ʔam be-jɑ:y-e to: . ke ni:stam
                                               sarɑ:y-e to: ::
              na ʔaz havɑ:y-e delbarɑ:n . bari: šodam
                                               barɑ:y-e to:
                    (Xɑqani)

* 6.2.11   - ᴗ - ᴗ - ᴗ - ᴗ - ᴗ -

           tɑ: to bɑ: mani: zamɑ:ne bɑ: man ast ::
              šu:r o kɑ:m-e jɑ:vedɑ:ne bɑ: man ast
                    (Sɑye)

* 6.2.08(2) - ᴗ - ᴗ - ᴗ - - | - ᴗ - ᴗ - ᴗ - -

           ʔei šekaste bɑ:l-e bolbol . kon co man feɖɑ:n
                                               o ɖolɖol ::
              to ʔalam-caši:de hasti: . man setam-
                                               kaši:de hastam
           cf. 5.3.08(2)   (Farroxi)
```
```

+ 7.1.11   ◡ - ◡ - - ◡ - ◡ - - -   <u>munsariḥ</u> musaddas <u>maxbūn</u> al-
                                    sadrayn maṭwī al-ḥašawayn
                                    <u>maqṭū</u>ⵆ al-ⵆarūḍ wa l-ḍarb

                   nabi:niy az man rahi: be-joz xedmat ::
                       nadɑ:ram az to: ṭamaⵆ be-joz di:dɑ:r
                       (al-Moⵆjam)

o 8.1.08(2)   ◡ - ◡ - - - ◡ - | ◡ - ◡ - - - ◡ -   <u>rajaz muṯamman maxbūn</u>
                                                          <u>wa sālim</u>

* 9.1.10   ◡ - - ◡ - - ◡ - ◡ -

                   roxat del be-dozdad nehɑ:n šavad ::
                       delam bar to z-i:n bad-gomɑ:n šavad
                       (Ouḥadi)

* 9.1.11   ◡ - - ◡ - - ◡ - ◡ - -

                   nadɑ:rad bar ɑ:n zolf-e mošk-bu:ʔi:
                       nadɑ:rad bar ɑ:n ru:y-e lɑ:le-ʔi: zi:b
                       (Abū Manṣūr ⵆamɑre Marvazi)

* 9.2.10   - - ◡ - - ◡ - ◡ - -   <u>munsariḥ musaddas aḥadd</u>

                   domm-e: salɑ:mat gerefte xɑ:mu:š ::
                       pi:ci:de bar ⵆɑ:fiyat co fažḍand
                       (Rabenjani)

+ 9.2.12   - - ◡ - - ◡ - ◡ - - ◡ -   <u>munsariḥ musaddas muxtalif al-</u>
                                                         <u>ajzā</u>

                   ʔei delbar-e: jɑ:n-fazɑ:y tondi: makon ::
                       bɑ: ⵆɑ:šeqɑ:n xoš-sarɑ:y tondi: makon
                       (al-Moⵆjam)

                   (So interpreted in <u>al-Moⵆjam</u>; but it could also
                   be regarded as a <u>mustazād</u> form of 1.2.07)

o 9.3.11   - ◡ - - ◡ - ◡ - - ◡ -

+ 9.3.12   - ◡ - - ◡ - ◡ - - ◡ - -

                   cand gu:yam be-man makon bad negɑ:rɑ: ::
                       tɑ: ze ⵆešqat ⵆayɑ:n na-gardad nehɑ:nam

(Meʕyaːr)

* 9.4.10   ◡ − − ◡ − ◡ − − ◡ −

s̱anaːʔi: s̱anaː-ye xod-ra: sazaːst ::
jamaːlaš be-jaːn kamaːl u: bahaːst
(ʕali Heravi)

+ 9.7.12   ◡ − ◡ − − ◡ − − ◡ − ◡ − muḍāriʕ musaddas maqbūḍ sālim
                                                        al-ḥašawayn
hami: konam mehrabaːni: be-jaːy-e to: ::
jafa: makon gar tavaːni: be-jaːy-e man
(al-Moʕjam)

* 9.7.08(2) ◡ − ◡ − − ◡ − − │ ◡ − ◡ − − ◡ − − muḍāriʕ mutamman
                                                        maqbūḍ

be-cašmat ei roušanaːʔi: . ke bi: to bas
                                        bi:-qeraːram ::
        be-jaːnat ei zandagaːni: . ke bi: to jaːn
                                        mi:sepaːram
                (Šarafoddin Šafrave Eṣfahani)

o 9.8.11   − ◡ − − ◡ − − ◡−◡ −

+ 10.4.11   − ◡ − − ◡ − − − ◡ − − mušākil musaddas maḥḍūf

ʔei be-sar mi: beyaːr u: baːz barboṭ ::
morḍ-e farbeh beyaːr u: baːz barboṭ
(al-Moʕjam)

* 10.6.11   − − ◡ − − − ◡ − − ◡ − munsariḥ musaddas marfūʕal-
                                                        ḥašw

pi:caːn daraxti: naːm-e ʔu: naː-ravaːn ::
cu:n sarv-e zarri:n por ʕaqi:q-e: yaman
(Farroxi)

+ 11.1.08   ◡ − − − − ◡ − − muḍāriʕ murabbaʕ sālim

delam bord aːn gol-setaːnaš ::
ze zolfein-e: del-setaːnaš
(al-Moʕjam)
(bi-ẕouq, "tasteless", according to Šams-e Qeis)

+ 11.1.12   ⌣ – – – – ⌣ – – ⌣ – – –   muḏāriˁ musaddas sālim

be-gi:ti: dar ʔaz mosalmɑ:n va ʔaz kɑ:fer   ::
    na-bi:nad kas cu:n soleimɑ:n-e ben nɑ:ṣer
    (al-Moˁjam)

(bi-zouq, "tasteless", according to Šams-e Qeis)

+ 11.1.16   ⌣ – – – – ⌣ – – ⌣ – – – – ⌣ – –   muḏāriˁ mutamman sālim

be-sonbol cu:n mar saman-rɑ: be-pu:šɑ:ni:di:
                                  neku:ʔi: ::
    beyafzu:di: ʔei mošaˁvez ze ke: ʔɑ:mexti:
                                  neku:ʔi:
    (al-Moˁjam)

(bi-zouq, "tasteless", according to Šams-e Qeis)

+ 11.8.08   – ⌣ – – – – ⌣ –   ḡarīb murabbaˁ sālim

ru:y dɑ:ri: ʔei saˁtari: :: hast ku:ʔi: cu:n
                                  moštari:
    (al-Moˁjam)

o 12.1.08(2) ⌣ – – ⌣ – ⌣ ⌣ – | ⌣ – – ⌣ – ⌣ ⌣ –

* 12.1.09(2) ⌣ – – ⌣ – ⌣ ⌣ – – | ⌣ – – ⌣ – ⌣ ⌣ – –   muqtaḏab
                                      mutamman maxbūn maṭwī

to ʔɑ:n mɑ:h-e zohre-jabi:ni: . va ʔɑ:n sarv-e
                                  lɑ:le-ˁazɑ:ri: ::
    ke bar lɑ:le ḏɑ:liye-sɑ:ʔi: . va ʔaz
        ṭorre ḏɑ:liye-bɑ:ri:
    (Xɑju)

*12.2.07(2) – – ⌣ – ⌣ ⌣ – | – – ⌣ – ⌣ ⌣ –   basīṭ mutamman maxbūn
    ʔei zolf-e delbar-e man . por band o por
                                  šekani: ::
        gɑ:hi: co vaˁde-ye ʔu: . gɑ:hi: co pošt-e
                                  mani:
    (Amir Moˁezzi)

o 12.3.08(2) – ⌣ – ⌣ ⌣ – ⌣ – | – ⌣ – ⌣ ⌣ – ⌣ –

+ 12.4.08(2) ⌣ – ⌣ ⌣ – ⌣ – – | ⌣ – ⌣ ⌣ – ⌣ – –

bed-ɑːn malek-ol-moluːkiː   .   ke har do jahɑːn
                                 be-ʔamraš ::
    šodand be-hiːc ciːziː   .   be-goftan-e kɑːf
                                 o nuːniː
              (Meʕyɑːr)

+ 13.1.09 $--\cup\cup---\cup-$ <u>hazaj musaddas axrab majbūb</u>

    ʔaz ʔɑːdamiyɑːn hamcuːn pariː ::
    cuːn bar go<u>z</u>ariː del miːbariː
              (al-Moʕjam)

o 14.6.12 $---\cup---\cup-\cup\cup-$ <u>sarīʕ musaddas maṭwī maksūf al-</u>
                                           <u>ʕarūḍ wa l-ḍarb</u>

+ 14.7.11 $--\cup---\cup-\cup\cup-$ <u>sarīʕ musaddas maxbūn maṭwī</u>
                                           <u>maksūf</u>

    ʔaz ʕešq-e ʔuː man dar jahɑːn sämaram ::
    miːsuːzad az hejrɑːn-e ʔuː jagaram
              (al-Moʕjam)

<u>Summary</u>

Pattern	1	2	3	4	5	6	7	8	9	10	11	12	13	14	Total
*	11	20	22	37	13	4	0	0	5	1	0	2	0	0	115
+	4	9	9	14	16	0	1	0	3	1	4	1	1	1	64
o	5	2	2	9	5	0	0	1	2	0	0	2	0	1	29
Total	20	31	33	60	34	4	1	1	10	2	4	5	1	2	208

It must be emphasised that these figures refer only to
the number of different metres registered, and have no
bearing on the relative popularity of the patterns.   This
will be discussed in the following chapter.

The following table shows the distribution of the Arabic
buḥūr between the various patterns:

Pattern	1	2	3	4	5	6	7	8	9	10	11	12	13	14	Total
hazaj	-	10	12	-	9	2	-	-	-	-	-	-	1	-	34
rajaz	-	11	4	-	8	-	-	1	-	-	-	-	-	-	24
ramal	-	9	7	2	2	-	-	-	-	-	-	-	-	-	20
mutaqārib	12	-	-	1	-	-	-	-	-	-	-	-	-	-	13
mutadārik	3	-	1	-	1	-	-	-	-	-	-	-	-	-	5
basīṭ	-	-	-	-	-	-	-	-	-	-	-	1	-	-	1
madīd	-	-	1	-	-	-	-	-	-	-	-	-	-	-	1
mujtatt	-	-	-	7	1	-	-	-	-	-	-	-	-	-	8
muḍāriʕ	-	-	-	11	-	-	-	-	2	-	3	-	-	-	16
munsariḥ	2	-	-	8	2	-	1	-	2	1	-	-	-	-	16
muqtaḍab	-	-	-	4	1	-	-	-	-	-	-	1	-	-	6
sarīʕ	-	-	4	-	1	-	-	-	-	-	-	-	-	2	7
xafīf	-	-	-	4	-	-	-	-	-	-	-	-	-	-	4
qarīb	-	-	-	5	-	-	-	-	-	-	1	-	-	-	6
ḍarīb	-	-	-	2	-	-	-	-	-	1	-	-	-	-	3
mušākil	-	-	-	4	-	-	-	-	-	1	-	-	-	-	5
unclass.	3	-	4	12	8	2	-	-	6	-	-	3	1	-	39
Total	20	30	33	60	34	4	1	1	10	2	4	5	1	2	208

Apart from the pattern and the length of line, the other
factor that may influence the poet in his choice of metre may
be the opening pattern.   The choice may be categorised as
follows.   The percentages are those of actual use as derived
from the statistics in Chapter IV.

A.   ⏑ ⏑ – ⏑ – ⏑   5.3
     ⏑ ⏑ – – ⏑ ⏑   3.1   20.29%
     ⏑ ⏑ – – ⏑ –   4.5

B.   ⏑ – ⏑ ⏑ –   12.4
     ⏑ – ⏑ – ⏑ ⏑   4.1
     ⏑ – ⏑ – ⏑ –   5.4, 6.1
     ⏑ – ⏑ – – ⏑   5.6, 7.1, 9.7
     ⏑ – ⏑ – – –   8.1   30.71%
     ⏑ – – ⏑ ⏑ –   3.2
     ⏑ – – ⏑ –   1.1, 4.6, 9.1, 9.4, 12.1
     ⏑ – – – ⏑   2.1
     ⏑ – – – –   11.1

C.   – ⏑ ⏑ – ⏑ –   5.2
     – ⏑ ⏑ – – ⏑   3.4, 4.4
     – ⏑ – ⏑ ⏑ –   4.2, 12.3
     – ⏑ – ⏑ – ⏑   4.8, 6.2
     – ⏑ – ⏑ – –   5.5   20.14%
     – ⏑ – – ⏑ –   1.3, 9.3, 9.8, 10.4
     – ⏑ – – – ⏑   2.4
     – ⏑ – – – –   11.8

D.   – – ⏑ ⏑ – ⏑   5.1
     – – ⏑ ⏑ – –   3.3, 13.1   28.75%
     – – ⏑ – ⏑ ⏑   12.7
     – – ⏑ – ⏑ –   4.7
     – – ⏑ – –   1.2, 2.3, 9.2; 10.6, 14.7

E.   – – – ⏑ –   2.2, 14.6   Not significant statistically

Bearing in mind that verses in group A may, under the rule
mentioned earlier, start with either a short or a long
syllable (with statistically an 80% preference for the
latter), we see that there is roughly a two-to-one preference
in favour of verses beginning with a long syllable. Another
noticeable tendency is for verses that start with one or two
long syllables (Groups C and D) to do so with respectively a
monosyllable or a dissyllable (or two monosyllables).

5.1.13 <u>ja:ʔi:</u> ke go<u>z</u>arga:h-e del-e: maḥzu:n-ast ::
                  ʔa:nja: do haza:r ti:re ba:la: xu:n-ast

        <u>leili:</u>-ṣefata:n ze ḥa:l-e ma: bi:xabar-and ::
                  <u>majnu:n</u> da:nad ke ḥa:l-e majnu:n cu:n-ast
                                        (Rudagi)

2.4.15 <u>ta:</u> be-bordi: ʔaz del u: ʔaz cašm-e man ʔa:ra:m o
                                              xa:b ::
                  <u>gah</u> ze del dar ʔa:teš-e: ti:zam gah az cašm
                                              andar a:b
        ʕešq-e to: ba: ca:r ci:zam ya:r da:rad hast ci:z ::
                  <u>mar</u> mara: har sa:ʕati: z-i:n ḍam jagar gardad
                                              kaba:b
                                        (Farroxi)

Reference has already been made to the "doubled" metre,
and it was pointed out that the fourteen and sixteen-syllable
metres (twelve and ten-syllable in the case of Pattern 1)
could often be indistinguishable from the doubled eight and
seven-syllable (six and five-syllable) metres. Since in most
of the doubled metres the final syllable before the break is
open to the same alternatives as those available to the final
syllable of the hemistich, that is to say, it may be either

long or overlong, it may be of interest to see to what extent
the normal pattern is violated where the possibility of
following it exists.   This would be the case when, if the
pattern calls for a long syllable (or two shorts) followed
at the beginning of the second half by a long syllable, the
last syllable before the break is overlong; or vice-versa,
if the pattern calls for an overlong (i.e. a long and a
short), a single long syllable is used.   The following
table of random samplings covers some of the principal
metres involved.   Some examples are given of possible
patterns.

Standard Pattern: — ◡ | —

—◡ | — : ba:z bar a:vard ʕešq .
              sar be-ma<u>sa</u>:l-e nahang   4.4.07(2)
— | — : ta: šekanad zouraq-e: .
              ʕaql be-darya:-ye ʕešq   4.4.07(2)

Standard Pattern: — | —

— | — : ba:z a:madam dar šu:reši: .
              ha:<u>da</u>: jonu:nol- ʕa:šeqi:n   2.3.08(2)

           peika:n-e parra:n a:madan ◡ . ◡ d az la:-maka:n-e:
                                       la:-maka:n 2.3.08(2)

—◡ | — : tabri:z-e xoš-xa:n-e: man ast .
              ḥobbol-vaṭan ʔa:n-e: man ast   2.3.08(2)

Standard Pattern: — | ◡ ◡

— | ◡ ◡ : to darya:-ye ʔela:hi: .
              hame-ye: xalq co ma:hi: 3.2.07(2)
—◡ | ◡ : makon ya:r o makon ya:r .
              marou ʔei bot-e ʕayya:r   3.2.07(2)
— | ◡ : rox-e: farrox-e xod-ra: .
              ma-pu:ša:n be-yaki: ba:r   3.2.07(2)

⌐ | ⌣ ⌣ :   šah-e šams-e di:n-e tabri:z   .
                 ce šavad ?agar be-faẓlat   5.3.08(2)

Standard Pattern: ⌣ ⌣ | –

⌣ ⌣ | –   :   cu:n šamⵏ gahi: gerye ?o .
                 gah xande hami: dɑ:ram   3.3.07(2)

                 mi:ram be-talxi-ye: ḍam o   .
                 nɑ:zam be-mošreb-e: ⵏešq   4.7.07(2)

– | –   :   mɑ:?i:m o šu:r o masti: .
                 masti:y o mei-parasti: 4.7.07(2)
                 z-i:n sɑ:n ke mɑ: šodasti: . m az mɑ:
                            degar ce ?ɑ:yad   4.7.07(2)

⌐ | –   :   dɑ:ru:-ye ṣeḥḥat-e: ⵏešq   .
                 dar ḥekmat-e: ?azal ni:st   4.7.07(2)

The following table based on random samplings indicates the extent to which each of these different variants is found in the poets.

	Standard Pattern	% following pattern		% violating pattern	
1.2.05(2)	– ⌣ | –	⌐ | –	30	– | –	70
2.3.08(2)	– | –	– | –	94.5	⌐ | –	2
		⌐ | v	3.5		
3.2.07(2)	– ⌣ | ⌣	⌐ | ⌣	76.5	– | ⌣	4.5
		– ⌣ | ⌣	12		
		– | ⌣ ⌣	5.5		
		– – | ⌣	1.5		
3.3.07(2)	⌣ ⌣ | –	– | –	91	⌐ | –	3
		– –	6		
4.4.07(2)	– ⌣ | –	⌐ | –	49.5	– | –	50.5
4.7.07(2)	⌣ ⌣ | –	– | –	91	⌐ | –	3
		⌐ | v	6		

5.2.08(2)	– | –	– | – 98	
		⌣|v – 2	
5.3.08(2)	– | ⌣ ⌣	– | ⌣ ⌣ 92	
		⌣|v ⌣ 3.5	
		⌣ ⌣ 4	
		– ⌣ ⌣ .5	

The figures show that it is quite common for a long
syllable to precede the break where the pattern would call
for an overlong, e.g. 1.2.05(2), 4.4.07(2).   The reverse
process, however, where an overlong syllable takes the place
of a standard pattern long syllable, e.g. 2.3.08(2), 3.3.07
(2), is much less common.   We may also note an intermediate
case, where the final syllable of the first half is overlong,
but is followed at the beginning of the second half by a word
beginning with a vowel (v) so that the final letter of the
word before the break really belongs to the second half (e.g.
the second example under 2.3.08(2) and the third example
under 4.7.07(2) above).   The following is an example of the
same combination in the metre 5.3.08(2):

rox-e roušan-e: to ʔei du: .   st be-mošk-na:b ma:nad

Frequently the break is additionally marked by the use of
an internal rhyme, changing with each bayt.   In the following
example the first bayt, the maṭlaʕ, carries the general rhyme
at the end of each miṣrāʕ, in accordance with the normal rule,
but thereafter the poem rhyme figures only at the end of each
bayt, which has also three separate rhymes.

ru:zi: bas xorram ast   .   mei gi:r   4.4.07(2)
az ba:mda:d   ::

hi:c bahɑ:ne namɑ:nd . ʔi: zad kɑ:m-e: to dɑ:d
xɑ:ste dɑ:ri:y o sɑ:z . bi:-q̊amiyat hast bɑ:z
ʔeimaniy u: ʕezz o nɑ:z . farroxiy u: di:n o dɑ:d
rafte ʔo farmu:dani: . mɑ:nde ʔo farsu:dani:
bu:d hame: bu:dani: . kelk forou ʔi:stɑ:d
(Manucehri)

It has already been pointed out that the pattern is only the "standard" form of the metre. The rhythm and shape of the verse can be, and usually is, modified by a variety of licences, which fall basically into two categories. The first consists of alternative scansions of particular syllables, words, or phonetic groups; the principal of these have already been listed in Chapter One. The second includes metrical variations that are permissible for any given combination of syllables, no matter what the metre.

In addition to the four optional changes already listed at the beginning of this chapter (⌣ ⌣ = –, – ⌣ = –⌣, initial ⌣ ⌣ = – ⌣, final – = –⌣), two other variations are sometimes found:

(e) Some of the older poets add or elide a short initial syllable (xazm):

miyɑ:nkaš-e: nɑ:zokak co šɑ:ne-ye mu: :: 4.5.11
gu:ʔiy az yakdegar gosestasti: (Rudagi)

(f) In certain metres of Patterns 4 and 5 the ⌣ – ⌣ – section of the pattern may be replaced by – ⌣ ⌣ –:

ni:z ʔabɑ: ni:kovɑ:n . namɑ:yadat jang-e fand :: 4.4.07/5.6.07
laškar-e feryɑ:dani: . xɑ:ste nei su:dmand (Rudagi) 4.4.07(2)

ʔaz dast o zabɑ:n-e ke: bar ɑ:yad ::   5.1.10
   k-az ʕohde-ye šokraš be-dar ɑ:yad   3.3.10
                    (Saʕdi)

This change is of course normal in the rubāʕī metre
(5.1.13/3.3.13).

The extent to which one or more of these variants may be
employed in one and the same hemistich depends to a large
degree on the taste of the poet and the effect he is trying
to create.   In general a series of long or overlong
syllables is unlikely to be found in lyric verse; on the
other hand, in epic verse, it is quite common, as the
following two lines from the Šɑhnɑme illustrate:

   k-az ɑ:mi:xtan rang nɑ:madš su:d (8 syllables) 1.1.11

   be-padru:d kardanš raftand pi:š (8 syllables)

The following bayt by Ḥɑfeż illustrates the minimum and
maximum syllabic lengths of the metre 4.1.15:

   behi:c dour na-xɑ:hand yɑ:ft hošyɑ:raš (10 syllables)
   :: coni:n ke ḥɑ:feż-e mɑ: mast-e bɑ:de-ye
                    ʔazal-ast (15 syllables)

The following tables, based on random samplings, show the
frequencies of the various possible forms of a small selection
of metres.   As indicated, the letters A, B, C, etc., denote
substitutions of an overlong syllable for the sequence - ᴗ,
while the numerals 1, 2, 3, etc., are used to designate the
substitution of a long for two shorts.   200 sample hemistichs have been examined in each case, except for metres
1.1.11, 2.1.16, 2.4.15, and 3.3.14 (100 samples each), and
5.1.13/3.3.13 (400 samples).   The alternative long/overlong

ending has been ignored, as having no statistical significance.

1.1.11   ◡ − − ◡ − − ◡ − − ◡ −   Range: 11-8 syllables
                 ⌣   ⌣   ⌣
                 A   B   C

I	II	III	IV		
11 syl.	10 syl.	9 syl.	8 syl.		
52	A: 8	AB: 3	ABC: 1	_Total_	A: 15
	B: 15	AC: 3			B: 23
	C: 14	BC: 4			C: 22
% 52	37	10	1		

2.1.16   ◡ − − − ◡ − − − ◡ − − − ◡ − − −   Range: 16-13 syllables
                 ⌣   ⌣   ⌣
                 A   B   C

I	II	III	IV		
16 syl.	15 syl.	14 syl.	13 syl.		
66	A: 13	AB: 0	ABC: 0	_Total_	A: 14
	B: 3	AC: 1			B: 4
	C: 16	BC: 1			C: 18
% 66	32	2	0		

2.4.15   − ◡ − − − ◡ − − − ◡ − − − ◡ −   Range: 15-11 syllables
             ⌣   ⌣   ⌣   ⌣
             D   A   B   C

I	II	III	IV	V	
15 syl.	14 syl.	13 syl.	12 syl.	11 syl.	
52	D: 6	DA: 2	DAB: 0	DABC: 0	_Total_
	A: 6	DB: 5	DAC: 0		A: 15
	B: 8	DC: 0	DBC: 0		B: 17
	C: 13	AB: 3	ABC: 0		C: 18
		AC: 4			D: 13
		BC: 1			
% 52	33	15	0	0	

3.1.11 $\overset{b}{\underset{\overline{a}}{\smile}} \smile - - \underset{2}{\smile} \smile - - \underset{4}{\smile} \smile -$ range: 11-8 syllables

$\underset{D}{} \underset{A}{} \underset{C}{}$

I		II		III		IV	
11 syl.		10 syl.		9 syl.		8 syl.	
b	a	b	a	b	a		a
16	40	D: –	9	AC: 1	10	DAC:	2
		A: 3	18	A4: 7	7	DA4:	3
		2: 3	9	2C: 1	3	D2C:	1
		C: 2	17	24: 0	2	D24:	0
		4: 9	23	DA: –	2		
				D2: –	3		
				DC: –	2		
				D4: –	7		
% 28		46.5		22.5		3	

	b	a	D	A	2	C	4
%	21	64.5	14.5	26.5	11	19.5	29

64.5 ‿ 14.5 = 79

Marked preference for long initial syllable. Tendency for last pair of shorts to be contracted, but rare for both pairs to be so.

3.1.15 $\overset{b}{\underset{a}{\smile}} \smile - - \underset{2}{\smile} \smile - - \underset{3}{\smile} \smile - - \underset{4}{\smile} \smile -$ Range: 15-11 syllables

$\underset{D}{} \underset{A}{} \underset{B}{} \underset{C}{}$

I		II		III		IV		V
15 syl.		14 syl.		13 syl.		12 syl.		11 syl.
b	a	b	a	b	a	b	a	a
4	32	D: – 8		AB: 1 4		ABC:0 2		DABC: 0
		A: 0 13		A3: 0 0		AB4:2 2		DAB4: 0
		2: 0 2		AC: 0 3		A3C:0 0		DA3C: 0
		B: 2 14		A4: 1 6		A34:0 0		DA34: 1
		3: 0 3		BC: 1 2		2BC:0 0		D2BC: 0

C: 3 19	B4: 3 6	2B4: 0 2	D2B4: 0
4: 6 35	3C: 0 1	23C: 0 0	D23C: 0
	34: 0 2	234: 0 0	D234: 0
	2B: 0 1	DAB: - 2	
	23: 0 0	DA3: - 0	
	2C: 1 0	DAC: - 2	
	24: 0 0	DA4: - 1	
	DA: - 5	D2B: - 0	
	D2: - 0	D23: - 0	
	DB: - 2	D2C: - 0	
	D3: - 0	D24: - 0	
	DC: - 2	DBC: - 1	
	D4: - 3	D3C: - 0	
		D34: - 0	

% 18	52.5	22	7	.5
b	a D	A 2 B 3 C 4
% 12	74.5 13.5	32.5 3 33.5 3.5 19.5 35
	88	

Marked tendency to start line with long syllable. Contraction of two shorts is rare except for last group.

3.3.14   -- ᴗ ᴗ -- ᴗ ᴗ -- ᴗ ᴗ --   Range: 14-11 syllables
             ᴸ2ᴶ ᴸ3ᴶ ᴸ4ᴶ
         ᴸAᴶ ᴸBᴶ ᴸCᴶ

| I | II | III | IV | |
14 syl.	13 syl.	12 syl.	11 syl.	Total %
39	A: 10	AB: 4	ABC: 2	A: 23
	2: 1	A3: 1	AB4: 0	2: 1
	B: 14	AC: 6	A3C: 0	B: 28
	3: 1	A4: 0	A34: 0	3: 2
	C: 14	2B: 0	2BC: 0	C: 30
	4: 0	23: 0	2B4: 0	4: 0
		2C: 0	23C: 0	
		24: 0	234: 0	

		BC: 8	
		B4: 0	
		3C: 0	
		34: 0	
% 39	40	19	2

4.1.15   ◡ – ◡ – ◡ ◡ – – – ◡ – ◡ – ◡ ◡ –   Range: 15-10 syllables
                 2̲   4̲
         ⌊A⌋⌊B⌋   ⌊C⌋⌊D⌋⌊E⌋

I	II	III	IV	V	VI
15 syl.	14 syl.	13 syl.	12 syl.	11 syl.	10 syl.
21	A: 7	AB: 2	ABC: 0	ABCD: 0	ABCDE: 0
	B: 11	A2: 1	ABD: 0	ABCE: 0	ABCD4: 0
	2: 3	AC: 2	ABE: 2	ABC4: 1	A2CDE: 0
	C: 2	AD: 5	AB4: 1	ABDE: 0	A2CD4: 0
	D: 4	AE: 1	A2C: 2	ABD4: 0	
	E: 7	A4: 7	A2D: 2	A2CH: 0	
	4: 40	BC: 0	A2E: 1	A2CE: 0	
		BD: 6	A24: 3	A2C4: 0	
		BE: 0	BCD: 1	A2DE: 0	
		B4: 11	BCE: 0	A2D4: 0	
		2C: 6	BC4: 2	ACDE: 0	
		2D: 0	2CD: 0	ACD4: 1	
		2E: 1	2CE: 0		
		24: 8	2C4: 3		
		CD: 2	ACD: 0		
		CE: 0	ACE: 0		
		C4: 8	AC4: 5		
		DE: 4	ADE: 0		
		D4: 8	AD4: 3		
			BDE: 0		
			BD4: 2		
			CDE: 0		
			CD4: 2		
			2DE: 1		
			2D4: 1		

% 10.5	37	36	15.5	1	0*

	A	B	2	C	D	E	4
%	22	19.5	16	18.5	21	8.5	53

Note the characteristic contraction of the second (4) pair of short syllables.

* An example of a ten-syllable hemistich is:

na ʔɑ:ftɑ:b na mahtɑ:b nu:r baxši:di: .... (ABCD4)

contrasted in the same poem (from the Divɑn-e Šams-e Tabriz) with

negar be-yu:sef-e kanʕɑ:n ke ʔaz kenɑ:r-e pedar ......

which has the full fifteen syllables.

<u>4.4.07(2)</u> - ᵕ ᵕ - - ᵕ -   - ᵕ ᵕ - - - ᵕ -   Range: 14-10 syllables

        ⌊2⌋   ⌊4⌋

     ⌊B⌋ ⌊C⌋   ⌊E⌋   ⌊F⌋

I	II	III	IV	V
14 syl.	13 syl.	12 syl.	11 syl.	10 syl.
77	B: 26	BC: 4	BCE: 0	BCEF: 0
	2: 3	BE: 4	BC4: 0	BC4F: 0
	C: 19	B4: 1	BCF: 2	2CEF: 0
	E: 12	BF: 5	BEF: 0	2C4F: 0
	4: 5	2C: 3	B4F: 0	
	F: 12	2E: 2	2CE: 0	
		24: 1	2C4: 0	
		2F: 2	2CF: 1	
		CE: 7	2EF: 0	
		C4: 1	24F: 0	
		CF: 8	CEF: 2	
		EF: 2	C4F: 0	
		4F: 1		
% 38.5	38.5	20.5	2.5	0

	B	2	C	E	4	F
%	21	6	23.5	14.5	4.5	17.5

Marked preference for the less modified forms. Contraction of two shorts in either half is rare.

4.5.11 $\begin{smallmatrix}b\\ \smile\\ a\end{smallmatrix}$ ᴗ – – ᴗ – ᴗ – ᴗ ᴗ –   Range: 11-7 syllables

⌐4¬

⌐B⌐ ⌐C⌐D⌐E⌐

I 11 syl.	II 10 syl.	III 9 syl.	IV 8 syl.	V 7 syl.
b a	b a	b a	b a	b
9 36	B: – 6	BC: – 3	BCD: – 0	BCDE: 0
	C: 4 9	BD: – 0	BCE: – 1	BCD4: 0
	D: 4 9	BE: – 2	BC4: – 3	
	E: 1 13	B4: – 8	BDE: – 0	
	4: 4 54	CD: 1 1	BD4: – 1	
		CE: 1 1	CDE: 0 1	
		C4: 4 7	CD4: 1 2	
		DE: 0 2		
		D4: 5 7		
% 22.5	52	21	4.5	0

	b	a	B	C	D	E	4
%	17	71 12	19.5	17	11	48	

(71 + 12 = 83)

4.7.14   – – ᴗ – ᴗ – ᴗ ᴗ – – ᴗ – ᴗ –   Range: 14-9 syllables

⌐4¬

⌐C⌐D⌐E⌐   ⌐F⌐A⌐

I 14 syl.	II 13 syl.	III 12 syl.	IV 11 syl.	V 10 syl.	VI 9 syl.
48	C: 6	CD: 6	CDE: 1	CDEF: 1	CDEFA: 0
	D: 16	CE: 5	CD4: 0	CDEA: 1	CD4FA: 0
	E: 15	C4: 2	CDF: 2	CD4F: 0	

4:	7	CF:	7	CDA:	2	CD4A:	0	
F:	14	CA:	6	CEF:	2	DEFA:	0	
A:	12	DE:	10	CEA:	3	D4FA:	0	
		D4:	3	C4F:	1			
		DF:	7	C4A:	1			
		DA:	4	CFA:	2			
		EF:	5	DEF:	1			
		4F:	1	D4F:	0			
		4A:	0	DEA:	0			
		FA:	1	D4A:	0			
		EA:	3	EFA:	1			
				4FA:	2			
				DFA:	2			

%	24	35	30	10	1	0

	C	D	E	4	F	A
%	24	28	24	8.5	24.5	20

4.7.07(2) — — ◡ — ◡ — — | — — ◡ — ◡ — —   Range: 14-10 syllables

⌐C⌐D⌐   ⌐F⌐A⌐

I	II	III	IV	V
14 syl.	13 syl.	12 syl.	11 syl.	10 syl.
40	C: 13	CD: 1	CDF: 1	CDFA: 0
	D: 8	CF: 2	CDA: 2	
	F: 10	CA: 1	CFA: 0	
	A: 9	FA: 5	DFA: 0	
		DF: 3		
		DA: 5		

%	40	40	17	3	0

	C	D	F	A
%	20	20	21	22

a. <u>5.1.13</u> $--\cup\cup$ a$-\cup-\cup--\cup\cup-$ Range: 13-9 syllables

   ⌊2⌋   ⌊4⌋   The rubāʕī metre.

   ⌊A⌋ ⌊B⌋⌊C⌋ ⌊E⌋

b. <u>3.1.13</u>   b$--\cup\cup$

              ⌊3⌋

              ⌊D⌋

I 13 syl.		II 12 syl.			III 11 syl.			IV 10 syl.			V 9 syl.	
a	b		a	b		a	b		a	b			a
29	26	A:	11	10	AB:	3	–	ABC:	0	–	ABCE:		2
		2:	4	0	AD:	–	0	ABE:	1	–	ABC4:		1
		B:	3	–	AC:	6	–	AB4:	6	–	2BCE:		0
		D:	–	14	A3:	–	0	ADE:	–	1	2BC4:		0
		C:	14	–	AE:	6	3	AD4:	–	5			
		3:	–	0	A4:	13	14	ACE:	4	–			
		E:	29	15	2B:	0	–	AC4:	4	–			
		4:	51	41	2D:	–	0	A3E:	–	0			
					2C:	0	–	A34:	–	0			
					23:	–	0	2BC:	0	–			
					2E:	1	3	2BE:	0	–			
					24:	7	2	2B4:	1	–			
					BC:	3	–	2DE:	–	0			
					BE:	4	–	2D4:	–	3			
					B4:	12	–	2CE:	0	–			
					DE:	–	3	2C4:	1	–			
					D4:	–	21	23E:	–	0			
					CE:	4	–	234:	–	0			
					C4:	16	–	BCE:	2	–			
					3E:	–	0	BC4:	1	–			
					34:	–	0						
% 7.25	6.5		28	20		19	11.25		5	2.25			.75
13.75		48			30.25			7.25			.75		

	A	2	B	C	D	3	E	4
%	22.5	5.5	9.75	14.5	11.75	0	17	49.75

Grouping of hemistichs in quatrains

a	a	a	a	a	a	a	a	b	b	b	b	b	b	b	b	
a	a	a	a	b	b	b	b	a	a	a	a	b	b	b	b	Total %
a	a	b	b	a	a	b	b	a	a	b	b	a	a	b	b	a: 58.5
a	b	a	b	a	b	a	b	a	b	a	b	a	b	a	b	b: 41.5
21	7	10	5	4	5	1	7	7	2	2	4	8	5	4	8	quatrains

Ignoring the alternation of the final syllable, there are
63 possible forms of the rubāʕī metre, of which 42 are
attested in the 400 hemistichs examined.

The "a" group (5.1.13) is rather more common than the
"b" group (3.3.13), but mixing of the two in one quatrain is
fairly evenly practised over the whole range of possible
combinations (with some favour towards quatrains entirely in
the "a" group).   12- and 11-syllable verses predominate.

Contraction of the first pair of shorts (2) is fairly
uncommon, of the last pair (4) quite usual.   Contraction of
the second pair (3) is almost unknown (none in the sample),
though reference may be made to the famous line by Xayyɑm:

   ʔuː dɑːnad ʔuː dɑːnad ʔuː dɑːnad ʔuː: (234)
and another is given in al-Moʕjam:

   goftɑː dɑːram goftam kuː goft iːnak   (234)
Farzɑd quotes two from either Xayyɑm or Ḥɑfeż:

   mɑːʔiːm dar iːn gonbad naː poxte na xɑːm   (A3)
   sadd-e: ramaqiː baːyad neṣf-e: nɑːniː: (34)

The following table shows the frequency of the "tree"
forms:

axrab tree:	a4	a	b3	b34	b4	b	Total
%	26.25	30.25	0	0	20	18	94.50

<u>axram tree:</u>   a24   a2   b23   b234   b24   b2

     %   2.25   1.25   0   0   1.25   .75   5.50

It will be seen that the axram tree (distinguished by modification 2) accounts for only one in twenty of the metres used.   The significant difference is between "a" and "b", where the proportion is roughly three to two.

<u>5.2.08(2)</u> $-\smile\smile-\smile-\smile-$ | $-\smile\smile-\smile-\smile-$ Range: 16-10 syllables

I	II	III	IV	V	VI	VII
16 syl.	15 syl.	14 syl.	13 syl.	12 syl.	11 syl.	10 syl.
		*	*	*	*	*
61	A: 14	AB: 6	ABC: 1	ABCF: 1		
	2: 1	AC: 3	2BC: 2	AEFG: 1		
	B: 15	AE: 10	2BE: 1			
	C: 10	AF: 2	ACE: 1			
	E: 18	2B: 1	ACF: 1			
	4: 3	2E: 1	ACG: 1			
	F: 13	2F: 1	2CG: 1			
	G: 5	BC: 3	AEF: 1			
		BF: 3	2EF: 1			
		BG: 2	24F: 1			
		CE: 4	EFG: 1			
		CF: 1				
		CG: 1				
		EF: 4				
		EG: 3				
		3F: 1				
% 30.5	39.5	23	6	1	0	0

* Only those combinations are given of which examples were found in the sampling.   It will be seen that both this and the following metre are less prone to modification than

others of similar pattern.

	A	2	B	C	E	4	F	G
%	21	5	17.5	15	23	2	16	7.5

<u>5.3.08(2)</u>   ◡ ◡ – ◡ – ◡ – – | ◡ ◡ – ◡ – ◡ – –   Range: 16–10 syllables
        └2┘   └4┘

└B┘└C┘ └D┘ └F┘└G┘

I 16 syl.	II 15 syl.	III 14 syl.	IV 13 syl.	V 12 syl.	VI 11 syl.	VII 10 syl.
		*	*	*	*	*
92	2: 0	2D: 1	2BC: 1			
	B: 16	BC: 2	BCF: 2			
	C: 21	BF: 4	BFG: 1			
	D: 4	BG: 4	CFG: 4			
	4: 0	DG: 1				
	F: 14	CF: 8				
	G: 18	CG: 7				
% 46	36.5	13.5	4	0	0	0

* Only those combinations are given of which examples were found in the sampling.

	2	B	C	D	4	F	G
%	1	15	22.5	3	0	16.5	17.5

This metre does not observe the normal rule regarding the lengthening of the first of an initial pair of short syllables.   On the other hand these are found contracted into one long, though rarely.   An overlapping overlong syllable is sometimes found at the break.

The following table summarises the range of syllabic length for all Persian metres.

4.7.6-4	1.3.9-6	1.1.11-8	1.1.12-9	1.1.14-11	1.1.16-11
3.3.6-5	4.5.	1.2.	2.3.	2.1.	4.6.
1.2.7-5	4.6.	2.4.	2.4.	2.3.	5.6.
2.4.	5.1.	3.1.	3.1.	3.2.	8.1.
4.2.	1.1.9-7	3.4.	3.4.	3.3.	9.7.
4.4.	2.3.	4.1.	4.6.	3.4.	12.1.
4.6.	2.4.	4.6.	14.6	5.3.15-9	12.4.
5.2.	3.3.	4.7.	2.1.12-10	4.1.15-10	1.2.16-12
5.6.	3.4.	5.1.	3.3.	4.2.	2.3.
2.1.7-6	13.1.	7.1.	11.1.	4.4.	2.4.
2.3.	4.8.10-6	9.1.	4.1.13-9	4.5.	3.1.
3.2.	1.1.10-7	10.4.	4.4.	4.6.	3.4.
3.3.	1.2.	10.6.	4.7.	4.7.	2.1.16-13
4.5.8-5	1.3.	14.7.	5.1.	5.4.	11.1.
4.7.	4.4.	2.1.11-9	5.4.	2.4.15-11	2.3.18-14
4.8.	4.6.	2.3.	2.3.13-10	3.1.	12.1.18-13
5.5.	4.7.	3.2.	2.4.	5.1.	4.8.20-12
1.1.8-6	5.1.	3.3.	3.1.	2.1.15-12	4.1.20-13
1.2.	9.2.	6.1.12-7	3.3.	2.2.	
2.3.	9.4.	1.3.12-8	3.4.	2.3.	
2.4.	2.4.10-8	4.1.	4.2.14-9	3.2.	
3.1.	3.3.	4.4.	4.6.	3.3.	
3.4.	3.4.	4.5.	4.7.	6.1.16-9	
4.1.	4.1.	4.7.	5.3.	4.5.16-10	
4.4.	6.2.11-6	5.2.	5.4.	4.7.	
5.1.	4.2.11-7	5.3.	5.6.	4.8.	
11.8.	4.5.	5.4.	1.2.14-10	5.2.	
2.1.8-7	4.8.	5.6.	1.3.	5.3.	
11.1.	5.2.	9.2.	3.1.	5.4.	
	5.6.	9.3.	4.4.	5.5.	
	9.3.	9.7.	5.5.	6.2.	
	9.8.		12.2	12.3	

The quantitative length of each metre can easily be
reckoned, but it may be helpful to have the following
equivalents in mind:

Pattern 1:   three-syllable section = 5 morae

Pattern 2:   four-syllable section = 7 morae

Pattern 3:   four-syllable section = 6 morae

Pattern 4:   eight-syllable section = 12 morae

Pattern 5:   eight-syllable section = 12 morae

Looking ahead to the statistics given in the following
chapter, we find that about 41% of all metres actually used
fall into the 15-syllable group, 24% into the 14-syllable
group, 18% into the 11-syllable group, and 10% into the 16-
syllable group.   These designations refer, of course, to
the "standard" form of the metre.

To determine the metre of a given poem, a few lines must
be scanned, allotting the quantities to the syllables in
accordance with the rules at the beginning of this chapter,
and bearing in mind the alternative quantities listed at
the beginning of Chapter One.   Sometimes several lines may
have to be scanned in this way before the pattern can be seen
clearly.   The following examples illustrate the process.

For ease of reference, a straightforward transcription
of the four passages is given first:

1.   mousem-e ʕeid o bahɑr-e xorram o šah-e gavɑn

     sɑye-e   abr o kenɑr-e sabze o baxt-e javɑn

     ....

     moṭrebɑ bar to-st guš ɑn mast-rɑ bešnou ze man

cand harfi dar bayαn-e šouq o urα bešnavαn   (Jαmi)

2. tα sar-e zolf-e to dar dast-e nasim oftαdast

del-e soudα-zade az qosse do nim oftαdast

cašm-e jαdu-ye to xod ʕein-e savαd-e sahar ast

liken in hast ke in nosxe saqim oftαdast   (Hafež)

3. soʔαl kardam o goftam jamαl-e ru-ye to-rα

ce šod ke murce bar gerd-e mαh jušidast

javαb dαd nadαnam ce bud ruyam-rα

magar be-mαtam-e hosnam siyαh pušidast   (Saʕdi)

4. ʔαnhα ke dar haqiqat-e asrαr mi-ravand

sar-gašte hamco noqte-ye pargαr mi-ravand

ham dar kenαr-e ʕarš sar-afrαz mi-šavand

ham dar miyαn-e bahr negunsαr mi-ravand   (ʕattαr)

1. mouse m‿e   ʕei d u:bahɑ:r‿e   xor‿ram mu: ʂɑ:‿h‿e ga‿vɑ:n
   ⌣ ‿e: ʕeid va   ‿ram va   vu: ‿h‿e: ja‿vɑ:n

   ⌣ −   −   ⌣ −   −   ⌣ −   −   ⌣ −   −   ⌣ −

   sɑ:ye ʔe ʔab r u:kenɑ:r‿e   sab ze va   bax t‿e ja‿vɑ:n
   sɑ:ye: ʔe: ʔabr va   sab‿ze: va bax‿t‿e:

   ⌣ −   ⌣ −   −   ⌣ −   −   ⌣ −   −   ⌣ −

   ....

   motre‿bɑ: bar to‿st gu:ʂ ɑ:n mas‿t‿ rɑ: be‿ʂnou ze man

   ⌣ −   −   ⌣   ʂ ʔɑ:n   t‿

   cand har fi: dar bayɑ:n‿e   ʂou q u: ʔu:- rɑ: beʂ‿na‿vɑ:n
                              ʂouq va   vu:

   ⌣ −   −   ⌣ −   −   ⌣ −   −   ⌣ −   −   ⌣ −

By elimination we get ⌣ − − − ⌣ − − − ⌣ − − ⌣ −, i.e. 2.4.15.

2. tɑ̌: sa ⌣r-e zol⌣f-e to dar dast-e na⌣si:⌣m of ʔof⌣tɑ:⌣dast
       ⌣r-e: ⌣f-e: to: dast-e: ⌣si:m of ʔof⌣tɑ:⌣dast

de⌣l-e sou⌣dɑ:-za⌣de ʔaz qoṣ̌ṣe do ni:⌣m of ʔof⌣tɑ:⌣dast
       ⌣l-e: de: ̣qo.ṣe: do: ni:m of ʔof⌣tɑ:⌣dast

caš⌣m-e jɑ:⌣du:-ye to xod ʕei⌣n-e sa⌣vɑ:⌣d-e saha⌣r ast
       m-e: ye: ⌣n-e: d-e: saha.⌣r ast

li⌣ke n i:n has⌣t ke ʔi:n nosxe sa⌣qi:⌣m of ʔof⌣tɑ:⌣dast
ken ʔi:n   ke: xe: ⌣qi:m of ʔof⌣tɑ:⌣dast

By elimination we get ͝ ͝ - - ͝| - ͝ - - ͝ ͝ , which is clearly 3.1.15.

3. so‿ʔɑ:‿l karda‿m u: gof‿tam ja‿mɑ:l-e ru:y-e to-rɑ:
      dam va   l-e:
      m o
      vu:

ce šod ke mu:r ce bar ger‿d-e mɑ:h ju:ši: dast
ce: ke: ce: d-e:

ja‿vɑ:b dɑ:d na‿dɑ:‿nam ce bu:d ru:yam‿rɑ:
               ce:

ma‿gar be‿mɑ:ta‿m-e hos‿nam si‿yɑ:h pu:ši: dast
            m-e:

By elimination we get ∪ ∪ − ∪ − ∪ − ∪ − ∪ ∪ −, which is 4.1.15.

4. ?ɑːn hɑː: ke:/ke   dar ha⏜qiːqa   t-e:/t-e   ?as⏜rɑːr   miː-ravand

sar⏜gaš te:/te   ham co   noq te:/te.   ye:/ye   par⏜gɑːr   miː-ravand

ham   dar   ke⏜nɑː: r-e:/r-e   ʕar⏜š   sa⏜raf / sar⏜ʔaf⏜rɑːz   miː-šavand

ham   dar   mi⏜yɑː⏜n-e:/n-e   bah⏜r   ne⏜guːn sa:r   miː-ravand

By elimination we get ‒ ‒ ⏑ ‒ ⏑ ⏑ ‒ ⏑ ‒ ⏑ ‒ ⏑ , i.e. 4.7.14.

IV. Statistical survey of use of metres

The purpose of this chapter is to assess on a statistical
basis the metres actually used by Persian poets throughout
the history of New (Islamic) Persian poetry. This is of
course an exercise whose limits are as boundless as the ocean
of Persian literature. The comparatively restricted scope
of the survey here presented finds its justification in the
fact that the figures, whether applied to the whole period,
to particular centuries, or to individual poets, show a remarkable degree of consistency. One is at liberty to assume
that expanding the statistical basis of the survey would not
lead to any significant change in the overall result. In
fact "snap" polls taken subsequently (and not included here)
confirm this impression. It can at least be said that the
figure of over 20,000 participating poems is some twenty
times better than the average political "opinion poll", with
the additional advantage that the voters do not change their
views the day after the poll.

The figures are based on the standard editions of the
individual poets (details of which are given in the Bibliography). No apology is offered for this procedure, since
textual accuracy is not at issue here, except in the case of

a few scattered fragments. The "anthology" which is the
subject of the first line of figures is a composite of the
three anthologies of early Persian poetry compiled by Saꟼid
Nafisi (in his work on Rudagi), Moḥammad Moꟼin and Gilbert
Lazard. The other poets have been selected more or less at
random to provide a coverage of the whole period up to, but
not including, the experimental and "free" verse of the
present day, which requires separate study.

The figures given under each head refer to the number of
separate poems, of whatever length and including incomplete
quotations and fragments, composed in each distinct metre.
The matter of the number of verses has not been taken into
account, since it is the poet's choice of metre that is
significant, rather than his longwindedness. <u>maṯnawīyāt</u>
and <u>rubāꟼīyāt</u> have been excluded, since the choice of metre
for both these forms is more or less restricted. Notes on
the metres used will be found in the Appendix dealing with
verse-forms.

Name	Date (A.D.)	Place	No. of poems	.09	1.1. .11	.12	1.2. .05(2)	1.3. .10	Total
1. Anthology	800–1000	–	1057		57	21			78
2. Rudagi	c.870–940	Samarqand	230		10	7			17
3. Gonsori	d.1040/50	Xorasan	76		6	3			9
4. Manucehri	d.c.1041	Damqan	98		4	3			7
5. Farroxi	d.c.1037	Seistan	239		4	10			14
6. Qatran	d.c.1060	Tabriz	345		10	11			21
7. Naser-e Xosrou	1003–1070	Marv	40		3	4			7
8. Lame'i	1030–1087	Boxara	79			2			2
9. Runi	d.c.1100	Neišapur	109		4	2			6
10. Mas'ud Sa'd Salman	d.1121/31	Gorgan	635		27	8			35
11. Sana'i	d.c.1150	Balx	885		8	11			19
12. Amir Mo'ezzi	d.1147	Neišapur	568		8	9			17
13. Ašraf	d.c.1160	Qazne	236		3	3			6
14. Xaqani	1106–1185	Širvan	956		15	27			42
15. Nežami	1141–1203	Ganje	91						0
16. Faryabi	d. 1201	Balx/Geraq	335		1	1			2
17. Gattar	1119–1234	Neišapur	824		1	3			4
18. Kamaloddin	d.c. 1237	Esfahan	344		6	9			15
19. Sa'di	1184–1291	Širaz	1688		106	6			112
20. Moulavi	1207–1273	Balx/Qonye	678		1		1		2
21. Homam	d. 1314	Tabriz	128						0
22. Ouhadi	d. 1337	Maraqe	510		15	5	1		21

Name	Date (A.D.)	Place	No. of poems	.09	1.1.11	.12	1.2.05(2)	1.3.10	Total
23. Gobeid Zakani	d. 1371	Qazvin/Širaz	316		19		1		20
24. Hafez	d. 1389	Širaz	530		1	1	3		5
25. Jami	1414–1492	Xorasan	1035		12	15	4		31
26. Baba Feqani	d. 1519	Širaz	620						0
27. Gorfi	d. 1590	Širaz	613		3	1			4
28. Tarzi Afšar	fl.1650	Tabriz	266		9	13	1		23
29. Sa'eb	d. 1677	Tabriz	2409		1	10			11
30. Gašeq	d. 1767	Esfahan	994		8	20	4		32
31. Qa'ani	d. 1853	Širaz	931		5	10			15
32. Foruqi	1804–1858	Bestam	265			1	1		2
33. La'li	1836–1907	Tabriz	393	1	11	8	1		21
34. Adib	1844–1930	Pišavar	85		4	1			5
35. Šuride	1857–1937	Širaz	155			1			1
36. Adibol-Mamalek	1860–1917	Kazerun	654		17	22			39
37. Iraj Mirza	1874–1925	Tabriz	83						0
38. Garef	1882–1933	Qazvin	159	1	1	1	1		4
39. Pur Da'ud	1885–1968	Rašt	38				1	1	2
40. Farroxi	1887–1939	Yazd	200			1			1
41. Gešqi	1894–1923	Hamadan	84						0
42. Parvin	1906–1941	Tabriz	174		2	8			10
			20155	2	382	258	19	1	662

	.08	2.1.			.11	.04(3)	2.3.		.05(2)	2.4.					Total
		.11	.12	.16			.13	.16		.11	.12	.13	.15	.16	
1.		60	1	33	1	1		4		39		1	21		161
2.		5		10				1		9			9		34
3.		10		2						3			7		22
4.		4		5				1		1			18		29
5.		5		6				1		2			19		33
6.		8		42						1			77		128
7.		2		1						2			4		9
8.		1		8				2					13		24
9.		7		1						3			4		15
10.		17		7				1		11			20		56
11.		36		59				14		39			214		362
12.		14		26				4		3			152		199
13.		13		6						6			30		55
14.		45		17				12		48			71		193
15.		11		6				2		4			9		32
16.		12		7						2	4		31		56
17.		90		14				9		169			46	1	329
18.		24		4						13			12		53
19.		167		40				14		52			67	3	343
20.		41		80				55		28			20		224
21.		13		6				3		7			23		52
22.	1	15	1	39				19		33			35	3	146

	2.1.				2.3.				2.4.						Total
	.08	.11	.12	.16	.11	.04(3)	.13	.16	.05(2)	.11	.12	.13	.15	.16	
23.		34		2				2		18				15		71
24.		27		25				2		9				39		102
25.		70		72				20		28				198		388
26.		6		128				13						92		239
27.		10		55				7		2				96		170
28.		35		22				2		8				14	1	82
29.		17		257				1		5				650		930
30.		29		109				26		7				91		262
31.		58		30				9		33				120		250
32.		5		7				1			2			16	6	37
33.		23		22				3		22	3			34	5	112
34.				5				10		7				17		39
35.		5		2						7						15
36.		44		22				7	1	11	4			73	11	173
37.		3		1						3				8	1	16
38.		7		4			1			1					1	14
39.		1						1		1						3
40.		1		11				1						63	7	83
41.		5		7						4				11	1	28
42.		9		3						7				13		32
	1	989	2	1203	1	1	1	247	1	648	13	1	2452	41	5601

	3.1.					3.2.						3.3.				3.4.		
	.11	.13	.07(2)	.15	.16	.07(2)	.15	.05(2)	.10	.11	.13	.14	.07(2)	.15	.05(2)	.11	.16	Total
1.	14			57			3		2	2	1	69	3			25		176
2.	3	2		12			2			2		14	4			8		47
3.												3						3
4.	1			14			1					11	1			2		30
5.	4	1		55			1					10	1			2		74
6.	1	2		20										1				24
7.				2								3				5		10
8.	1			6								12	3					22
9.	3			1								7						11
10.	7	1		8								33	3			20		72
11.	17			46	2		1					86	9			16	1	178
12.				38								58	9			3		108
13.	9			15		10						8				2		44
14.	33			33			1					25	22			8		122
15.	1			5								7	6			2		21
16.	3			23								9	2					37
17.	19			15								29	28			20		111
18.	22			18					1			3				4		48
19.	10			159	14			5	1			60	8			36		293
20.	4			37	15							25	91	3	1	19	22	229
21.				16								1	3					20
22.	2			53	5							20	17			3	2	102
23.	2			36								1	3			3		45

	3.1.					3.2.			3.3.						3.4.			
	.11	.13	.07(2)	.15	.16	.07(2)	.15	.05(2)	.10	.11	.13	.14	.07(2)	.15	.05(2)	.11	.16	Total
24.				143								19	5				1	168
25.	5			132	6							59	9				10	221
26.	1			37	2							52	2				1	95
27.	1			76				1				63	2					142
28.	1			23								10	2				2	39
29.	3			384	2							139					3	528
30.	7			136								98	5				3	249
31.	5		1	40	1							76	5				3	131
32.	3			66	1							28	8				5	111
33.	7			44								16	4				1	72
34.				6								2	1				1	10
35.	1			56	8							19	3				1	88
36.	6	3		47								23	9				2	90
37.	4			16								5	1				3	28
38.				36								7					3	46
39.	1			4				1				5	1					12
40.	1			34								28	7					70
41.				10								4	1				4	19
42.	17	9		6								2					5	39
	219	18	1	1965	56	10	9	6	4	4	1	1159	280	4	2	222	25	3985

		4.1.				4.2.		4.4.	
	.05(2)	.13	.15	.16	.05(4)	.14	.07(2)	.07	.10
1.		1	181			1			
2.	1		34	1					
3.			28						
4.			8						
5.			49						
6.			88	1					
7.			2						
8.			9						
9.			20	1					
10.		1	103					1	
11.			33	1					1
12.			107						
13.			25						
14.			59	5					
15.			4	1					
16.			103	2					
17.		10	14				20		
18.			92						
19.		1	295	14					
20.			46						
21.			18	2					
22.			54	7					
23.		1	66	1					
24.			128	3					
25.			124	11	1				
26.			76	12					
27.			123	4					
28.			31	2					
29.			441	9					
30.			126	30	1				
31.			158	14					
32.			28	4					
33.			61	1	1				

	4.1.					4.2.		4.4.	
	.05(2)	.13	.15	.16	.05(4)	.14	.07(2)	.07	.10
34.			8						
35.			13	4					
36.	1		152	4	1				
37.			11						
38.			55						
39.									
40.			11						
41.			11						
42.			37						
	2	14	3032	134	4	1	20	1	1

	4.4.				4.5.				4.6.	
	.12	.05/07	.13	.15	.11	.12	.04/11	.16	.11	.03/08
1.	2		40	3	158	1	1		1	5
2.			10	2	45					2
3.					6					
4.			3	3	1					
5.			6		25					
6.			10	2	12					
7.			3		3					
8.			1	2	2					
9.			1		33					1
10.			10	5	184	1				1
11.	1		7	18	120					
12.			7	2	13					
13.			2	1	25					
14.			29	34	168			1		
15.				4	2					
16.			10	4	40					
17.					90	1				
18.			4	2	57					
19.			16	23	297					
20.				22	5			6		

	4.4.				4.5.				4.6.	
	.12	.05/07	.13	.15	.11	.12	.04/11	.16	.11	.03/08
21.					3					
22.			7	18	24					
23.			1	6	28					
24.			3	1	9					
25.			2	10	53					
26.				4	6					
27.				7	15					
28.			2	2	27					
29.			9	3	12					
30.			1	28	13					
31.			34	7	174					
32.			9	9	4					
33.			9	4	36					
34.			2	7	1					
35.			6	2	1					
36.			39	2	65			1		
37.			4		8					
38.		1		3	7					
39.			8		2					
40.			3							
41.			5		1					
42.			1		14					
	3	1	304	240	1789	2	1	8	1	9

	4.6.		4.7.						
	.07(2)	.15	.07	.10	.02/08	.11	.02/09	.12	.06(2)
1.			1		3	28	12		
2.						5	2		
3.									
4.									
5.		1				1		1	
6.						1	3		
7.						1			
8.		1				1			

| | 4.6. | | 4.7. | | | | | | |
	.07(2)	.15	.07	.10	.02/08	.11	.02/09	.12	.06(2)
9.					2	1	1		
10.				4	4	14	10	8	
11.							2		
12.									
13.						1			
14.						4			
15.									
16.						1			
17.									
18.									
19.									
20.									
21.									
22.	1								
23.									
24.									
25.									
26.									
27.									
28.									
29.									
30.									
31.	1				1	2	2		4
32.									
33.									1
34.									
35.						1			
36.					1	4	1		1
37.						1			
38.									
39.									
40.									
41.									
42.						4	3		
	2	2	1	4	11	70	36	9	6

	4.7.			4.8.			
	.02/11	.14	.07(2)	.05(2)	.08(2)	.05(4)	Total
1.		142	23				603
2.		19	2				123
3.		8					42
4.		10	3				28
5.		27	4				114
6.		38	11				166
7.		4	1				14
8.		11	2				29
9.		11	1				72
10.		83	1				430
11.		55	10				248
12.		90	16				235
13.		51	1				106
14.		164	31				495
15.		4	3				18
16.		66	4				230
17.		48	45				228
18.		48	4				207
19.		146	21				813
20.		32	32				143
21.		18	10				51
22.		85	17		1		214
23.		53	13				169
24.		75	21		1		241
25.		149	13		1		364
26.		166	11				275
27.		119	8				276
28.		45	1				110
29.		430	21		1		926
30.		141	24				364
31.	1	90	10			1	499
32.		27	13		3		97
33.		46	7		1		167
34.		10	2				30

	4.7.			4.8.			
	.02/11	.14	.07(2)	.05(2)	.08(2)	.05(4)	Total
35.		8	3				38
36.		49	13				334
37.		8	1				33
38.		24		1	1		92
39.		1	1		2		14
40.		21	4		3	1	43
41.		14	1		1		33
42.		27					86
	1	2663	409	1	15	2	8800

	5.1.			5.2.		5.3.		5.5.	5.6.	
	.10	.11	.13	.11	.16	.15	.16	.07(2)	.07(2)	Total
1.	17	18								35
2.	6	3								9
3.										0
4.		2	1							3
5.					1		1			2
6.		6								6
7.										0
8.	2									2
9.	3	1								4
10.	27	15								42
11.	61	16					1			78
12.	3	5								8
13.	24	1								25
14.	70	17		9	1		5			102
15.	8			7			5			20
16.	9	1								10
17.	107	20		14			9	1		151
18.	20	1								21
19.	81	4		19			21			125
20.	21			39			20			80
21.	3			2						5

	5.1.			5.2.		5.3.		5.5.	5.6.	
	.10	.11	.13	.11	.16	.15	.16	.07(2)	.07(2)	Total
22.	11	3			5		8			27
23.	10				1					11
24.	5				6		3			14
25.	21				9		1			31
26.	4				7					11
27.	10				1		10			21
28.	7	2			2		1			12
29.	3	5			4		2			14
30.	42				17		28			87
31.	17	7			4		1		1	30
32.	4	3			8		3			18
33.	9	4	1		1		2	1	1	19
34.							1			1
35.	4	2			4		2			12
36.	11	4			1		1			17
37.	6									6
38.	2						1			3
39.	4		1					1	1	7
40.	1						1			2
41.	2		2							4
42.	5	2								7
	640	142	5	1	160	1	127	3	3	1082

	6.1.		6.2.	9.1.	9.2.	9.7.	10.6.	12.2.	
	.12	.08(2)	.08(2)	.11	.10	.08(2)	.11	.07(2)	Total
1.				2	1	1			
2.									0
3.									0
4.	1								1
5.					1		1		2
6.									0
7.									0
8.									0
9.	1								1

| | 6.1. | | 6.2. | 9.1. | 9.2. | 9.7. | 10.6. | 12.2. | |
	.12	.08(2)	.08(2)	.11	.10	.08(2)	.11	.07(2)	Total
10.									0
11.									0
12.								1	1
13.									0
14.		1						1	2
15.									0
16.									0
17.								1	1
18.									0
19.								2	2
20.									0
21.									0
22.									0
23.									0
24.									0
25.									0
26.									0
27.									0
28.									0
29.									0
30.									0
31.		4						2	6
32.									0
33.		2							2
34.									0
35.								1	1
36.								1	1
37.									0
38.									0
39.									0
40.			1						1
41.									0
42.									0
	2	7	1	2	2	1	1	9	25

The following table shows the percentage use made of each of the main patterns by individual poets. These proportions may be compared with the average percentages given at the end of the table.

Pattern	1	2	3	4	5	6-14
1. Anthology	7.4	15.2	16.6	57.0	3.3	.5
2. Rudagi	7.4	14.8	20.4	53.5	3.9	-
3. ᒼonsori	11.8	28.9	4.0	55.3	-	-
4. Manucehri	7.1	29.6	30.6	28.6	3.1	1.0
5. Farroxi	5.9	13.8	31.0	47.7	.8	.8
6. Qatran	6.1	34.2	6.9	48.1	1.7	-
7. Naṣer-e Xosrou	17.5	22.5	25.0	35.0	-	-
8. Lameᒼi	2.5	30.4	27.9	36.7	2.5	-
9. Runi	5.5	13.8	10.1	66.1	3.7	.8
10. Masᒼud Saᒼd	5.5	8.8	11.4	67.7	6.6	-
11. Sanaʔi	2.2	40.9	20.1	28.0	8.8	-
12. Amir Moᒼezzi	3.0	35.0	19.0	41.4	1.4	.2
13. Ašraf	2.5	23.3	18.6	45.0	10.6	-
14. Xaqani	4.4	20.2	12.8	51.8	10.7	.1
15. Neẓami	-	35.2	23.1	19.8	21.9	-
16. Faryabi	.6	16.4	11.4	65.6	3.0	-
17. ᒼaṭṭar	.5	39.9	13.5	27.7	18.3	.1
18. Kamaloddin	4.3	15.4	14.0	60.2	6.1	-
19. Saᒼdi	6.6	20.3	17.4	48.1	7.5	.1
20. Moulavi	.3	33.1	33.7	21.1	11.8	-
21. Homam	-	40.7	15.6	39.8	3.9	-
22. Ouhadi	4.1	28.6	20.0	42.0	5.3	-
23. ᒼobeid Zakani	6.3	22.5	14.2	53.5	3.5	-
24. Ḥafeẓ	.9	19.2	31.7	45.5	2.7	-
25. Jami	3.0	37.5	21.3	35.2	3.0	-
26. Baba Feḡani	-	38.5	15.3	44.4	1.8	-
27. ᒼorfi	.7	27.7	23.2	45.0	3.4	-
28. Ṭarzi Afšar	8.6	30.8	14.6	40.6	4.4	-
29. Ṣaʔeb	.5	38.6	21.9	38.4	.6	-

Pattern	1	2	3	4	5	6-14
30. ʕašeq	3.2	26.4	25.1	36.6	8.7	-
31. Qaʔani	1.6	26.9	14.1	53.6	3.2	.6
32. Foruɡi	.8	14.0	41.8	36.6	6.8	-
33. Laʕli	5.4	28.5	18.3	42.5	4.8	.5
34. Adib	5.9	45.8	11.8	35.2	1.2	-
35. Šuride	.6	9.7	57.0	24.7	7.7	.6
36. Adibol-mamalek	6.0	26.4	13.8	51.1	2.6	.1
37. Iraj Mirza	-	19.3	33.7	39.8	7.2	-
38. ʕaref	2.5	8.8	28.9	57.9	1.9	-
39. Pur Daʔud	5.3	7.9	31.6	36.8	18.4	-
40. Farroxi	.5	41.5	35.0	21.5	1.0	.5
41. ʕešqi	-	33.3	22.6	39.3	4.8	-
42. Parvin	5.8	18.4	22.4	49.4	4.0	-
Average	3.3	27.6	19.7	43.8	5.4	.2

The following table gives the metres in order of
popularity, expressed as percentages of the total.

Over 10%

4.1.15	15.0
4.7.14	13.2
2.4.15	12.2

5-10%

3.1.15	9.7
4.5.11	8.9
2.1.16	6.0
3.3.14	5.7

1-5%

2.1.11	4.6
2.4.11	3.2
5.1.10	3.2
4.7.15	2.0
1.1.11	1.9
4.4.13	1.5
3.3.07(2)	1.3
1.1.12	1.3
2.3.16	1.2
4.4.15	1.2
3.4.11	1.1
3.1.11	1.1

0.1-1%

5.2.16	.8
5.1.11	.7
4.1.16	.7
5.3.16	.6
4.7.11	.3
3.1.16	.3
2.4.16	.2
4.7.02/09	.2
3.4.16	.1
4.2.07(2)	.1
1.2.05(2)	.1
3.1.13	.1
4.8.08(2)	.1
4.1.13	.1
2.4.12	.1
4.7.02/08	.1
3.2.07(2)	.1

Less than 0.1%

3.2.15

4.6.03/08	4.4.12	9.2.10	4.4.10
4.7.12	5.5.07(2)	1.3.10	4.4.05/07
12.2.07(2)	5.6.07(2)	2.1.08	4.5.04/11
4.5.16	1.1.09	2.3.11	4.6.11
6.1.08(2)	2.1.12	2.3.04(3)	4.7.07
3.3.05(2)	3.4.05(2)	2.3.13	4.7.02/11
4.7.06(2)	4.1.05(2)	2.4.05(2)	4.8.05(2)
5.1.13	4.5.12	2.4.13	5.2.11
3.3.10	4.6.07(2)	3.1.07(2)	5.3.15
3.3.11	4.6.15	3.3.13	6.2.08(2)
3.3.15	4.8.05(4)	4.2.14	9.7.08(2)
4.1.05(4)	6.1.12	4.4.07	10.6.11
4.7.10	9.1.11		

The following table shows the percentage of each of the main poetic forms composed in each metre, compared with the overall percentage.   x = less than 0.1%.

Metre	Qaṣīda	Qazal	Qiṭ‛a, etc.	Stanzaic	Total
1.1.09		x			x
1.1.11	1.5	.6	5.0	.5	1.9
1.1.12	2.3	.6	1.8		1.3
1.2.05(2)		.2	x		.1
1.3.10			x	.5	x
1.	3.8	1.4	6.8	1.0	3.3
2.1.08		x			x
2.1.11	2.9	3.7	8.1	5.3	4.6
2.1.12		x	x		x
2.1.16	5.3	8.4	2.0	5.3	6.0
2.3.11		x			x
2.3.04(3)		x			x
2.3.13		x			x

Metre	Qaṣīda	Qazal	Qitˁa, etc.	Stanzaic	Total
2.3.16	1.2	1.8	.3	.5	1.2
2.4.05(2)			x		x
2.4.11	1.2	2.2	3.5	3.3	3.2
2.4.12	.1	.1	.2		.1
2.4.13		x			x
2.4.15	16.9	14.6	6.7	11.4	12.2
2.4.16	.2	.2	.3		.2
2.	27.8	31.0	21.1	25.8	27.8
3.1.11	.8	1.1	2.2	2.4	1.1
3.1.13	.4		x		.1
3.1.07(2)		x			x
3.1.15	6.9	13.5	5.0	11.0	9.7
3.1.16		.5	x		.3
3.2.07(2)		x	x		.1
3.2.15	x	x	x		x
3.3.05(2)		x			x
3.3.10			x		x
3.3.11			x		x
3.3.13			x		x
3.3.14	7.5	6.9	3.4	7.2	5.7
3.3.07(2)	.6	2.0	.5	1.4	1.3
3.3.15		x			x
3.4.05(2)			x		x
3.4.11	.6	.7	1.7	3.3	1.1
3.4.16	x	x			.1
3.	16.8	24.8	13.1	25.8	19.8
4.1.05(2)			x		x
4.1.13	x	x	x		.1
4.1.15	20.1	13.5	16.4	1.4	15.0
4.1.16	.2	1.1	.5	.5	.7
4.1.05(4)	x	x			x
4.2.14			x		x

Metre	Qaṣīda	Qazal	Qiṭʿa, etc.	Stanzaic	Total
4.2.07(2)			x		.1
4.4.07	x				x
4.4.10			x		x
4.4.12		x			x
4.4.05/07			x		x
4.4.13	2.2	.9	2.7	1.9	1.5
4.4.15	1.3	1.6	.5	2.9	1.2
4.5.11	7.8	2.9	22.1	10.0	8.9
4.5.12		x			x
4.5.04/11			x		x
4.5.16		x	x		x
4.6.11			x		x
4.6.03/08	x	x			x
4.6.07(2)		x		x	x
4.6.15	x		x	x	x
4.7.07			x		x
4.7.10	.1		x		x
4.7.02/08	.2	x	x		.1
4.7.11	.6	x	.4		.3
4.7.02/09	.4		.3		.2
4.7.12	x	x	.2		x
4.7.06(2)	.1		x	.5	x
4.7.02/11			x		x
4.7.14	13.7	14.8	10.3	17.0	13.2
4.7.15	1.4	2.4	1.0	.9	2.0
4.8.08(2)		x			x
4.8.08(2)	x	x			.1
4.8.05(4)	x	x	x	.9	x
4.	48.3	37.2	54.2	37.0	43.7
5.1.10	1.5	2.7	3.9	6.7	3.2
5.1.11	1.3	.3	.6	.5	.7
5.1.13		x	x	x	x
5.2.11			x		x

Metre	Qaṣīda	Qazal	Qiṭ٩a, etc.	Stanzaic	Total
5.2.16	.3	1.3	x		.8
5.3.15		x			x
5.3.16	.1	1.2	.2	.5	.6
5.5.07(2)			x		x
5.6.07(2)			x		x
5.	3.2	5.5	4.8	9.1	5.3
6.1.12	x				x
6.1.08(2)	x	x		1.3	x
6.2.08(2)		x			x
9.1.11			x		x
9.2.10			x		x
9.7.08(2)			x		x
10.6.11			x		x
12.2.07(2)	x		x		x
6–14.	.1	.1	x	1.3	.1
	100.0	100.0	100.0	100.0	100.0

The following table shows the relative use made of short
(under 13 syllables) and long (13 syllables and upwards)
metres in each of the poetic forms and overall.

Short	Qaṣīda	Qazal	Qiṭ٩a	Stanzaic	Total
1.	3.8	1.4	6.8	1.0	3.3
2.	4.2	6.0	11.8	8.6	8.2
3.	1.4	1.8	4.0	5.7	2.3
4.	9.2	2.9	23.0	10.0	9.6
5.	2.8	3.0	4.5	7.2	3.9
6–14.	x	–	–	–	x
	21.4	15.1	50.1	32.5	27.3

	Qaṣida	Q̇azal	Qiṭ ͨa	Stanzaic	Total
Long					
2.	23.6	25.0	9.3	17.2	19.6
3.	15.4	23.0	9.1	20.1	17.5
4.	39.1	34.3	31.2	27.0	34.0
5.	.4	2.5	.3	1.9	1.5
6–14.	.1	.1	x	1.3	.1
	78.6	84.9	49.9	67.5	72.7
	100.0	100.0	100.0	100.0	100.0

V. The sources of the Persian metrical system[*]

The poetry of the early Islamic period in Iran is marked by some obvious points of departure from the past. The language is coloured by Arabic (though less than contemporary prose); the sentiments are influenced by religious and philosophical ideas developed under Islam; even the new Arabo-Persian script has its effect on the poet's style. All these influences were absent before the Arab invasions of the 1st/7th century. Is it legitimate then to regard this poetry as a complete break with tradition, an entirely new development in Persian literature?

In seeking an answer to this question we are severely handicapped by the absence of source material. It is only in fact from the 3rd/9th century that we begin to find any substantial volume of Persian verse in the written records, and even this consists of small isolated fragments quoted in the body of historical, literary and lexicographical works of later date. Nevertheless it is possible to judge that by this time Persian versification had already reached a fairly well-developed stage, from the point of view of both prosody and subject-matter.

[*] Passages from this chapter have already appeared in IRAN, Vol. XIII, 1975.

There are several possible explanations for this sudden
leap into the light of day. Some scholars, both Western and
Iranian, maintain that poetry was not composed in Persian
prior to the Islamic era, and that the earliest efforts were
those modelled on Arabic verse, which so far as can be judged
had achieved a high degree of technical achievement at least
as early as the century preceding Muhammad's mission and the
Arab conquest of Iran. This theory is of course based on
the supposed identity of Arabic and Persian "classical"
metres, a view that is no longer tenable in the light of the
facts put forward in the preceding chapters. Nevertheless
it has been seriously argued, in explanation of the technical
maturity of their earliest work, that the Persians, having no
poetic tradition of their own, merely adopted that of the
Arabs. This proposition finds some support in a statement
by the 3rd/9th century Arab writer ꜤAmr b. Baḥr al-Jāḥiż to
the effect that the versification (kalām) of the Iranians
was not to be regarded as poetry (šiꜤr).[9] However a modern
scholar, Moḥammad Qazvini, is certainly going too far when
he argues that a verse in a "classical" metre cannot have
been composed earlier than the 3rd/9th century, because the
rules of the Arabic metrical system were only "laid down" by
al-Xalīl at the end of the 2nd/8th century.[10]

Quite apart from any technical questions of prosodic
systems, it is innately improbable that the Iranians, famous
now for more than a thousand years for the wealth and pro-
fundity of their poetic expression, were prior to that devoid

of any poetic instinct and started as mere imitators of the
literary genius of another culture.   We know in fact that
poetry was composed in Iran long before Islamic times.   The
Gathic hymns of the Avesta, dating from no later than the 7th
century B.C. and possibly much earlier, are clear enough
evidence that poetic genius was not a sudden mutation in the
Iranian character dating from an influx of foreign invaders,
but a trait as old as the history of the people themselves.
In Parthian and Sasanian times the evidence becomes still
stronger.   Benveniste has shown that the Pahlavi books
Draxt-i asūrīk, a religious polemic, and Ayyātkār-i Zarērān,
a secular epic, were almost certainly originally written in
verse, sometimes with rhyme or assonance, while the Manichaean
documents discovered in Ṭurfαn in Central Asia in the early
years of this century contain many hymns in metrical form.
Isolated samples of verse occur in other Middle Iranian
works.[11]

Apart from such concrete evidence, the historical works
of the early Islamic period constantly repeat the tradition
that poetry was sung and recited at the Sasanian court, as
well as on a more popular level.   al-Jāḥiż's statement
referred to above, that this was not true poetry, may be
discounted as the reaction of a protagonist of Arabism
against the claims of the Šuʿūbīya.   The names of famous
minstrels of Sasanian times are recorded - Bαrbod, Bαmšαd,
Nagisα - and we may be sure that what they sang was poetic in
form.   We even know something of the different types of

poetry composed.   The sarūd was a hymn addressed to a king,
or used by the priests in their rituals;   the cakāmak or
cāmak was a love-lyric or romantic story, while the tarānak
was a feasting or drinking song.   All these terms are still
in use, and the same classification could equally well be
applied to the poetry of Islamic times.

It seems clear that we must look for some explanation
other than a lack of poetic genius for the virtual absence
of recorded poetry prior to the 3rd/9th century.   The most
obvious one is that the written records were destroyed.
There is certainly reason to think that many Pahlavi manu-
scripts disappeared during and after the Arab conquest.   Nor
was this the end of it.   The library of the Samanid court is
related to have been destroyed in an accidental fire about
388/998, while Maḥmud of Qazne is said to have demolished the
Buyid library in 420/1029.   And we cannot overlook the
wholesale destruction of life and property during the Mongol
invasions of the 7th/13th century, in spite of what tradition
says about the efforts of rulers like Hulagu to preserve
libraries.

An alternative, equally likely, explanation is that
poetry was rarely committed to writing in Sasanian times.
The poets and singers we hear most of were court officials
whose task was to entertain the monarch, and their work was
not intended for an audience outside the court.   Popular
verse, on the other hand, would not - as indeed it scarcely
is even today - be considered of sufficient importance to be

preserved.   Moreover the art of writing was virtually a
monopoly of the Zoroastrian priesthood, and there is evidence
of their hostility towards poetry, an attitude shared by the
religious authorities in early Islamic times.[12]   Although
therefore poetry would have been preserved in the memories of
the professional reciters, the attitude of the priesthood and
- in Islamic times - the dominating status of Arabic as the
language of literature as well as of religion and science
would together have militated against efforts to make a more
permanent record.   Bausani, noting that this "second-class"
status of poetry continued into much later times, links it
with the constant reference by Ṣufi poets to rosvaʔi
ignominy), rendi (rascality), kofr (idolatry), even in a
religious context.[13]

All the same, if we look back over the rather meagre
remnants of pre-classical and pre-Islamic Persian poetry, we
find that the scene is not quite so featureless as might at
first glimpse appear.   The Russian orientalist N. Marr
takes the view (for which he claims the support of
Krachkovsky and Salemann) that the mutaqārib metre (1.1.11)
is derived directly from the eleven-syllable metres used for
much of the Middle Persian poetry that has survived.[14]   It
is certainly true that this metre is unknown in pre-Islamic
Arabic poetry, and is extremely rare in the poetry of the
Umayyad period.   It occurs more frequently in ʕabbāsid times,
a fact that suggests that the copying was from Persian to
Arabic.   Benveniste, quoted above (note 11), has pointed out

that parts of the two Pahlavi poems discussed by him seem to
be in a metre very close to it, and he even quotes a verse
from the former that must have been a prototype for one in
Daqiqi's part of the Šahnɑme:

    hac e:n xɑ:k axe:ze:t o kay gɑ:h niši:ne:t
                          (Ayyātkār-i Zarērān)

    to zi:n xɑ:k bar xi:z o bar šou be-gɑ:h (Šahnɑme)

    Rise from this land and sit on the royal throne!

Ibn Xurdādbih, author of the Kitāb al-masālik wa l-mamālik
(c. 230/844), quotes a popular verse (which he attributes to
one Abolyanbaqi ʕabbɑs b. Ṭorxɑn) which seems to have something of the mutaqārib rhythm:

        samarqand-i kandmand   be-zi:nat kiy afgand
        ʔaz cɑc ta bihi: hami:še ta xohi:

The verses are said to be a lament for the ruin of Samarqand,
and are interpreted by Zabihollɑh Ṣafɑ as follows:

    "O prosperous Samarqand, who has brought you to this
state? You are better than Cɑc, you are always good!"

    Another early verse of less certain authenticity is
quoted by Doulatšɑh in his Tazkeratoš-šoʕarɑ (892/1487), on
the authority of a late 5th/11th century poet, Abu Ṭaher
Xɑtuni, as having been inscribed on the ruins of Qaṣr-e
Širin. The metre is quite clearly Pattern 1, though the
original may well have been corrupted in transmission.

    hežabrɑ: be-geihɑ:n anušah be-zi:
    jahɑ:n-rɑ: be-di:dɑ:r-e to: šah be-zi:
    May the lion live prosperous on the earth!
    May the world gain a king at the sight of you!

Finally Christensen suggests that a fragment of a Zurvanite
hymn detected by Nyberg in the Pahlavi book the Bondahešn is
in something like this metre, though Nyberg himself regards
it as being nearer to the New Persian dūbaytī metre (2.1.11).[15]

Reference to the tables in the preceding chapter will
show that metres of this pattern were common by the early
Islamic period (over 7%), and in Chapter III examples are
quoted from Šahid Balxi (fl. 3rd/9th century), Mosʕabi (fl.
300), and Firuz Mašreqi (fl. 3rd/9th century).

Pattern 5 is even more clearly of Persian origin.   The
most noteworthy metre in this class is that used for the
rubāʕī (5.1.13).   Although the earliest extant example is by
Šahid Balxi, even the prosodists accept that it was developed
by the poets of Iran - though we should perhaps take with a
pinch of salt the legend recorded by Doulatšah that it was
originally inspired by the excited cry of the small son of
Yaʕqub b. Leis̲ as he was rolling nuts into a ditch:

ɢalṭa:n ɢalṭa:n hami:ravad tɑ: lab-e gav
It goes rolling rolling to the edge of the ditch!
Certainly no such metre is found in Arabic, even when the
quatrain form is consciously copied.   On the other hand,
according to Rempis, there is a discernible relationship with
the metre used for some parts of the Avestan Yasna.[16]   It is
reasonable too to suppose that the pattern as a whole is from
Persian sources;   other metres in the group are to be found
even earlier than the rubāʕī itself (Abu Salik Gorgani,
5.1.10;   Firuz Mašreqi, 5.1.11).   Krachkovsky, quoted by

Marr in the article referred to above (note 12) finds
similar metres in the Arabic poetry of the ʿabbāsid period
(he quotes an example from Abu l-Faraj Dimašqī, a 4th/10th
century poet), but is convinced that these were copied from
Persian rather than the reverse, since they are not found in
Umayyad times at all.

There is an obvious resemblance between Pattern 5 and
Pattern 4, the latter being the same sequence of syllables in
the reverse order.   As the statistics show, this pattern is
the favourite in Islamic Persian poetry, accounting for
nearly half of the total output, and one metre alone (4.1.15)
being chosen for 15%.   It is symbolic that one of the oldest
examples of "classical" Persian verse is in another metre of
this pattern (4.5.11), some lines written about 256/870 by
Ḥanẓale of Baḍḍis which are said to have inspired the
military career of a local chieftain:

> mehtari: gar be-kɑ:m-e ši:r dar ast
> šou xatar-kon ze kɑ:m-e ši:r be-juy
> yɑ: bozorgi:y o ʿezz o neʿmat o jɑ:h
> yɑ: co mardɑ:nt marg-e ru:yɑ:ru:y

> Even if chieftainship be in the mouth of a lion,
> Be reckless, seek it from the lion's mouth!
> Either greatness, glory, wealth and pomp,
> Or meeting death face to face like a man!

It is less easy to detect examples of Pattern 4 in pre-
classical poetry.   Some verses in the Draxt-i asūrīk might
be thought to fit:

> ēvom apartar hac tō draxt asūrīk

> I alone am superior to you, O Assyrian tree!

The Tarix-e Sistαn quotes a hymn recited by the Zoroastrian
priests at the fire-temple of Karkuy, which Ṣafα regards as
syllabic, but which could equally be fitted into a prototype
of this pattern:

froxte bα:dα: ru:š   xonide garšasb hu:š
May the light be kindled, may the soul of Garšasb be
                                        praised! etc.

Both patterns may be related to, possibly even derived
from, Pattern 3, features of which are seen in several pre-
classical verses.   The Tarix-e Sistαn, as well as three
Arabic sources, attributes to one Yazid b. Mofarreḍ, in about
the year 60/680, the following jingle:

ʔα:b ast o nabi:d ast   ҁoṣα:rα:t-e zabi:b ast
va donbe farbeh o pi:y ast   someiye ru:sbi:d ast

There's water and date-wine; there's dregs from dried
raisins; there's fat and a sheep's fat tail - and
Someiye is a tart!

In 108/726 a defeated general is said to have been thus
satirised by the people of Balx:

ʔaz xottalα:n α:madi:h   bα: ru: tabα:h α:madi:h
ʔα:vα:r bα:z α:madi:h   bi:-del farα:z α:madi:h

He's come back from Xotlαn; he's come with a sour face;
he's come back on the run;   he's come down sick at heart!

Several different versions are found of a verse attributed
to the Sasanian king Bahrαm Gur.   The attribution is unlikely,
but the bayt itself must be quite old, probably in the
following form:

man-am α:n ši:r-e šalanbe: va man-am babr-e yale:
I am that lion of Šalanbe, I am the roaming tiger!

A verse attributed to Abu Ḥafṣ Soġdi (4th/10th century), but
probably of much earlier date, also fits Pattern 3:

ʔɑ:hoy-e: ku:hi: dar dašt cegu:ne: davadɑ:
yɑ:r na:dɑ:rad̲ bi: yɑ:r cegu:ne davadɑ:

How does the mountain deer run in the valley?
He has no companion, how can he run without a companion?

As soon as we move into the Islamic period, we found
numerous examples of this pattern.   Almost contemporary with
the verse cited above by Ḥanżale Badġisi are three poems
recited before the Ṣaffarid ruler Yaʕqub b. Leis̲ shortly
after 251/865.   The first, by Moḥammad b. Vaṣif, is quoted
in Chapter III under metre 3.1.15.   The other two, by
Bassɑm Kurd and Moḥammad b. Moxallad, are both in 3.4.11:

har ke nabu:d u:y be-del mottaham
bar ʔas̲ar-e: daʕvat-e to: kard naʕam

All those who have no suspicion in their hearts
Have replied to your call - Yes!

*

joz to na-zɑ:d ḥavvɑ: v-ɑ:dam na-kešt
ši:r-nehɑ:di: be-del u: bar manešt

Eve never bore nor Adam begat one apart from you
Lion-like in heart and in greatness!

Pattern 2 comes nearest to an Arabic prototype;   but
even this has its Iranian forbears.   Metre 2.1.11, of which
an example is quoted in Chapter III from Maḥmud Varrɑq (fl.
256/870), is still commonly used today for the popular
dūbaytī, a quatrain form known in many Persian dialects;   and,
as the statistics show, it is equally frequent in all the
literary forms.   Adib Ṭusi differs from Benveniste in considering that most of the verses in the Draxt-i asūrīk can

be scanned in this way, while Nyberg suggests that a hymn to
Zurvān found in the Bondahešn is also of this type.[18]

Other examples of pre-Islamic and early Islamic verse have
recently come to light which, in the form they have reached
us, are less easy to fit into one of the standard patterns,
but which warrant further examination.   Three lines attributed to the Sasanian minstrel Barbod, and in any case almost
certainly dating from Sasanian times, are quoted in the kitāb
al-lahw wa'l-malāhī, a work attributed to the 3rd/9th century
writer Ibn Xurdādbih:[19]

> Qeiṣar mah manad o Xaqan xoršēd
> ʔan-e man xoday abr manad kamḍaran
> ka xᵛahad mah pōšad ka xᵛahad xoršēd

Another interesting discovery is a Persian translation of
a portion of the Qur'ān, possibly as early as the 2nd/9th
century, a unique manuscript of which was recently unearthed
during repairs to the Library at the Shrine of Emam Reza in
Mashhad.[20]   The editor claims it as "a bridge between
Persian syllabic and quantitative verse", and points out
that, apart from the use of rhyme and radīf, about a quarter
of the 2,000 hemistichs can be scanned according to the ʕarūḍ
system.   Most of them in fact seem to be in one or other
form of 5.1, though other patterns are present.

> do: ḥarf-e ḥadi:s man be-gu:yam
> mi: vɑ: gardam na man vaki:lam   (5.1.10)
>   *****
> ʔɑ:nɑ:n k-i:šɑ:n movaḥḥedɑ:n bɑ:šand
> bi: šakk i:šɑ:n beheštiyɑ:n bɑ:šand   (5.1.11)

While it is arguable that this translation is not in

verse but in an unusually regular form of rhymed prose, it
is nevertheless of considerable interest as a source for
examination of the relation between prosodic metres and the
rhythms of ordinary speech.

It remains to be considered whether we can throw any
light on the origins of these metres, now that we have satis-
fied ourselves that they are not copied from Arabic.   Our
task is complicated by two factors.   When we turn to pre-
Islamic verse, and particularly that of the Pahlavi books,
we find that the orthography is so obscure and inadequate
(only thirteen symbols are available to represent some two
dozen sounds, the indication of vowels is haphazard or non-
existent, and many words are represented by hozvareš
ideograms) that it is impossible to determine length and
quantity with any degree of accuracy.   As was noted above,
even scholars who accept the possibility of a quantitative
basis for Middle Iranian verse differ radically on how it
should be scanned.   The position is even more complex and
involved when it comes to Avestan verse.

Our second problem is that, until recently, specialists
in Iranian studies have tended to confine their researches
to one side or other of the Islamic watershed.   So far as
the examination of prosody is concerned, this has resulted
in two quite distinct approaches.   Islamic scholars, alerted
by the work of al-Xalīl, have recognised that New Persian
verse is quantitative, but largely ignore questions of stress
and syllable;   their colleagues on the other side of the

fence are convinced that Avestan and Pahlavi verse is
"syllabic", and that quantity does not enter into the matter.
Where it can be shown that a text is divisible into lines of
approximately equal syllabic length, this is accepted as
sufficient evidence that it is verse, and no further enquiry
is deemed necessary. Thus two entirely different types of
verse are observed, and it is easy to assume that there is no
connection between them. Lazard, for example, considers
that the fragments of early popular verse, such as those
quoted above from the Tarix-e Sistan and other works, which
"are not composed according to the principles of quantitative
metrics, on the Arabic model", are to be regarded as relics
of the "accentual" system of pre-Islamic poetry.[21]

The conventional view of the pre-Islamic metres is well
expressed by Benveniste when he writes: "The fundamental
character common to these three systems of versification,
Avestan, Pahlavi, and current, is in being based on the
syllabic principle and in excluding all considerations of
quantity." Thus the normal classification of the Avestan
metres is into lines of varying syllabic length ranging
generally from seven to ten syllables, broken by a caesura
into approximately equal halves. This caesura in fact seems
to be widely adopted as the basis not only of Avestan and
Middle Iranian verse, but also of Sanskrit. Yet it is
difficult to see what metrical role it can play, especially
as it means no more than the end of a word somewhere near
the middle of the line.

The inadequacy of the caesura as a metrical device,

coupled with the fact that in all this pre-Islamic verse the lines are seldom of equal syllabic length, persuaded some scholars to introduce the concept of "accentual" verse. As Henning puts it, writing of the Avestan metres, "the important point throughout is the number of stressed syllables...The favourite type of verse has lines of either three or four stressed syllables, the number of unstressed syllables being free...It seems to me that the verse of the Younger Avesta is in no way different from the Middle Iranian line of three stressed syllables." Henning offers a number of examples of Avestan verse-lines duly provided with three stress-accents; but one's confidence in this promising analysis is a little shaken when one finds that another scholar, Hertel, pursuing the subject on rather similar lines, accents the same verses not merely on different syllables, but with as many as four or five stresses.[22]

This rugged refusal to consider quantity as a factor in these metrical systems is all the more curious when it is remembered that the concept has never been questioned in the case of another major branch of Indo-European prosody, the Greek. If the Greeks understood this principle from the earliest times, why not the Iranians, and for the matter of that the Indians? Indeed Bīrūnī's discussion of Sanskrit and Arabic metres in his work on India suggests that in his time at any rate quantity was well recognised by Indian prosodists, and that their theories may even have had some influences on al-Xalīl. "Alkhalīl Ibn Aḥmad exclusively

drew from his own genius when he invented the Arabic metrics,
though, possibly, he may have heard, as some people think,
that the Hindus use certain metres in their poetry."[23]   To
speculate any further along these lines would be wholly
unprofitable, and we will content ourselves with drawing
attention to a curiosity.   Some of the Greek prosodists
give to the Ionicus a maiore (– – ◡ ◡) the name "persikos,
because the Persian histories were written in this metre,
both by Aeschylus and by others."   v. Wilamowitz-Moellendorf,
who quotes this passage, believes it may refer inter alia to
the opening passages of Aeschylus' The Persians, which are
certainly written in a pattern equivalent to our Pattern 3
(◡ ◡ – – ◡ ◡ – –...), a pattern we have already postulated as
being a possible source of the other classical Persian
metres.[24]

At this point it may be time to question the view that
verse can be purely syllabic.   The essence of rhythm is
contrast – a "regular swing of the pendulum".   A constant
syllabic length may or may not be a pre-requisite of
metrically balanced verses, but it is not enough by itself;
some pattern must be imposed on this, whether of quantity,
stress, pitch, or even vowel colour.   The basic element is
time, marked out in equal or proportioned lengths.   If stress
plays a part in the rhythm, there must still be a regular time
separation measured in some way.   But a purely quantitative
regular pattern does not need (though it may have) stress as
well.   One might pursue this matter further, but it is

sufficient to say that, whether the syllabic/accentual view
of pre-Islamic Persian verse is correct or not, this approach
is of little help in our discussion of the Islamic metres.
On the other hand, one is reluctant to accept Benveniste's
opinion that "the originality of the Persians in the matter
of poetic technique consisted in subjecting the Iranian
syllabic metre to the Arabic quantitative prosody."   We
have already seen that the supposed link with Arabic prosody
does not exist, and we are bound therefore to seek the
origin of the classical Persian metres in their immediate
predecessors.

The one thing we may be quite sure of is that, whenever
the present verse patterns were established (and this was
certainly no later than the beginning of the Islamic era),
the quantitative values of particular sounds and syllables
in Persian words already existed in Persian speech.   And
just as they came to form the basis of the subsequent stage
of Persian versification, so we can hardly suppose that they
played no part in what went before.   We may then draw two
main conclusions:

(a) there is some link between pre-Islamic and Islamic
prosody

(b) the traditional analysis of the pre-Islamic metres
along syllabic or accentual lines is inadequate.

From this it seems to follow that what we know so far of
the pre-Islamic metres will not help us much in our enquiry
into the Islamic metres, though the principles governing

the latter may well be worth consideration in further analysis
of the pre-Islamic metres.   For instance, the problem of the
variable syllabic length of parallel lines in Pahlavi (and
even Avestan) verse, which has puzzled many scholars, could
at least be examined in the light of the almost identical
variations that are found in classical Persian verses, and
which are easily explained on a quantitative basis.

We must now leave these historical speculations, and
proceed on the assumption that, if the basic "patterns" of
the classical Persian metres are founded on something
characteristic in Persian speech, we may expect to find
echoes of them in aspects of Persian literature, written and
oral, other than classical poetry.   First of all, though,
in support of the suggestion made earlier that Patterns 4
and 5 could be "derived" from Pattern 3, it is worth noting
that - apart from the well-known association of 3.3.13 and
5.1.13 in the rubāʕī - other such combinations are not
infrequently found, especially in early poetry.   An example
is given in the list in Chapter III of a verse (from <u>al-
Moʕjam)</u> which combines 3.3.09 with 5.1.09, while Saʕdi gives
an example of 3.3.10 with 5.1.10.

ʔaz dast o zabɑ:n-e ke: bar ɑ:yad
‑ ‑ ◡ ◡ ‑ ◡ ‑ ◡ ‑ ‑   (5.1.10)

k-az ʕohde-ye šokraš be-dar ɑ:yad
‑ ‑ ◡ ◡ ‑ ‑ ◡ ◡ ‑ ‑   (3.3.10)

The verse by Sanaʔi quoted under 5.2.04/12 occurs in a ġazal

the first bayt of which is quoted under 3.4.08(2).   Rudagi
has the following verse, combining 5 with 4:

ni:z ʔabɑ: ni:kovɑ:n namɑ:yadat jang-e fand

⌒ ᴗ − − ᴗ −   ᴗ − ᴗ − −   ᴗ −   (4.4.07/5.6.07)

laškar-e feryɑ:dani: xɑ:ste nei su:dmand

− ᴗ ᴗ − − ᴗ −   ⌒ ᴗ −   ⌒ −   (4.4.07(2))

The _Tarjomɑnol-balɑǧe_ quotes two verses by Abolḥasan ɑǧɑci
(4th/10th century) which combine Patterns 3 and 4:

nɑ:n-e nɑ:-kas batar az marg-e faji:ʔ

− ᴗ − − ᴗ ᴗ − − ᴗ ᴗ −   (3.1.11)

zoll-e tohmat batar az zoll-e niyɑ:z

− ᴗ − − ᴗ ᴗ − − ᴗ ᴗ −   (3.1.11)

hark beštɑ:ft bɑ:z pastar mɑ:nd

⌒ − ⌒ ⌒ − − −   (4.5.11)

zu:d bi:-ti:r mɑ:nd ti:r-andɑ:z

⌒ − ⌒ ⌒ − − −   (4.5.11)

This could be "corrected" by substituting _ze_ for _az_ in the
first two lines, but it is not so written in the original
manuscript dated 507/1113-4.

    In spite of the conservative nature of Islamic
literature, there seems to have been some experimentation.
Šams-e Qeis lists (with condemnation) three new "circles",
said to have been invented by Bahrɑmi Saraxsi, Bozorjmehr
Qɑsemi, and Abu ʕabdollah Qoraši:

1. al-dā ʔirat al-munꜤakisa

ṣarīm	⏑ – – – | – ⏑ – – | – ⏑ – –
kabīr	– – – ⏑ | – – – ⏑ | – – ⏑ –
badīl	– – ⏑ – | – – ⏑ – | – ⏑ – –
qalīb	– ⏑ – – | – ⏑ – – | ⏑ – – –
ḥamīd	– – – ⏑ | – – ⏑ – | – – – ⏑
ṣaḍīr	– – ⏑ – | – ⏑ – – | – – ⏑ –
aṣamm	– ⏑ – – | ⏑ – – – | – ⏑ – –
salīm	– – ⏑ – | – – – ⏑ | – – – ⏑
ḥamīm	– ⏑ – – | – – ⏑ – | – – ⏑ –

2. al-dā ʔirat al-munḍalita

bāꜤi̱t	⏑ – – – | – ⏑ – – | – – ⏑ –
qāṭiꜤ	– – ⏑ – | – – – ⏑ | – ⏑ – –
muštarik	– ⏑ – – | – – ⏑ – | ⏑ – – –
muꜤammam	– – – ⏑ | – ⏑ – – | – – ⏑ –
musattar	– – ⏑ – | ⏑ – – – | – ⏑ – –
muꜤayyan	– ⏑ – – | – – ⏑ – | – – – ⏑

3. al-dā ʔirat al-munꜤaliqa

maṣnūꜤ	⏑ – – – | – – ⏑ – | – ⏑ – –
mustaꜤmal	– – – ⏑ | – – ⏑ – | – ⏑ – –
axras	– – ⏑ – | – ⏑ – – | ⏑ – – –
mubham	– – ⏑ – | – ⏑ – – | – – – ⏑
muhmal	– ⏑ – – | ⏑ – – – | – – ⏑ –
maꜤkūs	– ⏑ – – | – – – ⏑ | – – ⏑ –

Some prosodists added two metres to al-Xalīl's al-dā ʔirat al-muxtalifa:

Ꜥarīḍ (mustaṭīl)	⏑ – – – | ⏑ – – | ⏑ – – – | ⏑ – –
Ꜥamīq (mumtadd)	– ⏑ – – | ⏑ – – | – ⏑ – – | ⏑ – –

There is no evidence that any of these metres were adopted by practicing poets.

According to Rypka, an experiment in syllabic verse is to be found in the dīwān of Ḥeidar Širazi, in a satire against

Xaju Kermani written about 750/1349; but there is no sign
of one in the British Museum manuscript of this work, and it
seems possible that Rypka misunderstood a footnote by Qasem
Qani which uses the word hijā?ī, meaning either "syllabic" or
"satirical" - in this case the latter.   Rypka also suggests
that the 12th/18th century poet Šehab Toršizi used "new verse-
forms"; but whatever this means, it cannot refer to new
metres, of which there are none in this poet's dīwān.[25]

   Mohammad Ishaque has given details of two experiments
carried out in 1930 in what he describes as "syllabic"
verse.[26] The first of these, two poems by Yahya Doulatabadi
written at the suggestion of E.G. Browne, are a conscious
imitation of what was supposed to be the syllabic system of
pre-Islamic verse.   The first is composed in five-line
stanzas, three lines of twelve syllables and two of seven,
divided approximately 7 + 5 and 4 + 3 respectively, no distinction being observed in respect of the quantity of the
syllables.

> sobhdam peimane šod az xoftan labriz
> jam-e bidari dar kaf kaj dar o mariz
> xab ba cašmanam andar jang o goriz
>   na xab budam na bidar
>   na mast budam na hušyar

The stanzas of the second poem consist of five eight-syllable
lines (4 + 4) and one ten-syllable.

> man dar Galam juyam adam   Gaqel dana kamel bina
> niku-xeslat niku-tinat   saheb-hemmat saheb-Gezzat
> šaxs-e rangin mard-e sangin   ?az har ce bovad in beh
>   dar Galam

Ishaque also identifies as syllabic a poem written by
ʕabdol-ḥosein Ɑyati in the same year, but there is clearly a
quantitative element in the metre, and in fact it can be
classified as 4.5.05(4) - not a previously known metre, but
possible within the system.

co be-dɑ:m-e: ʕešq   .   -e to oftɑ:dam . ze qoyu:d u:
ᴗ ᴗ ‒ ‒ ‒   ᴗ ᴗ ‒ ‒ ‒   ᴗ ᴗ ‒ ‒

                    sel   .   sele ʔɑ:zɑ:d-am
                     ‒   ᴗ ᴗ ‒ ‒ ‒

na-konam xod-rɑ: . be-jahɑ:n pɑ:-band . ke be-ʔɑ:zɑ:di:
ᴗ ᴗ ‒̈ ‒ ‒   ᴗ ᴗ ‒ ‒ ‒   ᴗ ᴗ ‒ ‒ ‒

                    . ze jahɑ:n zɑ:dam
                       ᴗ ᴗ ‒ ‒ ‒

Ishaque mentions, but without awareness of his importance
to the development of contemporary Persian poetry, Nimɑ Yušij
(1895-1958).   To him is owed the introduction into Persian
literature of "free verse" - <u>šeʕr-e ɑzɑd</u> - widely used by
contemporary poets, and in recent years taking a number of
different forms.   For the purposes of our present study,
however, the most interesting facet is that (widely adopted
by the majority of the "free verse" poets, including Nimɑ
himself) in which the traditional patterns are retained,
and the "freedom" consists in varying the length of the line
(and omitting rhyme).   Since no one would suggest that
these poets are bound by tradition in retaining this feature,
we can only conclude that the patterns are so natural to
Persian speech that it is hard even for a revolutionary
poet to abandon them.   In a volume of šeʕr-e ɑzɑd published
in 1961, out of 47 poems by sixteen poets, only four (by two

poets) do not use one or other of the patterns, and though
the picture has changed a little since then, it is still
substantially the same.   A few samples follow, with dates:

Nima Yušij

4.7.   qoqnu:s morq̇-e xoš-xa:n a:va:ze-ye: jaha:n
(1937)   − ⌣̄ − ⌣ − − − − ⌣ −   ⌣ −

       ʔa:va:re ma:nde ʔaz vazeš-e: ba:d-ha:-ye sard
       − − ⌣ − − ⌣ − ⌣ ⌣ − ⌣̄ − ⌣ −

       bar ša:x-e xeizora:n
       − − ⌣ − ⌣ −

       be-nšaste ʔast fard
       − − ⌣ ⌣̄ ⌣̄

       bar gerd-e ʔu: be-har sar-e ša:xi: parandaga:n
       − − ⌣ − ⌣ − ⌣ ⌣ − − ⌣ − ⌣ −

2.4.
(1941) morq̇-e ʔa:mi:n dard-ʔa:lu:di:-st k-a:va:re: be-ma:nde:
       − ⌣ − − ⌣̄ − − ⌣̄ − − − ⌣ − −

       rafte ta: ʔa:n-su:-ye ʔi:n bi:da:d-xa:ne:
       − ⌣ − − − − − ⌣̄ − − −

       ba:z gašte: roq̇bataš di:gar ze ranju:ri: na su:-ye
       ⌣̄ − − − − ⌣ − − − − − ⌣ − −

                         ʔa:b o da:ne:
                         − ⌣ − −

       noubat-e: ru:z-e: goša:yeš-ra:
       − ⌣ − − − ⌣ − − −

       dar pay-e: ca:re: be-ma:nde:
       − ⌣ − − − ⌣ − −

3.1.
(1946) ʔu: ze raft-a:madan-e: mouj be-ja:n šu:ri:de:
       − ⌣ − − ⌣ ⌣ − ⌣̄ ⌣ − − −

       ʔa:mad andi:še be-ka: raš ba:ri:k
       − ⌣ − − ⌣ ⌣ − − − −

       goft ba: xod ce šabi:
       ⌣̄ − − ⌣ −

bɑ: hame: xande-ye mahtɑ:b-aš bar man tɑ:ri:k
  – ◡ – – ◡ ◡ – – – – – –

cašm-e ʔi:n azraq
  – ◡ – – –

man be-rɑ:h-e:xod bɑ:yad be-ravam
  – ◡ – – – – – ◡ ◡ –

6.1.
(1956) ti ti:k ti ti:k
  ◡ – ◡ –

dar i:n kenɑ:r-e sɑ:ḥel u: be-ni:me šab
  ◡ – ◡ – ◡ – ◡ ◡ – ◡ – ◡ –

nok mi:-zanad
  – – ◡ –

siyu:li še:
  ◡ – ◡ –

ru-ye: šiše:
  ◡ – ◡ –

Mohammad ʕali Eslɑmi (Nodušan) (b. 1925)

1.3. ʔu: nešaste: marɑ: dar barɑ:bar
  – ◡ – – ◡ – – ◡ –

cu:n ʕoqɑ:bi: žiyɑ:n bar sar-e: ku:h
  – ◡ – – ◡ – – ◡ – –

zolf bogšu:de dar bɑ:d-e xɑ:var
  ⌣ – – ◡ – – ◡ – –

del por az yɑ:d
  – ◡ – –

šɑ:d o nɑ:-šɑ:d
  – ◡ – –

tɑ:ji ʔaz xande-ye: ṣobḥ bar sar
  – ◡ – – ◡ – ⌣ – –

Nɑder Nɑderpur (b. 1929)

2.3. ʔu: bu:d o man dar xɑ:ne-ye: man
  – – ◡ – – – ◡ –

v-ɑ:n ɑ:teš-e: sorx
  – – ◡ – –

mi:-su:xt dar kɑ:šɑ:ne-ye: man
- -◡ - - - ◡ - -

ʔaz pošt-e ʔa:teš ṭarḥ-e ʔandɑ:m-e: boland-aš
- - ◡ - - - ◡ - - - ◡ - -

raqsande cu:n du:d
- - ◡ - -

pi:cande cu:n mɑ:r
- - ◡ - -

mi:-goft bɑ: har pi:c o tɑ:b afsɑ:ne-ye: man
- -◡ - - - ◡ - - - - ◡ - -

Even those poets who appear to have abandoned quantitative
metres altogether sometimes have reminiscences of them in
their verse.   A passage in one of the best-known poems of
Foruǧ Farroxzɑ:d (1934-1967) has something of the Pattern 3
rhythm:

hame-ye: hasti-ye man ʔa:ye-ye tɑ:ri:ki:st
◡ ◡ - - ◡ ◡ - - ◡ ◡ - - -

ke to-rɑ: dar xod tekrɑ:r-konɑ:n
◡ ◡ - - - - -◡ ◡ -

be-saḥar-gɑ:h-e šegeftan-hɑ: vu: rostan-hɑ:-ye:
◡ ◡ - - ◡ ◡ - - - - - - - -

                              ʔabadi: xɑ:had bord
                              ◡ ◡ - - - - -

man dar i:n ɑ:ye to-rɑ: ʔɑ:h kaši:dam ʔɑ:h
- ◡ - - ◡ ◡ - -◡ ◡ - - -

man dar i:n ɑ:ye to-rɑ:
- ◡ - - ◡ ◡ -

be-daraxt u: ʔɑ:b u: ʔɑ:teš peivand zadam
◡ ◡ - - - - - - - -◡ ◡ -

To complete this investigation it would be necessary to
examine the rhythms of popular poetry and songs, folk poetry,
and prose writing from various periods, all of which would
expand this study well beyond the scope envisaged for it.

These lines of research must be left to some future occasion,
and we will content ourselves now with a glance at a curiosity
of post-classical Persian prose writing which is not without
its bearing on the questions we are discussing.   This is the
Persian bahr-e tawīl, which has nothing whatever to do with
the Arabic metre of the same name, but is a form of prose-
writing in which a consistent pattern (generally our Pattern
3) is maintained indefinitely.   Although an example of it is
attributed rather doubtfully to the poet Amir Xosrou of Delhi
(651/1253-724/1324), it is probably a much later development.
One of the most skilful practitioners was the Ɑẕarbɑyejɑni
poet Ṭarzi Afšar (11th/17th century), though one's attention
is liable to be distracted by his remarkable grammatical and
syntactical experiments:

šokr lellɑh ke be-kohli:d marɑ: di:de, ze xɑ:k-e: dar-e
⌣‿ – –   ⌣ ⌣ – ⌣‿   ⌣ – – ⌣ ⌣ – – ⌣ ⌣

qoumi:, ke ze ʔoulɑ:d-e rasu:land, bar aflɑ:k-e qabu:land,
– –   ⌣ ⌣ –   ⌣ ⌣ – ⌣‿   ⌣ – – ⌣ ⌣ – ⌣‿

goru:hi: hame pɑ:ki:ze va xoš-su:rat o ni:ku:-siyar u: pɑ:k-
⌣ – –   ⌣ ⌣ – ⌣ ⌣ – ⌣ – – ⌣ ⌣ – ⌣ ⌣ ⌣‿

serešt u: malaki:-xu:y . yɑ:ftam ʔaz ʔaṣar-e: ṣohbatašɑ:n
⌣ – – ⌣ ⌣ – ⌣‿   ⌣‿ – – ⌣ ⌣ – ⌣ ⌣ –

feiẕ-e farɑ:vɑ:n o beru:n az had o ʔandɑ:ze va darsi:dam o
– ⌣ ⌣ – – ⌣ ⌣ – – ⌣ ⌣ – – ⌣ ⌣ – – ⌣ ⌣

ʕelmi:dam o fahmi:dam, agar bogzarad ayyɑ:m-e man, i:n nouʕ,
– – ⌣ ⌣ – – ⌣ ⌣ – ⌣ – – ⌣ ⌣ – – ⌣ ⌣ – ‿

be-mɑ:tam ʕolamɑ:-rɑ:...
⌣ – – ⌣ ⌣ – –

    Some characteristics will be noticed: the sequence ⌣ ⌣
is never replaced by –, though at the beginning of a sentence
it may become – ⌣; sentences end on – ‿, though breaks within

the sentence may come anywhere.   Ṭarzi Afšar does not as a
rule introduce rhyme or assonance, but that this is also
common may be seen from this extract from a satire on Fatḥ
ʕali Šᵃh (reg. 1211/1797-1250/1834) by the Baxtyari poet
Farroxi Borujani Cahᵃr Maḥali:[27]

gu: xodɑ: du:st-e ḥari:fi: vɑ neku: ru:-ye žari:fi: ke
‾   ᵕ ‾   ‾   ᵕ ᵕ ‾   ‾   ᵕ ᵕ ‾   ‾   ᵕ ᵕ ‾   ‾ ᵕ

bovad ʕɑ:qel o farzɑ:ne va mastɑ:ne va rendɑ:ne ravad xedmɑt-e ʔɑ:n
ᵕ ‾   ‾   ᵕ ᵕ ‾   ᵕ ᵕ ‾   ᵕ ᵕ ‾   ‾   ᵕ ᵕ ‾   ᵕ ᵕ ‾ ‾ ᵕ

ri:š-e do dandɑ:ne zami:n bu:se dehad ʕarz konad pɑ:dšahɑ:
‾   ᵕ ᵕ ‾   ‾ ᵕ ᵕ ‾   ‾   ᵕ ᵕ ‾ ᷉᷉· ‾   ᷉᷉᷉ ᵕ ‾

qebl-gahɑ: moḥtaramɑ: mohtašamɑ: žell-e ʔalɑ:hɑ: na coni:n
᷉᷉ ᵕ ᵕ ‾   ᷉·᷉ ᵕ ᵕ ‾   ‾ ᵕ ᵕ ‾   ‾   ᵕ ᵕ ‾   ‾ ᵕ ᵕ ‾

ast bozorgi:y o jahɑ:ndɑ:riy o ʔɑ:ʔi:n-e salɑ:ṭi:n-e
᷉᷉ ᵕ ᵕ ‾   ‾   ᵕ ᵕ ‾   ‾   ᵕ ᵕ ‾   ‾   ᵕ ᵕ ‾   ‾   ᵕ

gozašte: ke ʔagar bi:-xabari: saxt...
ᵕ ‾ ‾   ‾   ᵕ ‾   ‾   ᵕ ᵕ ‾   ‾

So far our investigations have been limited to the
written literary form, and it will now be of interest to see
how far the theoretical quantitative pattern is reflected in
the reading and recitation of classical poetry, an art which,
as anyone who has heard it will readily appreciate, owes
almost as much to tradition as the writing of it.   The
following passages, in several different metres and patterns,
were recorded in 1957 by two members of the staff of the
Persian Service of the BBC, Sayyed Abolqasem Ṭaheri and
Ḥasan Balyuzi, and were subsequently analysed by sonograph
apparatus in the Phonetics Department of Edinburgh University.
By this means it was possible to time each syllable to the
nearest 1/100 second.   The resulting figures show that, in

spite of variations in speed of reading for dramatic effect
and so on, the general relationship 1:2:3 for the syllables
⌣ : — : —⌣ represents what happens in practice.

Read by Abolqasem Ṭaheri

1.1.12

⌣	—	—	⌣	—	—	⌣	—	—	⌣	—	—
ba	si:	ranj		di:	dam	ba	si:	gof	te	xa:n	dam
20	44	62		21	42	22	33	35	14	24	42
ze	gof	ta:	re	ta:	zi:	yo	ʔaz	pah	la	va:	ni:
17	26	34	14	34	38	22	28	28	13	28	41
be	can	di:n	ho	nar	šas	to	do:	sa:l		bu:	dam
14	32	24	17	34	31	17	23	45		20	39
ke	tu:	še:	ba	ram	za:š		ka:	ru:	ne	ha:	ni:
20	37	27	23	35	56		37	15	19	29	44
be	joz	has	ra	tu:	joz	va	ba:	le:	go	na:	han
18	30	.35	18	35	32	18	31	16	16	27	46
na	da:	ram	ko	nu:	naz	ja	va:	ni:	ne	ša:	ni:
22	26	28	22	16	30	23	30	32	15	32	37
be	ya:	de:	ja	va:	ni:	ko	nu:n	mu:	ye	da:	ram
26	22	12	15	32	27	23	21	32	15	23	27
ba	ri:n	bei	te	bu:	ṭa:	he	re:	xos	ra	va:	ni:
17	30	28	31	27	32	15	16	30	16	25	40
ja	va:	ni:	ma	naz	ku:	da	ki:	ya:d		da:	ram
26	26	24	16	23	26	16	28	37		24	29
da	ri:	ġa:	ja	va:	ni:	da	ri:	ġa:	ja	va:	ni:
21	25	29	21	25	23*	20	22	23	19	20	24

(Ferdousi)

1.2.05(2)

—	—	＇	—	—	—	—	＇	—
yɑː	rab	ʔa	mɑːn	deh	tɑː	bɑːz	biː	nad
38	31	10	33	26	*28	50	23	30
caš	meː	mo	heb	bɑːn	ruː	yeː	ha	biː	bɑːn
34	17	17	24	52	*20	16	19	20	44

(Hɑfeż)

* pauses: line 1 – 9, line 2 – 30.

2.1.11

＇	—	—	—	—	—	—	—	—	—	—
ya	kiː	rɑː	cuːn	be	biː	niː	koš	te	yeː	duːst
17	27	26	33	17	19	20	33	14	16	74
be	diː	gar	duːs		tɑː	naš	deh	be	šɑː	rat
20	20	30	45		30	26	30	20	29	44

(SaʕdI)

2.4.15

—	＇	—	—	—	—	—	—	＇	—	—	—	＇	—
ʔei	sa	nɑː	ʔiː	jahd	kon	tɑː	piː	še	sol	tɑː	neː	za	miːr
30	24	26	26	62	48	36	30	21	32	30	14	23	38
ʔaz	riː	ga	bɑːn	tɑːj	sɑː	ziː	vaz	bo	neː	dɑː	man	sa	riːr
28	21	19	33	50	41	40	38	28	18	37	34	27	48
tɑː	be	diːn	tɑː	juː	sa	riː	raz	bah	re	mah	ruː	yɑː	ne	ɢeib
30	17	38	40	27	19	29	29	40	17	36	30	27	19	56
har	za	mɑː	niː	ʕa	nou	siː	ruː	ʕeqd	ban	diː	bar	za	miːr
30	23	34	34	30	18	39	25	*54	35	29	27	20	53

3.1.16

bɑː 34	co 22	niːn 34	tɑː 44	juː 18	sa 27	riː 30	raz 32	bah 45	re 20	dɑː 40	rol 18	mol 31	ke 20	sar 41
ban 45	de 10	pɑː 34	yeː 19	sar 37	šo 21	mor 24*	tɑː 39	juː 17	sa 24	riː 19	reː 13	ʔar 22	da 15	šiːr 48
diːv 57	ham 29	kɑː 29	seː 22	bo 18	vad 29	bar 28	sof 42	re 18	tɑː 34	vah 34	mu 18	xi 28	yɑːl 40	
dar 33	mi 24	yɑː 26	neː 15	diː 33	no 15	ʕaq 31	lat 35	dar 32	sa 24	far 31	bɑː 22	šad 29	sa 20	fiːr 50

(Sanɑʔi)

* pauses: line 4 - 39, line 6 - 10.

—	ˊ	—	—	—	ˊ	—	ˊ	—	ˊ	—	—	ˊ	—	—
kiːst 64	kuː 49	dɑː 42	de 16	ma 20	naz 36	ʔaːn 48	bo 18	te 17	bad 27	xuː 44	be 18	se 16	tɑː 32	nad 36
de 19	le 17	diː 30	vɑː 34	ne 16	ʔa 16	zaːn 34	šuː 46	xe 20	pa 26	riː 26	ruː 38	be 18	se 17	tɑː 30	nad 33

(Šuride)

3.1.11

—	ˊ	—	ˊ	—	ˊ	—	ˊ	—	ˊ	—	ˊ	—	ˊ	—	—
šaː 40	he 16	diː 22	goft 74	be 15	šam 38	kem 40	ʕiː 39	šab 43
da 25	ro 18	diː 25	vɑːr 47	mo 19	zei 27	yan 32	kar 27	dam 35
diː 28	sa 21	baz 27	šouq 57	na 20	xof 29	tam 31	yak 33	dam 50

du:x 59   tam 40   jɑ: 38   me 18   va 19   bar 27   tan 41   kar 26   dam 39

do 20   se 21   har 32   ze 16   ga 22   lu: 22   ban 31   dam 30   ri:xt 56

bas 44   ta 20   mu: 23   bɑ:z 59   be 16   gar 27   dan 36   kar 26   dam 37

kas 38   na 22   dɑ: 31   nest 104   ce 20   seḥ 41   rɑ: 30   mi: 28   zi: 30

be 18   pa 31   ran 38   daz 27   na 24   xo 20   su: 31   zan 31   kar 29   dam 36

ṣaf 29   ḥe 19   ye: 16   kɑ:r 49   ga 19   haz 28   su: 30   sa 23   no 13   gol 56

be 17   xo 22   ši: 47 *   sa 24   fe 17   gol 28   šan 33   kar 29   dam 30

* pause: 38.

(Parvin Eʿtesami)

—   ʾ   —   ʾ   —   ʾ   —   ʾ   —   ʾ   —

ḥab. 37   ba 23   zɑ: 31   ʔaz 34   ha 24   vɑ: 30   ye 18   nei 29   šɑ: 37   bu:r 56

ke 25   bo 18   vad 36   mɑ: 31   ye 15   ʔe: 17   ne 20   šɑ: 36   to 17   so 27   ru:r 44

sob. 34   ḥe 24   ʔu: 40   ʔas. 31   le 16   noz 31   ha 20   tas 28   to 17   sa. 22   fɑ: 51

4.5.11

(see p. 214)

šɑ: 42	me 17	ʔu: 33	far 34	ʕe 26	ʕeš 25	ra 15	tas 19	to 19	ho̤ 16	bu:r 55
ʔaz 25	pa 19	ye: 18	ʔen 35	qe 17	tɑ̤: 39	ʕe 17	nas 33	le 16	me 13	han 49
so̤b 28	he̤ 23	ʔu: 20	rɑ: 36	ta̤ 25	bi: 23	ʕa 13	te: 18	kɑ: 34		fu:r 50
ta̤ 18	ra 22	bʔaz 48	xɑ: 33	ko 17	xeš 30	te 20	ʔu: 24	ža̤: 33	her 38
ka 22	ra 16	ban 29	dar 22	se 21	reš 21	te 19	ʔu: 23	mas 39	tu:r 51
bɑ: 27	ša̤ 22	daz 33	yom 37	ne 15	xɑ: 33	ke 23	ʔu: 29	ṭɑ̤: 41	ʕen 42
ni: 44	še 17	ʕaq 26	rab 45	be 34	faz̤ 31	le 18	ye: 16	zan 35	bu:r 37

(Qɑʔani)

* pause: 37.

5.1.13/3.3.13

	—	›	ʔ↲	—	›	—	›	—
gu: yand 31 60		ka 23	sɑ:n be 53 *12	hešt 65		bɑ̤: hu:r 37 48	xo 24	šast 54
man mi: gu: 29 19 24	›		yam ke 38 22	ʔɑ: 36	be 11	ʔan gu:r 31 36	xo 22	šast 52
ʔi:n naqd 26 52	›		gi: ro 30 24	das *33	ta 17	zɑ:n nes ye 18 31 15	be 20	dɑ:r 43

kɑ:	vɑ:	ze	do	hol	ša	ni:	da	naz	du:r	xo	šast
33	28	16	24	30	19	20	28	27	36	27	56

(ʕomar Xayyɑm)

* pauses: line 1 – 40, line 3 – 24.

ʔaf	su:s	ke	sar	mɑ:	ye	ze	kaf	bi:	ru:n		šod
22	65	17	30	27	17	17	36	26	25		41
vaz	das	te	ʔa	jal	ba	si:	ja	gar	hɑ:	xu:n	šod
30	33	16	16	41	17	25	17	26	27	40	40
kas	nɑ:	ma	da	zɑ:n	ja	hɑ:n	ke	por	sam	az	vei
44	36	15	14	29	14	26	16	18	29	24	40
kah.	vɑ:	le	mo	sɑ:	fe	rɑ:	ne	don	yɑ:	cu:n	šod
25	39	14	13	32	19	22	12	30	28	38	41

(ʕomar Xayyɑm)

Read by Ḥasan Bɑlyuzi

1.1.11

ʼ	ʼ			ʼ				ʼ			
ma	rɑ:	ju:	de	ʔu:	tɑ:	ze	da:	rad	ha	mi:	
19	40 *	20	12	60 *	25	15	18	20	15	20	
ma	gar	ju:	da	šʔab	ras	to	man	kešt	zɑ:r		(see p. 214)
18	46	27	32	70	36	28	53	65	93		
ma	gu:	yak	su	ʔaf	kan	ke	xod	ham	co	ni:n	
21	47	35	25	25	40	21	49	31	18	49	

be 26	yan 25	di: 22	šo 38	di: 31	de: 30	xe 27	rad 41	bar 36	go 18	ma:r 43
?a 8	ba: 36	bar 37	qu 20	ba: 39	jes 35	ta 19	ne: 15	ṣa: 50	?e 16	qe: 38
?a 14	ba: 46	qol 36	qo 18	le: 18	ra?d 63	dar 36	ku:h 66	sa:r 60		
na 20	ma: 40	he: 20	se 36	ya: 30	mi: 38	na 23	he: 19	fa 32	lak 41	
ke 32	?i: 31	nat 39	qo 39	la: 26	mas 28	to 20	?a:n 50	pi:š 50	ka:r 46	
na 17	cu:n 50	pu: 44	re 36	mi: 34	re: 18	xo 28	ra: 26	sa:n 39	ke 22	?u: 52
ça 18	ṭa: 38	ra: 30	ne 17	šas 33	te: 19	bo 17	vad 31 *	ker 15	de 29	ga:r 45

(Rudagi)

* pauses: line 1 – 60,27, line 10 – 44.

2.1.16

?	—	—	?	—	—	?	—	—	—	—	—	?	—	—	—
ma 17	nam 28	?ei 24	bar 56	qe 28	ra: 45	me: 18	to: 44	ba 22	ra: 34	ye: 25	sei 42	de 33	da: 45	me: 18	to: 45
ga 27	hi: 36	bar 32	rok 45	ne 40	ba: 48	me: 16	to: 42	ga 25	hi: 39	beg 38	ref 26	te 42	ṣah ra: 44 30	ra: 44	ra: 22
he 18	la: 24	zoh 32	re 16	ye: 22	zah 34	ra: 44 * 20	be 20	kaš 48	?a:n gu: 42 32	še 30	zah ra: 40 36	ra: 44

ta 13, qɑ: 38, zạ: 38, ʔi: 26, ne 19, hɑ: 32, das 36, ti: 30, da 19, ri:n 33, jaz 36, be: 35 *, de 20, le: 15, mɑ: 30, rɑ: 20

ce 22, dɑ: 31, nad 35, dɑ: 52, me 19, bi: 30, cɑ: 42, re: 30, fa 25, ri: 26, be: 24, mor 29, ɋe 24, ʔɑ: 23, vɑ: 26, re: 34

ce 21, dɑ: 34, nad 38, yu: 37, se 21, fe: 20, meṣ 43, ri:ḷ 34 *, ɋa 25, mu: 23, dar 38, de: 26, zo 21, lei 20, xɑ: 36, rɑ: 25

co 22, šah 37, re: 20, lu:ṭ 76, vi: 26, rɑ: 25, nam 22 *, co 17 *, caš 37, me: 23, lu:ṭ 70, hei 38, rɑ: 33, nam

sa 28, bab 33, xɑ: 34, ham 33, ke 29, vɑ: 38, por 30, sam 41 *, na 21, dɑ: 45, ram 46, zah 42, re 20, vu: 37, yɑ: 36, rɑ: 28

(Moulavi – Šams-e Tabriz)

* pauses: line 3 – 64, line 4 – 48, line 6 – 50, line 7 – 75, line 8 – 47.

2.3.16

xɑ: 38, kam 34, pa 16, se: 23, far 36, su: 35, da 14, gi: 34, ri: 28, zi:d 57, — , — , — , dar 34, mei 29, dɑ: 32, ne 12, ʔu: 31

bɑ: 36, šad 44, sa 26, man 32, de: 16, xi:š 58, — , rɑ: 37, ru: 24, zi: 27, ba 18, — , ra:n 33, jou 28, la:n 30, de 11, had 30

(Jami)

2.4.11

ni:st 81, ʔom 30, mi: 24, ʔom 36, dam 48, ke 20, — , dar 27, rɑ: 43, he: 20, — , rɑ: 43, de 26, lam 43

šah 34, ne 17, ye: 12, mi:d 47, — , rɑ: 42, kɑ: 47, ri: 14, ra 16, sad 44

(Xɑqɑni)

3.1.15

–	›	–	–	›	›	–	–	›	›	–	–	›	›	–
?et 30	te 20	fa: 35	qam 45	be 12	sa 25	re: 35	ku: 38	ye 48	ka 25	si: 45	of 33	ta: 35		dast 81
ke 20	da 21	ra:n 31	ku:y 93		co 29	man 44	koš 48	te 49	ba 27	42	?of 25	27		dast 73
xa 23	ba 16	re: 16	ma: 40	be 16	ra 14	sa: 38	ni:d 42		be 17	mor 37	qa: 35	ne 16	ca 24	man 34
ke 18	ha 18	ma: 29	va: 31	ze 16	šo 19	ma: 33	dar 21	qa 20	fa 20	si: 23	of 21	ta: 24		dast 62
be 14	de 22	la: 30	ra:m 54		be 20	gu: 36*	?ei 37	na 17	fa 20	se: 20	ba: 40	de 14	sa 26	har. 41
ka: 35	re 13	ma: 31	ham 28	co 20	sa 24	har. 30	ba: 31	na 14	fa 20	si: 27	?of 20	ta: 24		dast 56
band 66		bar 28	pa:y 64		ta 28	ham 32	mol 45*	ce 20	ko 20	nad 32	gar 32	na 20	ko 21	nad 33
?an 38	ga 21	bi: 25	ni:st 60	be 16	ke 16	dar 32	vei 42*	ma 18	ga 18	28	19	22		dast 62
hi:c 44		kas 54	?ei 31	ke 16	ha 17	vas 33	ba:x 43		ta 20	ne: 16	ma: 29	na 18	ko 21	nad 33
ma 21	ga 19	ra:n 27	kas 49*	ke 32*	be 19	da: 36	me: 22	ha 21	va 15	si: 27	?of 19	ta: 22		dast 51
sa? 37	di 17	ya: 34	ha: 38	le 31	pa 28	ra: 28	kan 42	de 18	ye 20	gu: 65	ya:n 60	da: 36		nad 33

ke(14) ha(21) me:(23) ʕomr(52) be(16) cou(31) ga:(28) ne(15) ka(22) si:(24) ʔof(18) ta:(22) dast(40)

* pauses: line 5 – 104, line 7 – 21, line 8 – 45, line 10 – 13.

(Saʕdi)

3.3.14

– ʔei(45) ru:(32) ye(18) to(49) rax(36) šan(37) de(12) ta(21) raz(43) qeb(35) le(15) ye(23) zar(36) došt(90)

– bi:(40) ru:(39) ye(17) to(60) cu:n(62) zol(41) fe(20) to(65) gu:(54) žast(70) ma(21) ra:(27) pošt(84)

– ʕeš(28) qe:(18) to(23) ma(18) ra:(32) koš(42) to(16) ha(21) va:(19) ye:(21) to(29) ma(20) ra:(23) su:xt(60)

– jou(23) re:(21) to(23) ma(23) ra:(24) xas(44) to(24) ja(23) fa:(30) ye:(15) to(26) ma(23) ra:(25) košt(83)

– har(28) cand(57) ha(22) me:(35) jou(48) to(16) ja(20) fa:(34) ye:(19) to(23) ka(20) ši:(25) dam(44)

– har(39) gez(43) na(20) ko(22) nam(32) meh(31) ro(24) va(20) fa:(32) ye:(20) to(36) fa(24) ra:(20) mošt(68)

– bar(33) xi:(37) zo(22) be(24) ya:(49) ta:(50) ze(27) ro(23) xu:(48) zol(43) fe(24) to(35) ʔem(29) šab(60)

– por(40) la:(42) le(15) ko(22) nam(39) da:(38) ma(19) no(26) por(39) mošk(69) ko(28) nam(29) mošt(70)

(Amir MoʕEzzi)

4.1.15

#	Scansion of the hemistich (syllable : duration)
1	ʔa ⏑ 11 · gar — 32 · ce ⏑ 22 · bɑː — 50 · de ⏑ 21 · fa ⏑ 23 · rah — 27 · bax — 39 · šo ⏑ 26 · bɑːd — 78 · gol ⏑ 46 · bi: — 33 · — zast 81
2	be ⏑ 22 · bɑːn — 28 · ge ⏑ 26 · čang — 78 · ma ⏑ 21 · xor ⏑ 38 · mei — 38 · ke 15 · moh — 38 · ta 24 · seb — 48 · ti: 42 · zast 65
3	ṣo ⏑ 29 · rɑː — 34 · hi: ⟩ 66 · yi: 22 · o 22 · ḥa 25 · ri: 28 · fi: 31 · ga 20 · rat 26 · be 20 · čang — · of — · tad 32
4	be ⏑ 18 · ʕaql — 42 · ce 22 · nu:š 62 · ke 20 · ʔay 25 · yɑːm 51 · fet — 33 · ne 7 · ʔan 30 · gi: 24 · zast 62
5	da ⏑ 17 · rɑːs — 52 · ti: 22 · ne 14 · mo 16 · raq 23 · qaʕ 36 · pe 22 · yɑː — 30 · le 13 · pen 30 · hɑːn 28 · kon 41
6	ke ⏑ 14 · ham — 35 · čo 21 · čas 44 · me 18 · ṣo 26 · rɑː 32 · hi: 42 · za — 24 · mɑː 29 · ne 14 · xu:n 35 · ri: 24 · zast 65
7	be ⏑ 19 · ʔɑː — 31 · be 18 · di: 27 · de 18 · be 19 · šu: 35 · ʔi:m 43 · xer — 37 · qe 22 · hɑː 40 · ʔaz 34 · mei 28
8	ke ⏑ 22 · mou — 31 · se 23 · me: 19 · va 22 · ra 22 · ʕo 66 · ʔi:m 52 · gɑː 36 · re 11 · par 40 · hi: 28 · zast 62
9	ma ⏑ 23 · juːy — 49 · ʕei 20 · še ž 20 · xo 30 · šaz 53 · dou 58 · re 40 · bɑːž ž 71 · gu: 28 · se 24 · pehr 70
10	ke ⏑ 23 · sɑ̣ — 63 · fe 29 · ʔi:n 33 · sa 30 · re 14 · xom 40 · jom 40 · le 40 · dor 36 · di 21 · yɑː 25 · mi: 22 · zast 62

(Hɑfeż)

5.1.13/3.3.13

ı	›	›	›	—	ı›	› ı	›	ı	ı	›	›	—
gof 31	tam 30	ke 41	la 38	bat 56	goft 91		la 26	bam 53	ʔa: 27	be 16	ḥa 20	ya:t 90
gof 25	tam 28	da 14	ha 20	nat 45*	goft 74		za 31	hi: 32	hab 54	be 17	na 21	ba:t 38
gof 29	tam 36*	so 27	xa 23	ne: 16	to 24	ci:st 55	ha: 25	feẓ 65*	gof 30			ta:: 36
ša: 49	di: 28	ye 20	ha 23	me: 16	la 18	ti: 26	fe 17	gu: 28	ya:n 30	sa 21	la 14	va:t 60

(Ḥafeẓ)

sei 38	la:b 44	ge 19	reft 62	ne 14	ger 32		vi: 22	ra: 26	ne 14		ye 14	Somr 59
va: 35	ḍa: 36	ze 17	po 28	ri: 20	ne 14	ha:d 56	pei 32	ma: 24	ne 14	ye 11	Somr 29
bi: 23	da:r 48	šo 44	vei 32	xa: 47	je 41*		xoš 45	xoš 45	be 25	ka 19	šad 40
ham 34	ma: 28	le 17	za 22	ma: 30	ne 35*	raxt 62	az 22	xa: 26	ne 13	ye 16	Somr 59

(Ḥafeẓ)

* pauses: line 2 – 82, line 3 – 15,22, line 7 – 59, line 8 – 36.

Analysis of these figures shows that, while there is often a fairly wide range in the time-length of lines in the same metre, the average length of each speech element (as measured in <u>morae</u>) remains fairly constant for each speaker. The first table gives the average length of line in each metre, and from this the average length of the <u>mora</u>. All measurements are given in hundredths of a second.

Pattern	Syll. in line	Morae	Time Range (inc. pauses)	Aver. Time (speech only)	Aver. mora
Read by Taheri					
1.1.	12	20	275-359	298	15
1.2.	05(2)	18	278-293	266	15
2.1.	11	19/20	294-296	295	16
2.4.	15	26/27	397-490	435	16
3.1.	16	24/25	420-483	451	18
3.1.	11	16/18	255-344	305	18
4.5.	11	16/18	263-351	293	17
5.1. 3.3.	13	20/21	305-447	334	16
Read by Balyuzi					
1.1.	11	18	303-428	339	19
2.1.	16	28	472-598	500	18
2.3.	16	28	450-453	452	16
2.4.	11	19	309-362	336	18
3.1.	15	22/24	326-529	407	18
3.3.	14	22/23	370-600	472	21
4.1.	15	22/23	344-519	433	19
5.1. 3.3.	13	20/21	316-520	388	19

The next table shows the average length of each category of syllable for the two speakers, from which it will be seen that the ratio 1:2:3 is maintained fairly closely overall:

	'				ا				؟		
	No.	Total Lgth	Av.	Range	No.	Total Lgth	Av.	Range	No.	Total Lgth	Av.	Range
Taheri	190	3722	20	10–31	367	11566	32	12–56	46	2506	55	36–104
Balyuzi	275	6084	22	7–65	430	14473	34	14–70	71	4496	63	42–93

If a similar analysis were to be made of normal speech,
it would be found that the average difference between these
syllables, especially where the "long" vowels ($\underline{a}$, $\underline{i}$, $\underline{u}$) are
concerned, is considerably less.   Indeed, what distinguishes
these vowels today from the corresponding "short" ones ($\underline{a}$, $\underline{e}$,
$\underline{o}$) is not their quantitative length, but the different
position of articulation.   However the orthography is
derived from the writing of the vowels in Arabic, where the
distinction is precisely one of length and hardly at all of
articulation.   Are we to deduce from this that at the time
the Arabic script was applied to Persian a difference of
quantity rather than quality existed in the Persian vowels
also?   Or was the use, for example, of the Arabic alif
(wāw, yā?) the only available way of indicating what was not
in fact a longer sound, but simply a different one that did
not exist in Arabic and therefore had no accepted orthography
in that language?   The early Persian grammarians, dominated
by concepts of Arabic grammar, do not help us very much.
Avicenna, in the maxārij al-hurūf,[28] states with some
diffidence that the "long" alif was twice the length of the
"short" fatha: "walākinnī aᶜlamu yaqīnan anna l-alifa l-
mamdūdata l-muṣawwata taqiᶜa fī ḍaᶜfin aw adᶜāfi zamāni
l-fatha. wa anna l-fathata taqiᶜa fī aṣḍara l-azminati
llatī yaṣiḥḥu fīhā l-intiqālu min ḥarfin ilā ḥarf." ("But I
know for certain that the long vowel alif occupies about
double the time-length of the fatha, and that the fatha
occupies the shortest time possible for transfer from one

sound to another.")   However, though in this treatise
(e.g. Chapter 5) he implies at certain points that he is
discussing Persian as well as Arabic, we cannot rely on this
statement as evidence in the particular case under discussion.
The rules of prosody on the other hand give grounds for
supposing that the distinction of length did exist at the
time that the Persian metres took on their present characteristic patterns, for it is hardly to be supposed that such an
elaborate system could have been developed on the basis of a
purely orthographic circumstance that bore no relation to the
spoken word.

One other piece of evidence may be noted at this point.
A commonly exploited poetic licence is the "shortening" of
the "long" vowels, for instance cɑ:h - cah, rɑ:h - rah,
ni:ku: - neku:, di:gar - degar, ku:h - koh, bu:d - bod,
xɑ:mu:š - xamoš.   The significant point is that this change
in quantity involves in modern Persian a change in quality
as well.   At what stage this change of quality took place
it is hard to say.   It was certainly established as early
as Ḥafeż (d. 792/1390), who rhymes hamrah (for hamrɑh), gah
(for gɑh), cah (for cɑh), etc., with Arabic muvajjah,
muraffah;   but there is little evidence of such a licence
before his time, though Sanɑʔi (d.c.545/1150) admits veilah
(Ar. waylah), zah (from Persian root zɑ), and xah-xah
(onomatopaeic) into a series of rhymes consisting otherwise
of the shortened ending -ah for -ɑh.   It is obvious too that,
since the final syllable of a verse may be long or overlong

without affecting the metre, there would be no point in
using the shortened form in the rhyme unless it were intended
to introduce some originally short rhymes.

It will have been noticed that the average length of the
"long" syllable in the table above is somewhat less than
double that of the "short" syllable.   This is partly
accounted for by the fact that the first category includes
syllables that are naturally short, though optionally
available to fill the place of a long syllable.   If these
are as far as possible excluded, the average length of a
"long" syllable is found to be increased by 1/100 second.
The three syllables principally concerned are the iḍāfa,
the hā? maxfī, and wāw meaning "and".   The table on p. 211,
based on the sonograph readings, shows that in practice the
first is unaffected by its metrical position, the second
seems on average to gain a little length in the "long"
position (though the available cases are insufficient to
establish a statistically sound average), while in the case
of the third one speaker makes no difference and the second
does in fact double the length (though again the numbers are
statistically too small).

It may be of interest to compare these figures with
statistics of the placing of these syllables in classical
poetry.   The following figures have been obtained by
counting the number of the particular syllable in question
(iḍāfa, hā? maxfī, wāw) in selected passages of about 100
bayts, dividing them according to whether they are to be

Lgth	Taheri No. of »	Taheri No. of ǀ	Balyuzi No. of »	Balyuzi No. of ǀ
10	1			
11	1	1	2	
12	1	1	2	1
13		2	1	
14	2	1	4	3
15	1	6	1	5
16	5	2	4	5
17	7	3	4	2
18	1	1	3	6
19	2		2	2
20	4		4	2
21	1		1	2
22				2
23	2		1	2
24	1		2	1
25				1
26	1		1	1

Lgth	Taheri No. of »	Taheri No. of ǀ	Balyuzi No. of »	Balyuzi No. of ǀ
7			1	
12			1	
13			2	
14	2		5	
15	3			
16	3		2	1
17	2		2	
18	3		3	
19	1		6	1
20	2		3	
21	1		5	
22	1	1	1	
23	1			1
25	1			
27		1		
29			1	
30				2

Lgth	Taheri No. of »	Taheri No. of ǀ	Balyuzi No. of »	Balyuzi No. of ǀ
13	1			
15	1	1		
16			2	
17	4	1		
18	1	2		
19	2	1	2	
20	1		2	
22	1			
23	1		2	
24			2	
26			1	
28				
35		1		
37			1	1
38			1	
48				1
66				1

Lines	31	17	42	32		Lines	19	2	44	9	12	7	12	3
28						32			2					
29	1					34				1				
30	1			1		35			1					
31	1					38			1					
32	1					40			1					
33	1					41			2					
35	1		1			42			1					
36	1					49			1					
40				1										
48				1										
No.	31	17	42	32		**No.**	19	2	44	9	12	7	12	3
Total Lgth	559	271	899	627		**Total Lgth**	336	49	952	260	218	145	282	151
Av. Lgth	18	16	21	20		**Av. Lgth**	18	25	22	29	18	21	24	50

scanned short or long, and adjusting the figures to allow
for the relative frequency of short and long places (excluding
the first and in the case of iḍāfa and wāw the last syllable
of each line on grammatical grounds - iḍāfa and hā? maxfī
cannot appear in these positions, and wāw can only come at
the beginning of a line as a consonant in conjunction with a
word beginning with a vowel: v-az, v-agar, etc.).   In each
case the adjusted proportion for the short scansion is given
first:

iḍāfa	Šahnāme:	1.44:1
	Masnavi:	1.62:1
	Ḥafeż:	2.00:1
hā? maxfī	Šahnāme:	21.00:1
	Masnavi:	8.33:1
	Ḥafeż:	always short except at the end of a line
wāw	Šahnāme:	1.52:1
	Masnavi:	1.45:1
	Ḥafeż:	5.00:1

No distinction is made here between the forms o/va, uː/vuː,
since the latter of each of these pairs, while found always
after vowels, is only occasionally used after consonants:
      cuːn xariːd uːrɑː va barxordɑːr šod...
      šah ṭabiːbɑːn jamʕ kard az cap va rɑːst...
      rang-e ruː vuː nabż o qɑːruːreː be-diːd...
                              (Masnavi)
The option of retaining or omitting ḥamza at the beginning of words, whether Persian or Arabic, has already been

mentioned.   An examination of the three texts already
used gives the following figures:

	hamza retained	hamza dropped
Šahname	38	67
Masnavi	70	71
Hafeż	66	74

In the recorded passages hamza was incorrectly read in
two cases only: 1.1.11, 1.2 - inserted between ju:daš and
abr;   4.5.11, 1.7 - inserted between tarab and az.   At the
same time, it should be said that in the reverse situation
hamza was often slurred over when the metre required its
insertion.

It has already been pointed out that after a "long"
vowel the letter n has no value for prosodic purposes, but is
regarded rather as nasalisation (ġinna) not increasing the
length of the syllable.   Our sonograph analyses however show
that in modern speech this n is pronounced as a distinct
consonant, though without in general increasing the length
of the syllable as much as a full extra consonant would do.

	Aver. long	Aver. overlong	-a:n	-i:n	-u:n
Taheri	32	55	37	26	33
Balyuzi	34	63	44	34	63

A great many other licences are permitted to poets,
apart from those mentioned in Chapter I and in this chapter.
Although these are all indicated in the orthography, it may
be useful to provide a list with a few examples.   It will
be seen that in general they consist in the elision, addition,

transposition or substitution of consonants or vowels, and
the abbreviation and contraction of words.

A. CONSONANTS

(i) Elision

(a) Initial: (h) hi:c - i:c

(b) Internal: (g) ʔagar - ʔar

                    (d) badtar - batar

                    (v) ʔɑ:varam - ʔɑ:ram

                    (h) cehel - cel

                    (y) taǧyi:r - taǧi:r

                    (r) farvardi:n - farvadi:n

(c) Final: (h) gavɑ:h - gavɑ:

                    (t) modɑ:rɑ:t - modɑ:rɑ:

(ii) Addition (to a large extent restoration or survival of
            obsolete consonants):

                    (y after vowel) pɑ: - pɑ:y

                                     ru: - ru:y

                    (t after consonant) pɑ:dɑ:š - pɑ:dɑ:št
                                          (also pɑ:dɑ:šn)

(iii) Transposition (qalb):

                    darvi:š - daryu:š (DaRWiYŠ - DaRYuWŠ)

                    hu:šyɑ:r - hoši:vɑ:r (HuWŠYaʔR - HuŠiYWaʔR)

B. VOWELS

(i) Elision

(a) Initial: ʔaz - ze

                    ʔagar - gar

                    ʔɑ:hang - hang

(b) <u>Final</u>:   va, be, ze, ke, ce, na, when followed by a

word beginning with a vowel:

va ʔagar - vagar - var

ke ʔaz - kaz

ʔaz ʔɑ:n - ze ʔɑ:n - zɑ:n

ʔaz ʔɑ:n ke - zɑ:nk

har ce ʔaz - harcaz

goft ʔaz c-andɑ:m kardi ʔebtedɑ: (Moulavi)

:   hā? maxfī before word beginning with vowel:

gerefte ast - gereftast

goft makšu:f u: barahn-u: bi: ɖalu:l

(Moulavi)

:   Arabic words ending in short vowel:

ʔa lastu - ʔalast

(ii) <u>Addition</u>:

(a) <u>Initial</u>:   bɑ: - ʔabɑ

bar - ʔabar

zi:rɑ: - ʔazi:rɑ:

(b) <u>Final</u>:   (ɑ:) goftɑ:, davadɑ:, ʔɑ:škɑ:rɑ:, xošɑ:

(i:) ḥeirɑ:ni:, ʔarmaɖɑ:ni:

(e) maʕšu:qe (not feminine)

(iii) <u>Shortening of long vowel</u> (examples given above):

bi:hu:de - bi:hode

gouhar - gohar

(iv) <u>Lengthening of short vowel</u>:

ʔoftɑ:dam - ʔu:ftɑ:dam

ʔomi:d - ʔu:mid

(v) <u>Transposition</u>:

ʔafgandan - fegandan

šotor - ʔoštor

C. ABBREVIATION OF WORDS

xorši:d - xor, ši:d

vali:ken - li:ken, li:k, vali:k, vali:

cu:n - con, co

It is misleading to speak (as Noeldeke does[29]) of these
poetic licences as artificialities invented by the poets to
facilitate the application of alien metres to the Persian
language.   They are far more likely to be natural features
of the language, "frozen" in some cases into the poetic
tradition, but in many others still common in ordinary speech.
For instance, the use of the contraction <u>bog̲zarad</u> for <u>be-</u>
<u>go̲zarad</u> in both verse and colloquial speech shows that this
is not a convention forced on the poets by the exigencies of
the metre, but a feature natural to the language.

The same considerations apply to a number of grammatical
and syntactical licences, notably the mobility of the pronominal suffix, which, apart from having numerous other uses
than the possessive characteristic of standard prose, may be
attached to virtually any convenient word in the line.   This
may result in baffling combinations like: <u>kat</u> = <u>ke ʔat</u> =
<u>ke torɑ:</u>, <u>bedu:yam</u> = <u>be-ʔu: marɑ:</u>, <u>tam</u> = <u>to-ʔam</u> = <u>to marɑ:</u>,
<u>ʔɑ:ncet</u> = <u>ʔɑ:nce-ʔat</u> = <u>ʔɑ:nce be-to</u>.   The uses of the suffix
may be summarised as follows:

(a) subjective use:

har koja: xu:bi:st man moula:yam-aš (Adib Pišavari)

(b) objective use:

gereft-aš

(c) indirect object:

mi:-dehad-am

(d) prepositional:

yaki: ḥa:jatastam ze nazdi:k-e ša:h (Ferdousi)

(e) possessive attached to verb:

to gofti: be-sangast-aš a:gonde pu:st (Ferdousi)

(f) possessive attached to other word:

ke gar ze pa:y dar a:yad kas-aš nagi:rad dast (Saʕdi)

The flexibility that this licence (which is common in
colloquial Persian too) provides is well illustrated by this
last verse, the second half of which (here scanned as 4.1.15)
may be fitted into no fewer than three other patterns by
merely moving the pronominal suffix, without changing the
meaning:

.... kas nagi:radaš dast

                    −   ∪ − ∪ −   ⌒

            kas nagi:radš dast

                    −   ∪ − ⌒   ⌒

            kas nagi:rad dastaš

                    −   ∪ − −   − −

Another particle that is frequently displaced is the
verbal prefix hami:, mi:.   So we may get:

mi:-nad(e)hi: for nami:dehi:

mi: na:rami:d for nami:ya:rami:d

mi: bar xoru:ši:d for bar mi:-xoru:ši:d

ʔaz-i:n dar soxan cand ra:nam hami: (Ferdousi)

Unusual combinations with be- are also found: benadham for
nadeham.

Arabic and other foreign phrases do not necessarily
follow the correct rules of scansion:

sala:m ˤaleika
ᵕ −   − − ᵕ

tama:man ḥoqqe-ba:z u: ša:rla:ta:nand   (Iraj Mirza)
ᵕ − −   − ᵕ − − − ᵕ − −

In spite of all these complications, it is exceedingly
rare for a false quantity to be found in the work of a
recognised poet (one must of course allow for the possibility
of correction by an over-enthusiastic editor).   Those that
do occur seem often to have some phonetic explanation, if not
justification.   Examples are:

hast honar zarre-i: be-vaḥdat-e xi:š   (Jami)
− ᵕ − − ᵕ − ᵕ − ᵕ ᵕ ⁓

ʔaz du:zax ast ce parva: neya:zmandtara: (Şaʔeb Tabrizi)
ᵕ − ᵕ ⁓ ᵕ − − ᵕ ⁓ ⁓ ᵕ −

ḋaẓab namu:d seti:z ˤaql qahrama:n dar xa:b (Şaʔeb Tabrizi)
ᵕ − ᵕ ⁓ ᵕ − ⁓ − ᵕ − − −

va:ˤeż tora: pa:ye-ye gofta:r-e boland ast (Şaʔeb Tabrizi)
− ᵕ ᵕ − ᵕ − − − ᵕ − −

ze xa:b-e ḋeflat har a:n di:de-i: ke bi:da:r ast (ˤaref)
ᵕ − ᵕ − ᵕ ᵕ − ᵕ − ᵕ − −

sang-tara:ši: bu:d ʔandar ku:h-e ṭu:r (ˤobeid Zakani)
− ᵕ − − ⁓ − − − ᵕ −

Lazard quotes a number of other instances in early Persian
poetry, where this kind of thing is commoner than in later,
more strictly controlled classical verse.[30]   In all these
cases it will be seen either that one consonant is "weak" (h,
ˤ, ŋ for ng), or there is a combination such as z/d, z/t,

offering to the ear the possibility of assimilation.

The question of accent has been largely ignored by writers on Persian prosody.   This has been partly because of the difficulty of defining it, partly because of a feeling that it does not in fact play a significant role in the Persian metre.   The only writer who has devoted much attention to the matter is P.N. Xɑnlari, who gave it a section of his standard work on Persian prosody.   For fuller details, inquirers are referred to the book itself. Here it is sufficient to say that Xɑnlari divides the metres into two- or three-syllable feet, and maintains that in a rhythmical poem one stress and no more should fall in each foot.   As an example he gives a line by Amir Moʕezzi:

Ɂei sɑ|:rbɑ:n|manzel|makon|joz dar|diyɑ:|r-e yɑ:|r-e man

He contrasts this with two lines by Nɑṣer Xosrou, which he considers to be unrhythmical because they do not observe this rule:

Ɂaz mard mɑ:|nad mell̲k har|gez joz|pesar|yɑ: dox|tareš

monker|šodaš|nɑ:dɑ:n|vali:ken ni:|st dɑ:|nɑ: monkeraš

The first of these three lines (all in metre 2.3.16) has eight accents, two on the first syllable of the foot and six on the second.   The second line also has eight accents, but two of the feet have two accents and two have none;   while the third line has only seven accents.   However, as Xɑnlari

himself points out, the distribution of accents evenly over
two- or three-syllable feet seems to stem primarily from the
fact that the accent in Persian falls mainly on the last
syllable of the word (less often on the first), and that the
bulk of Persian words (about 87% according to Xɑnlari's
figures) are of one, two or three syllables.   Rypka, working
on quite different lines with the mutaqārib metre of the
Šɑhnɑme (1.1.11), finds a regular accent on each three-
syllable foot; but this could be explained in the same way.
A verse by Ṭarzi Afšɑr provides a good example of the
difficulty of pinning down the natural accent to a metrical
function:

    kašad su:ye: morɑ:d az ṣabr kɑ:r ɑ:heste ʔɑ:heste
    ◡ ‒   ‒   ‒   ◡ ‒   ‒   ‒   ◡̰   ‒   ‒   ‒   ◡   ‒   ‒   ‒

    be-dargɑ:he: šahɑ:n yɑ:band bɑ:r ɑ:heste ʔɑ:heste
    ◡   ‒   ‒   ‒   ◡ ‒   ‒   ‒   ◡̰   ‒   ‒   ‒   ◡   ‒   ‒   ‒

The natural stress in ʔɑ:hesté falls on the final
syllable.   Thus, if we take the traditional foot mafāʕīlun
(◡ ‒ ‒ ‒) as the basis, we find two stresses in the last foot;
while if we take Xɑnlari's two-syllable feet, we find
stresses in each of the last two feet, but none on the one
before that.

    ...kɑ:r ɑ:heste ʔɑ:heste:

    ◡ ⸍ ‒   ‒ | ⸍ ‒   ‒   ⸍
    ◡ ⸍|‒   ‒ | ⸍ ‒| ‒   ⸍

The answer to this problem is probably that there can be
only one type of regular rhythm in a verse.   Either there
is a regular beat, falling at equal intervals of time and

separated by a variable number of syllables; as we saw
earlier, this seems to be the case with Arabic verse, and it
is probably the explanation of the shape of some popular and
colloquial Persian verse. Or there is a regular quantitative pattern, in which case the accent falls where it pleases,
and there may well be a variable number of accents to the
line. Our investigation suggests that the classical Persian
metres fall into this latter category. This would probable
be confirmed by a phonetic analysis of verse readings, but
in any case it must be remembered that the artistry of the
poetry reader or reciter lies in his deviations from the
norm. As Xanlari once put it, a good verse-reader is like
a virtuoso on the violin. This is perhaps the answer to
the modern "free verse" poets who claim to have found the
only way to break the shackles of tradition. The 60,000
verses of the Šahname are all in the same metre, but the
reciter can build as much dramatic effect into it as if it
were in no metre at all.

Appendix I. Rhyme

It has hitherto been widely assumed that rhyme, like the
metres of Persian verse, was copied from the Arabs.   The
case is certainly somewhat stronger where rhyme is concerned,
since it appears to be the exception rather than the rule in
Middle Persian verse.   Nevertheless, examples are by no
means infrequent; the Zurvanite hymn from the bondahešn
cited by Nyberg is one instance, while many of the verses in
the ayyātkār-e Zarērān show, if not strict rhyme, assonance
(bošn - borz, mēx - arvēš, zarēr - konēt, etc.).   Nearly all
the examples quoted in Chapter V of pre-classical verse also
use rhyme - the Karkuy hymn, the Yazid b. Mofarreq jingle,
the lament for Samarqand.   However all these pieces are too
short to enable us to judge whether the most characteristic
feature of Islamic verse, the monorhyme, was present.   This
is certainly found in pre-Islamic Arabic poetry, and also in
the earliest examples of "classical" Persian poetry.
Christensen suggests that the monorhyme at least must have
been copied from Arabic, since only that language has the
facility of forming words of similar pattern in sufficient
quantity to sustain the rhyme throughout poems of the length
of the qasīda.[31]   But in fact investigation reveals that

the overall ratio in rhyming words is four to five Persian
against one Arabic, while even in long qasīdas, depending on
the rhyme chosen, the ratio is rarely lower than two to one.
Thus out of the first 200 rhyming words in Lazard's anthology
of early Persian verse, 169 are Persian and 31 Arabic.   The
philosophical qasīda by Abol-heisam Gorgani, reproduced in
the same work, has 60 Persian rhymes in -α:r to 30 Arabic.
The qasīdas of Manucehri show about the same ratio, though
those of his contemporary ʿonsori seem to be weighted a
little more in favour of Arabic, depending on the rhyme
chosen:

-α:	19 Persian, 18 Arabic
-α:b	10 Persian, 34 Arabic
-ar (ni:st)	20 Persian, 13 Arabic
-α:r (ast)	26 Persian, 14 Arabic
-α:n (bovad)	31 Persian, 15 Arabic

It is also worth noting that certain archaic pronunciations -
for instance, x^Vard, x^Vaš, etc., for later xord, xoš - which
were already dying out in late Sasanian times, were retained
by convention in poetry for many centuries; the possible
implication is that such rhymes as zard - x^Vard had become
well-established in the pre-Islamic period, while these
pronunciations were still current.   That they had already
disappeared in ordinary usage by early medieval times is
strongly suggested by the fact that examples do occur
against the weight of tradition in which the "new" pronunciation is observed in the rhyme, for instance:

yaki: šab ʔaz šab-e: nouru:z xoštar

ce šab k-az ruz-e ʕeid andu:h-koštar

(Nežami, 536/1141 - 600/1203)

One feature of classical Persian rhyme, the <u>radīf</u>, is
purely Persian;   Rašidoddin Vaṭvaṭ (d. 573/1177-8) writes in
the Ḥadạyeqos-seḥr: radif kaleme-ʔi bạšad yạ bištar ke baʕd
az ḥoruf-e ravi ạyad dar šeʕr-e parsi...va ʕarab-rạ radif
nist....[32]   It may be defined as a word or words supple-
menting and following the rhyme proper and recurring without
change at the end of each line (though forming of course an
integral part of it and of the metre).   That it appeared in
Persian verse at an early date may be assumed from its
presence in, for example, the jingle from Balx quoted in
Chapter V (though here it is preceded by assonance rather
than rhyme), and the verse by Abu Ḥafṣ Ṣoǵdi, to say nothing
of early classical poetry like the verse by Maḥmud Varrạq
(quoted in Chapter III under 2.1.11).

The radīf may consist of anything from a monosyllabic
particle

zahi fozu:de jamạ:l-e: to zi:b o ʔa:rạ:-<u>rạ:</u>

šekaste sonbol-e zolf-e: to mošk-e sạ:rạ:-<u>rạ:</u>

(Rudagi)

to a complete phrase or sentence

xalvat-gozi:de-rạ: be-tamạ:šạ: ce ḥạ:jat-ast

cu:n ku:y-e du:st hast be-ṣaḥrạ: ce ḥạ:jat-ast

(Ḥạfež)

Prosodists and even poets have composed verse in which

virtually the entire miṣrāʕ consists of radīf and rhyme
proper (ḡāfiya - see below).

ʔei du:st ke del ze bande bar dɑ:šte-ʔi:

ni:ku:st ke del ze bande bar dɑ:šte-ʔi:

(al-Moʕjam)

sarv-rɑ: gol-bɑ:r nabvad v-ar bovad nabvad coni:n

sarv-e gol-roxsɑ:r nabvad v-ar bovad nabvad coni:n

di:dam-aš vei bar sar-e: golbɑ:r o goftam rɑ:sti:

sarv dar golbɑ:r nabvad v-ar bovad nabvad coni:n.......

(Xɑju)

A variant on the radīf is the ḥājib, in which the
repeated word precedes instead of following the ḡāfiya:

solṭɑ:n malek ast o dar del-e: solṭɑ:n nu:r

har ru:z be-ru:y-e ʔu: konad solṭɑ:n su:r

hargez naravad bar u: va bar solṭɑ:n zu:r

cašm-e: bad-e xalq az-u: va ʔaz solṭɑ:n du:r

(Masʕud Saʕd Salmɑn)

An ingenious variant introduces a rhyme before as well
as after the ḥājib:

ʔei šɑ:h-e zami:n bar ɑ:smɑ:n dɑ:ri: taxt

sost ast ʕadu: tɑ: to kamɑ:n dɑ:ri: saxt

ḥamle: sabok ɑ:ri:y o gerɑ:n dɑ:ri: raxt

pi:ri: to be-tadbi:r o javɑ:n dɑ:ri: baxt

(Amir Moʕezzi)

The double rhyme is sometimes found without the radīf (dū l-
ḡāfiyatayn):

xodɑ:vandɑ: dar-e: toufi:q bogšɑ:y

neža:mi:-ra: rah-e: taḥqi:q benma:y

deli: deh ku: yaqi:nat-ra: be-ša:yad

zaba:ni: k-a:fari:nat-ra: sara:yad

(Nežami)

Turning to the q͞afiya or rhyme proper, we find that this
may consist of anything from one to four syllables (it is
rarely more).   Several examples of monosyllabic (e.g. 4.4.07
(2), 4.7.14) and dissyllabic (e.g. 2.3.16, 3.3.07(2), 4.1.15,
5.1.13) rhymes have already been given.   The Šahna͞me provides
plenty of examples of the longer rhymes:

na gašt-e: zama:ne: be-farsa:yadaš

na ʔi:n ranj o ti:ma:r bagza:yadaš   (3 syllables)

bedi:n gu:ne ʔaz carm-e pu:yandaga:n

be-pu:ši:d   ba:la:-ye gu:yandaga:n   (4 syllables)

However the elaborate terminology devised by the Arab
prosodists to describe the various possible combinations is
based, like the scansion, not on syllables but on letters.
The one essential element in all rhymes is the raw͞i, which
is defined as being the last letter of a word in its basic
form, that is, without the addition of a suffix or
inflection.   This, together with a preceding vowel, may be
the only element in the rhyme, or it may be preceded by one
or two letters, and followed by anything up to six.   Each
of these letters, together with the vowels accompanying them,
have distinctive names according to their position.   When
the raw͞i is itself the last element in the rhyme, it is known
as muq͞id;   when it is followed by one or more letters, it is

muṭlaq or mawṣūl.

(a) **Preceding the rawī.**   Six different combinations are
possible:

(i) **tawjīh:**   a short vowel.   This must be constant when the
rawī is muqīd, but may vary when the latter is muṭlaq (though
on the whole this is avoided).   In this form the rawī is
known as **mujarrad.**

rawī muqīd mujarrad

    gahi: ze mošk zanad bar gol-e: šegofte raqam

    gahi: ze qi:r kašad bar mah-e: do hafte qalam

                    (Amir Moˤezzi)

In the above rhyme M̲ is the rawī and a̲ the tawjīh.

(ii) **ridf mufrid:**   alif, wāw, or yāʔ when they stand for a
long vowel.   The preceding short vowel is known as the **ha̲dw.**

rawī murdaf bi 1-ridf al-mufrid

    ʔɑ:n pi:r-e mɑ: ke ṣobḥ leqɑ:ʔi:st xeẓr nɑ:m

    har ṣobḥ bu:y-e cašme-ye xeẓr ayadaš ze kɑ:m

                    (Xɑqɑni)

The three elements in the rhyme, -a-ʔ-M, are respectively
the ha̲dw, the ridf and the rawī.

(iii) **ridf zāʔid:**   in Persian verse only, one of the
following six letters: x̲, r̲, s̲, š̲, f̲, n̲ may be inserted as a
sākin letter between the ridf and the rawī, in which case
it is known as the **ridf zāʔid** (sometimes **ridf mud̲āˤif**),
while the normal ridf becomes the **ridf aṣlī.**

rawī murdaf bi 1-ridf al-murakkab

    ru:dagi: cang bar gereft o navɑ:xt

bɑ:de ʔandɑ:z ku: saru:d andɑ:xt

(Rudagi)

The four elements in the rhyme, -a̲-ʔ-X̲-T̲, are respectively
the ḥad̲w, the ridf aṣlī, the ridf zā̲ʔid, and the rawī.

(iv) q̲a̲y̲d̲: any other sākin letter preceding the rawī, the
preceding short vowel being known as the ḥad̲w.

<u>rawī muqīd bi l-qayd</u>

    dar ʕahd-e to ʔei negɑ:r-e del-band

    bas ʕahd-e to beškanand o sougand

(Saʕdi)

-a̲-N̲-D̲: ḥad̲w, qayd, rawī.

The letters most commonly used in this position are b̲, x̲,
r̲, z̲, ṣ̲, š̲, g̲, f̲, n̲, ḥ̲. Occasionally h̲ is found rhymed with
ḥ̲. The ḥad̲w does not vary when the rawī. is muqīd, but may
do so when it is muṭlaq.

(v) t̲a̲ʔ̲s̲ī̲s̲: an alif standing for the long vowel (the preceding fatḥa is known as the <u>ras</u>), separated from the rawī
by a variable mutaḥarrik letter.

<u>rawī muʔassis</u>

    dɑ:rɑ:-ye jahɑ:n noṣrat-e di:n xosrov-e kɑ:mel

    yahyɑ bn-e mozaffar malek-e: ʕɑ:lam-e ʕɑ:del

(Ḥɑfeż)

-a̲-ʔ-[ ]-i̲-L̲: ras, taʔsīs, [...], tawjīh (or išbāʕ - see
below), rawī.

(vi) d̲a̲x̲ī̲l̲: an <u>invariable</u> letter standing between the
taʔsīs and the rawī; the following short vowel is called
the išbāʕ.

rawī mu?assis

    gar to: be-safar šodi: nega:rɑ: šɑ:yad

    mɑ:hi:y o mah az safar šodan nɑ:sɑ:yad

                        (Masʕud Saʕd Salmɑn)

-a̲-?̲-Y̲-a̲-D̲: ras, ta?sīs, daxīl, išbāʕ, rawī. Some prosodists describe the intervening letter as the daxīl even
when it is variable.

Summary

	Vowel	Letter	Letter	Vowel	Letter	Letter	Letter
mujarrad	–	–	–	tawjīh	–	–	rawī
RaQ–				a			M
murdaf (a)	–	–	–	ḥadw	ridf	–	rawī
					mufrid		
N–				a	?		M
murdaf (b)	–	–	–	ḥadw	ridf	ridf	rawī
					aslī	zā?id	
NaV–				a	?	X	T
muqīd	–	–	–	ḥadw	qayd	–	rawī
DiLB–				a	N		D
mu?assis(a)	ras	ta?sīs	*	tawjīh	–	–	rawī
K/ʕ–	a	?	M/D	i			L
mu?assis(b)	ras	ta?sīs	daxīl	išbāʕ	–	–	rawī
Š–	a	?	Y	a			D

Each of the above combinations may constitute the complete rhyme, or may be followed by up to six more letters
(which are of course repeated without change at the end of
each line). These are not to be confused with the radīf;

they are suffixes attached to but not forming an integral
part of the main word.

(i) waṣl, preceded by the majrā: The waṣl is generally the
yāʔ-i maṣdar, yāʔ-i waḥdat, or yāʔ-i xitābī; the pronominal
suffixes -am, -at, -aš; the hāʔ maxfī; the -n of the
infinitive, etc.

      toxm gašt ei ʕajab magar soxanam

      ke parɑ:kande bar zami:n feganam

                   (Masʕud Saʕd Salmɑn)

-a-N-a-M: tawjīh, rawī, majrā, waṣl.

(ii) xurūj, preceded by the nifād (the term used for all the
remaining short vowels that may occur in the qāfiya):

      gar ce ṣɑ:heb velɑ:yat-e: zamiyam

      pi:švɑ:y-e: pari:y o ʔɑ:damiyam

                   (Neżami)

-a-M-i-Y-a-M: tawjīh, rawī, majrā, waṣl, nifād, xurūj.

(iii) mazīd:

      xɑ:kiyɑ:ni: ke zɑ:de-ye: zamiyand

      dadagɑ:ni: be-ṣu:rat ɑ:damiyand

                   (Neżami)

-a-M-i-Y-a-N-D: tawjīh, rawī, majrā, waṣl, nifād, xurūj,
                                   mazīd.

(iv) nāʔira (fourth and any subsequent letters):

      gar rɑ:y-e šɑ:h cu:n falak-e: canbari:sti:

      rɑ:y-aš bar ɑ:n falak co mah u: moštari:sti:

                  (Amir Moʕezzi)

-a-R-i-Y-S-T-i-Y: tawjīh, rawī, majrā, waṣl, xurūj, mazīd,
                             nifād, nāʔira.

Summary

Rhyme	Letter rawī	Vowel majrā	Letter waṣl	Vowel nifāḏ	Letter xurūj	Vowel nifāḏ	Letter mazīd	Vowel nifāḏ	Letter nāʔira
-aNaM	N	a	M						
-aMiYaM	M	i	Y	a	M				
-aMiYaND	M	i	Y	a	N		D		
-aRiYSTiY	R	i	Y		S		T	i	Y

The examples cited above are all based on the simplest
form of the rawī, the mujarrad (i.·e. preceded only by the
short vowel tawjīh).   It is unnecessary to give examples of
all the twenty other possibilities;   the following verses
show examples of the full-length rhyme (i.e. as far as the
nāʔira) for each of the other forms of the rawī (rawī under-
lined).

rawī muṭlaq bi l-taʔsīs maς al-xurūj wa l-mazīd wa l-nāʔira:

ṭɑ:lebi:maša:n   -   rɑ:ḍebi:maša:n   -aʔL/ḌiBiYMaša?N*

... bi l-taʔsīs wa l-daxīl...

šamɑ:yelastaša:n   -   mɑ:yelastaša:n   -aʔYiLaSTaša?N*

...bi l-ridf al-mufrid...

    pi:š-e voju:d-e: hame ʔɑ:yandagɑ:n

    pi:š-e baqɑ:-ye: hame pɑ:yandagɑ:n   -aʔYaNDaGaʔN
                    (Nežɑmi)

...bi l-ridf al-murakkab...

    marɑ: ṣu:ratgari: ʔɑ:mu:xtastand

    qobɑ:-ye: jɑ:n degar jɑ: du:xtastand   -uWXTaSTaND
                    (Nežɑmi)

...bi l-qayd...

    kašmakaš har ce dar u: zandagi:st

    pi:š-e xodɑvandi-ye ʔu: bandagi:st   -aNDaGiYST
                    (Nežɑmi)

The obvious weakness of this terminology is that it makes
_no clear distinction between sākin and mutaḥarrik letters,

---

* No examples have been found in the poets;   these words
are suggested by Habib Yaqmaʔi.[33]

or, to put it in Western terms, it does not indicate the
number of syllables contained in the rhyme, let alone the
scansion. Thus rhymes extending the full length to include
the naʔira may be either three or four syllables, and may be
quite different in pattern. Both the following rhymes have
the rawī bi l-ridf al-mufrid and the full complement of
following letters:

$$\text{ʔa:yandaga:n} \quad - \quad \text{pa:yandaga:n}$$
$$\overline{-} \ \ \overline{-} \ \ \smile \ \ \overline{-} \qquad\qquad \overline{-} \ \ \overline{-} \ \ \smile \ \ \overline{-}$$

$$\text{pu:ši:dand} \quad - \quad \text{(xo)ru:ši:dand}$$
$$\overline{-} \ \ \overline{-} \ \ \smile \qquad\qquad \overline{-} \ \ \overline{-} \ \ \smile$$

Another classification found in the prosody books, that
still does not throw much light on this problem and is indeed
rather obscure of purpose, is reckoned on the basis of the
number of mutaḥarrik letters at the end of the line:
(i) mutarādif: the last two letters are both sākin. This is
found in the ʕilal qaṣr, waqf, tasbīḍ, and idāla - fuʕu:l,
fuʕu:la:n, fa:ʕila:n, mafʕu:la:n, faʕili:ya:n, mustafʕila:n,
etc.

ni:sti:ʔa:nke zani: ši:še-ye hasti: bar sang
var na dar pa:t feta:di: falak-e: mi:na:-rang
                        (Xaju)

(ii) mutawātir: the two sawākin are separated by one
mutaḥarrik. This arises in any foot ending in a sabab
xafīf preceded by another sabab xafīf or a watad majmūʕ,
e.g. mafa:ʕi:lun, fa:ʕila:tun, mafʕu:lun, fuʕu:lun, faʕlun,
etc.

be-ti:ḍam gar kašad dastaš na-gi:ram

va gar ti:ram zanad mennat paẕi:ram

(Ḥafeż)

(iii) <u>mutadārik</u>: the two sawākin are separated by two
mutaḥarrikāt.   This arises in any foot ending in a watad
majmūˤ preceded by a sabab xafīf, e.g. fa:ˤilun,
mustafˤilun, mafa:ˤilun, etc.

 bɑ:z   ɑ:y sɑ:qiyɑ: ke havɑ:-xɑ:h-e xedmatam

 moštɑ:q-e bandagi:y o doˤɑ:-gu:y-e doulatam

(Ḥafeż)

(iv) <u>mutarākib</u>: the two sawākin are separated by three
mutaḥarrikāt.   This occurs in:

 ṭayy and xazl - muftaˤilun, mufa:ˤalatun.

 xabn, xabn wa ḥaḏf, ḥaḏad, xabl wa kasf - faˤilun.

 (in the Arabic mutaqārib metre only) - fuˤu:lu faˤal.

 man ke bɑ:šam ke bar ɑ:n xɑ:ṭer-e ˤɑ:ṭer goẕaram

 loṭf-hɑ: mi:koniy ei xɑ:k-e darat tɑ:j-e saram

(Ḥafeż)

(v) <u>mutakāwis</u>: the two sawākin are separated by four
mutaḥarrikāt, e.g. faˤilatun preceded by a rukn ending in a
sākin letter.   This involves a sequence of three short
syllables, and cannot occur in Persian verse.

 The following are regarded as faults by the prosodists:

(i) <u>iqwā?</u>: variation in the haḏw or the tawjīh.

 ʔaz ḍoṣṣe-ye hejrɑ:n-e to del por dɑ:ram

 peivaste ʔaz ɑ:n di:de be-xu:n tar dɑ:ram

(Ḥabib Yaḍmɑ?i)

In Arabic prosody this fault is called <u>sinād</u> (see (iii)

below), the term iqwā? being used for variation in the majrā
between i and u, while isrāf designates variation in the
majrā between a and i/u.

(ii) ikfā?:   variation in the rawī between two letters of
similar sound or classification, e.g. ehtiya:ṭ and eʕtema:d
(two dentals);   šak and sag (Arabic and Persian letters).

    hami: gorz bα:ri:d bar xu:d o tark

    co bα:d-e: xazα:n bα:rad az bi:d barg

                              (Ferdousi)

In Arabic the term ijāra or ijāza is used to designate
similar variations in other letters of the rhyme.

(iii) sinād: variation in the ridf, whether aṣlī or zā?id.

    namα:?i:m mα: ?α:nce ni:kα:n konand

    xeradmand mardα:n o pα:kα:n konand

                              (Ḥabib Yaqmα?i)

    šahryα:r andar pay-e: ?u: ?asb tα:xt

    tα: ke ?u:-rα: dar biyα:bα:ni: be yα:ft

                              (Ḥabib Yaqmα?i)

The first of these is permissible in Arabic, and the term
sinād is used instead for

    (a) the rhyming of a qāfiya murdafa with a ḍayr murdafa,
e.g. muhibb and habi:b.

    (b) the rhyming of a mu?assisa with a ḍayr mu?assisa,
e.g. manzil and mana:zil.

    (c) variations in the hadw, tawjīh, or išbāʕ (see (i)
above).

(iv) Īṭā?:   repetition of the rhyming word or part of word.

(a) <u>jalī</u>:   where there is no change in meaning, e.g.
niːkuːtar/ziːbɑːtar, fosuːngar/setamgar.

dar in zamɑːne botiː niːst ʔaz to niːkuːtar

na bar to bar šamaniː ʔaz rahiːt mošfeq-tar

(Abu Salik Gorgɑni)

Infinitive endings, e.g. goftan/šaniːdan.

ʔei nehɑːdeː bar miyɑːn-eː farq-e jɑːn-eː xiːštan...

...cuːn šaviː biːmɑːr behtar gardiy az gardan zadan

(Manucehri)

Plural endings (also known as <u>šāyigān</u>), e.g. yɑːrɑːn/
duːstɑːn, kɑːʔenɑːt/ṣefɑːt, ḋonce-hɑː/lɑːle-hɑː.

diːdɑːr-e to ḥall-e moškelɑːtast

ṣabr az to xalɑːf-e momkenɑːtast

(Saʕdi)

Adjectival endings, e.g. geryɑːn/xandɑːn, siːmiːn/
zarriːn.

ḥɑːsedam guːyad cerɑː bɑːšiː to dar dargɑːh-e šɑːh

ʔiːnt boḋzi ʔɑːškɑːrɑː ʔiːnt jahliː rɑːstiːn

  ...

bɑːš tɑː sɑːl-eː degar noubat kerɑː xɑːhad bodan

tɑː kerɑː miːbɑːyadam zad bar sar-eː vei puːstiːn

(Manucehri)

Indefinite <u>-ī</u>, e.g. mardiː/duːstiː.

Verbal endings, e.g. barad/dehad.

It is regarded as permissible to use such rhymes not
more than two or three times in a qaṣīda, and at intervals
of not less than seven abyāt.

(b) <u>xafī</u>:   where there is a difference in meaning, e.g.

α:b/golα:b.   This is regarded as permissible.

(v) <u>ḍulū</u>: the rawī is mutaḥarrik in one verse and sākin in

the other.

    ṣalα:ḥ-e kα:r kojα: vu: man-e: xarα:b kojα:

    be-bi:n tafα:vot-e rα:h az kojα:-st tα: be-kojα:

                        (Ḥafeż)

(vi) one word overlaps the qāfiya and the radīf.

(vii) <u>taḍmīn</u>:   the rhyming word overlaps into the next

miṣrā؏.   This was done for humorous effect in the poem by

Qα?emmaqαm Farαhαni which begins:

    sayyedα: dast o pα: mazan ke be-؏oun-

    n-e ?elα:hi: ḥosein-e ben mostou-

    fi: samα:?i:l-e tafreši: z-i:n ṭou-

    r be-ku:šad hami: be-<u>z</u>ouq o be-šou-

    q...etc.

(viii) <u>qāfiya ma؏mūla</u>:   simple and compound words are rhymed.

    bu:y-e: gol o bα:ng-e morḍ bar xα:st

    hengα:m-e nešα:ṭ o ru:z-e sahrα:-st

                (Sa؏di)

(ix) otiose letter rhymed with ordinary:

    do cašm-e: to hastand fattα:n o jα:du:

    del u: di:n negah dα:št bα:yad ze har do:

                (Amir Mo؏ezzi)

(x) alteration of a word for the sake of the rhyme:

    (a) change of letter:

    ?α:b-e ?angu:r o ?α:b-e ni:lu:fel (for ni:lu:far)

mar marα: ʔaz ʕabi:r o mošk be-del

                 (Ḥabib Yaǧmaʔi)

(b) addition of letter:

xα:s̩ dar band-e lezzat u: šahavα:t

ʕα:m dar band-e hazl o torrα:hα:t (for torrahα:t)

                 (Sanαʔi)

(c) deletion of letter:

(d) addition or deletion of tašdīd:

gu:sfandα:n ku: beru:nand az ḥesα:b

z-anbohi:šα:n kei betarsad ʔα:n qas̩α:b (for qas̩s̩α:b)

                 (Moulavi)

(e) grammatical irregularity:

xande-ye to: gα:he xašm xande-ye ši:r-e: nar ast

har ke na-geryad ʔaz α:n xande ze ši:r ašyar ast (Arabic

      elative a̱šyar from Persian ši̱r) (Qαʔani)

(xi) iqʕād: variation of the ʕarūḍ, e.g. between saḥīḥ and

maqtūʕ, especially in the kāmil metre (not found in Persian

verse).

(xii) tajrīd: similar variation of the ḍarb (not found in

Persian verse).

(xiii) wāw/yāʔ maʕrūf wa majhūl: the classical poets

considered it a fault to rhyme these vowels with each other.

    be-bα:ǧ-e lahv-e to rα:meš co ʔarǧavα:n xandi:d

    ze šα:x-e madḥ-e to doulat co ʔandali:b saro̱:d

    hamiše tα: šavad az bα:ǧ dašt mošk-α:gi:n

    hamiše tα: šavad az mehr ku:h zar-ʔandu̱:d

                 (Masʕud Saʕd Salmαn)

rɑ:ẓiy-am gar marɑ: be-har di:nɑ:r

be-dehad ru:zgɑ:r ni:m pešḙ:z

ʔablahi: kon bar-u: ke barre-foru:š

barre nafru:šadat be-ʕaql o tami:z

                              (Masʕud Saʕd Salmɑn)

yā̆ʔ maʕrū̆f is found rhymed with yā̆ʔ al-imā̆la:

ʔei ravɑ: karde fari:bande jahɑ:n bar to fari:b

mar to-rɑ: xɑ:nde va xod ru:y nehɑ:de: be-naši:b

ʔi:n jahɑ:n-rɑ: be-joz az xɑ:biy o bɑ:zi: ma-šomor

gar moqarr-i: be-xodɑ: vu: be-rasu:l u: be-keti:b

                              (for keta:b)

                    (Nɑṣer-e Xosrou)

     With the complete disappearance in modern times of any
distinction in the pronunciation of these two pairs of
vowels, this rule has to a large extent been abandoned.
(xiv) dāl and d̠āl: in classical Persian dāl was only used
after a consonant (in practice r̠, z̠, n̠), and d̠āl after a
vowel.   Since however dāl frequently occurs after a vowel
in Arabic, the possibility of rhyming the two arose once the
distinctive pronunciation of Persian d̠āl disappeared.   It was
nevertheless regarded as a fault by the purists.

     gahi: por ʔɑ:b cašm-aš z-ašk-e šɑ:di:

     gahi: por xu:n ze bi:m-e: nɑ:-morɑ:di:

                    (Jɑmi)

(xv) Attention has already been drawn to the practice of
rhyming words beginning with x^v according to their original
pronunciation, rather than with the vowel-sound subsequently

acquired.   To ignore this is considered a fault by strict
followers of tradition.

    saram α:xer be-sotu:ni: bar xord

    Ɂu:ftα:dam be-zami:n xα:bam bord

                       (ʕešqi)

Contrast with

    jahα:n-e: fari:bande-rα: gard kard

    rah-e: su:d peimu:d o mα:ye: na-x^{v}ard

                     (Ferdousi)

Apart from the taɁsĪs, other cases of assonance and semi-
rhyme are commonly found that have no official terminology:

    doxtar u:rα: deham be-Ɂα:zα:di:

    Ɂarjomand-aš konam be-dα:mα:di:

                    (Nežαmi)

    bα:z nα:n-rα: zi:r-e dandα:n ku:ftand

    gašt ʕaql u: jα:n o fahm-e: su:dmand

                   (Moulavi)

    har ce Ɂα:mad ze daxl-e dehqα:nα:n

    ṣarf mi:-šod be xarj-e mehmα:nα:n

                    (Nežαmi)

    farq-ast miyα:n-e Ɂα:nke yα:r-aš dar bar

    tα: Ɂα:nke do cašm-e Ɂentežα:r-aš bar dar

                   (Saʕdi)

The use and arrangement of rhymes in the various verse-
forms will be discussed in Appendix II, but the following
technical terms may be mentioned here.

    (a) <u>muṣarraʕ</u>: a bayt in which the ʕarūḍ and the ḍarb

rhyme. This is the rule for the first bayt (the maṭlaʕ) of
all verse-forms except the qiṭʕa (and the musammaṭ, which is
not composed of bayts).

(b) muqaffā: the ʕarūd and darb do not rhyme. This is
the normal practice for the ḡazal and the qaṣīda.

(c) musajjaʕ: in "doubled" metres there may be a
separate rhyme (for each bayt) at the end of each of the
first three half-hemistichs (this does not· apply to the
maṭlaʕ when this is muṣarraʕ):

> ce bu:y-ast i:n ce bu:y-ast i:n magar ʔa:n ya:r mi:ya:yad
>
> magar ʔa:n ya:r-e golroxsa:r ʔaz golza:r mi:ya:yad
>
> šabi: ya: parde-ye: ʕu:di: . va ya: mošk-e: ʕaber-su:di:
>
> va ya: yu:sef bedɑ:n zu:di: . ʔaz ɑ:n bɑ:zɑ:r mi:ya:yad

>   (Moulavi)

Appendix II. Verse forms

All verse-forms in classical Persian poetry are character-
ised by one common feature: the same metre (pattern and
length of line) is preserved throughout the poem. This
rule is observed up to the present day by poets writing in
the traditional style, though of course the "free verse"
poets have abandoned it altogether, nor is it observed by
those, like ʿešqi (1894-1923), writing in metrical but non-
classical forms like the taṣnif, an irregular verse form
designed for setting to music.

Subject to this over-riding requirement, Persian verse-
forms may be divided into three main categories: poems in
which each couplet has its own rhyme, poems in which the
same rhyme is preserved throughout, and stanzaic poems in
which the rhyme varies to a greater or less extent with
each stanza.

I. RHYMED COUPLETS: matnawī (muzdawaj).

In spite of the Arabic form of the name, the matnawī is
purely Persian in origin and use, and owes nothing to
Arabic versification. Each miṣrāʿ rhymes with its partner,
and the rhyme changes for each bayt (indeed it is considered
bad style to repeat the same rhyme too frequently). The

ma<u>t</u>nawī is therefore capable of expansion to any length, and
so is pre-eminently suitable for epics, romances, and didactic,
philosophical and mystical poems.   Many of the most famous
poems in Persian (the <u>Šahname</u> of Ferdousi, over 50,000 verses,
the <u>Xamse</u> or five romances of Nežami, the "spiritual"
Ma<u>s</u>navi-ye maʕnavi of Jalaloddin Rumi Moulavi, the <u>Haft</u>
<u>ourang</u> or seven romances of Jami, etc.) have been composed
in this form.

According to the prosodists, it is possible to tell the
nature of a ma<u>t</u>nawī poem from the metre in which it is
composed: metre 1.1.11 is used for <u>razm</u> (heroic epics) and
<u>bazm</u> (festive poems), 2.1.11 and 5.1.10 for <u>ʕešq</u> (love poems),
2.4.11, 3.1.11 and 3.4.11 for <u>pand</u> (homilies) and <u>taṣavvof</u>
(Sufism), and 4.5.11 for <u>bazm</u>.   Traditionally these were
the only metres in which a ma<u>t</u>nawī might be composed, and a
favourite ploy was to compose a set of seven poems (<u>sabʕa</u>)
using each of them.   In fact the choice of neither metre
nor subject was strictly observed, at any rate in early
classical times.   Rudagi uses 4.7.11, Daqiqi 4.7.02/09,
and the late classical Jami 2.1.16.   Abu Šakur's philosophical <u>Ɑfarin-name</u> (336/947-8) is in metre 1.1.11, while
Ḥakim Meisari's medical treatise the <u>Daneš-name</u> (370/980-1) -
the earliest full-length ma<u>t</u>nawī we have - is in 2.1.11.
Rudagi chose 2.4.11 for his version of <u>Kalile va Demne</u>.
Moreover, at least two romantic poems from Qaznavid times
were composed in metre 1.1.11 - ʕonṣori's <u>Vameq o ʕazra</u>
and ʕayyuqi's <u>Varqe va Golšah</u>.   A fragment of a <u>Šahname</u>

composed by Masʕudi Marvazi towards the end of the 3rd/9th
century is in 2.1.11, and some verses by Rabenjani from a
poem of the same class is in 4.5.11.   The earliest surviving
maṯnawī fragments, by Šahid Balxi and Farɑlɑvi, are less
easily identifiable as to subject, and are in 1.1.11 and
4.5.11.   Although there is no direct evidence of a maṯnawī
form in Pahlavi literature, it is worth noting that all the
conventional metres for this form are of the short eleven-
syllable (in one case ten-syllable) type.   This strongly
suggests a connection with the poetry of the Pahlavi books,
where the eleven-syllable line is also the norm, though the
metrical pattern is less clear.

II.   MONORHYME   (a) ǵazal.

The ǵazal is a short poem in lyric form, with anything
from five to seventeen couplets, and - as the figures in
Chapter IV show - may be composed in any metre.   It has
the rhyme-scheme common to most forms of this class, a
single rhyme common to both halves of the first bayt (the
maṭlaʕ) and the second miṣrāʕ of all subsequent abyāt.

The following terms may be noted at this point:

maṭlaʕ: the first bayt of a poem.

maqtaʕ: the last bayt of a poem, especially in the
ǵazal, in which the maqtaʕ usually, since the time of Saʕdi
(1184-1291) at any rate, contains the "signature" of the
poet (taxalluṣ).

radd al-maṭlaʕ: repetition of the second miṣrāʕ of the
poem at the end.

ḥusn al-maṭlaᶜ: the second bayt of the poem.

ḥusn al-maqṭaᶜ: the penultimate bayt of the poem.

bayt al-ḡazal, šāh-bayt: the best bayt of the poem.

The origin of the ḡazal has been the subject of much speculation. Traditionally it has been regarded as stemming from the erotic section of the qaṣīda (the tašbīb), and in favour of its Arabic origin is the name, which appears to be Arabic, though it is interesting to note that the first recorded use of the word in the sense of "love-song" occurs in a poem attributed to the Umayyad poet Waddāḥ, who if he existed at all was probably of Persian origin.[34] Yet this form is so typically Persian that one hesitates to accept its foreign derivation without question. We are told of the existence of a lyric form (the cakāmak) in pre-Islamic times, and it seems not unreasonable to suppose that this would have survived as an influence, if not a form, in later periods. The Tājīk scholar A.G. Mirzoev takes the view that the form in general was based on popular folk-songs, but that its development as a technical form, which was not complete until the time of Saᶜdi, may possibly have been influenced by Arabic models.[35] If so, we may assume that the ḡazals of the Sāmānid and Ḡaznavid period owed nothing to alien sources. However it was not at this period as popular as it later became. Farroxi, generally looked on as the master of the ḡazal at this period, has no more than 28 in his dīwān, while Manucehri and ᶜOnṣori number barely a dozen each.

(b) qaṣīda.

The qaṣīda is generally held to have been of Arabic
inspiration, and certainly of all the Persian poetic forms
this comes nearest to its Arabic parallels. It is a comparatively long poem, ranging according to the authorities from
thirteen couplets to as many as two hundred. The earliest
qaṣīda-writers from whom we have any substantial body of work
- ʿonsori, Manucehri, and Farroxi - seem to favour poems of
40 to 50 bayts, though Manucehri has a fair number of shorter
ones, while Farroxi has one, celebrating Maḥmūd of Qazne's
successful campaign against Sumnat in India (415/1024-417/
1026), that runs to 175 couplets.

The qaṣīda normally falls into two parts - the nasīb,
consisting usually of the tašbib or taḍazzul (erotic prelude),
and the maqṣad or maqsūd, the central element of which is the
madīha or šarīṭa, the panegyric section in praise of the
poet's patron. In the Arabic qaṣīda the theme of the
tašbib is nearly always a lament over the deserted encamp-
ment of the beloved, a natural Arabian setting that was
sometimes copied rather self-consciously by the Persian
poets. For the most part however the Persian qaṣīdas open
with a lyrical description of spring or autumn, or a welcome
to one of the great Persian festivals (both purely Persian
themes); or the poet may praise his mistress, or the joys
of wine-drinking. The transitional point between this and
the panegyric section, the main purpose of the poem, when
the poet turns his attention more or less abruptly (but as

neatly as possible) to the mamdū̱h, the object of his eulogy,
is known as the taxallu̱s or iqti̱dāb (Persian gurīzgāh).

xojaste bɑ:šad ru:y-e: kasi: ke di:de bovad

xojaste ru:y-e bot-e: xi:š bɑ:mdɑ:d pagɑ:h

ʔagar na-bu:di: bar man xojaste di:dan-e to:

xodɑ:y šɑ:d na-kardi: marɑ: be-di:dan-e šɑ:h

Happy is the face of one who has seen the happy face of
his beloved in the early morning; if I had not had the
happiness of seeing you, God would never have blessed
me with the sight of the king!

                                        (Farroxi)

The qasīda ends with the duʕā? (prayer for the patron's
wellbeing) and the husn al-talab (polite request for favours,
sometimes couched in general terms, and sometimes quite
specific). The last two bayts of the poem just quoted run
as follows:

dehad vali:y-e to-rɑ: kardgɑ:r pɑ:dɑ:šan

dehad ʕadu:-ye to-rɑ: ru:zgɑ:r bɑ:dafrɑ:h

bozorg bɑ:d be-nɑ:m-e: bozorg-e to: šeš ci:z

negi:n o tɑ:j o kolɑ:h u: sari:r o majles o gɑ:h

May the Creator grant reward to your friend!
May Fortune grant punishment to your enemy!
May six things be great in your great name -
Ring, crown, helmet, throne, court and palace!

A qasīda consisting of both prelude and panegyric is
called tamhīdī (making preparation); one that introduces
the madīha at once is xatābī (addressed), muqtadab

(extempore), maḥdūd (restricted). The tašbīb is also sometimes found as a separate poem, from which circumstance no
doubt arose the belief that it was the origin of the ḡazal.

As with the ḡazal, the metres used range over the whole
metrical system. The following additional technical terms
may be noted:

bayt al-qaṣīda: the best couplet in the poem.

ḏāt al-maṭāliʕ(muṣarraʕ): a qaṣīda divided into a number
of sections, each of which continues with the same metre and
rhyme, but opens with a fresh maṭlaʕ.

tāj: a couplet towards the end introducing the poet's
name.

(c) mustazād.

In this form, which is really a variant of the ḡazal or
short qaṣīda, though other forms such as the rubāʕī are also
adapted in this way, an additional phrase repeating the
pattern of the main metre is added to each miṣrāʕ or bayt.
Called the ziyāda, it may have the same rhyme as the main
poem or a separate rhyme of its own. It is usually stipu-
lated that it should supplement, but not be essential to
the understanding of, the verse itself; but this rule is
not always observed. The metre normally used for this
rather rare form is 3.3.14, though 3.1.15 and 3.4.11 are
also found; the Haft qolzom quotes several rubāʕiyāt,
including the following by Amir Xosrou of Delhi (651/1253-
725/1325):

tɑ: xaṭṭ-e moʕanbar ze rox-at bi:ru:n jast

ʔaz bɑ:de-ye ʔašk-e xi:š har ʕɑ:šeq-e mast

                 rox golgu:n kard

dar ju:y-e jamɑ:l-e to: magar ʔɑ:b na-mɑ:nd

k-ɑ:n sabze ke zi:r-e ʔɑ:b bu:di: peivast

                 sar bi:ru:n kard

Xɑju (689/1290-754/1353) has an example in 3.1.11:

to ma-pendɑ:r ke bar ṭarf-e caman

cu:n rox u: qɑ:matat ei si:mi:n-tan

               gol o šemšɑ:di: hast

dar dahɑ:n-e: to na-gonjad soxani:

gar ce ši:ri:n dahan-at gɑ:h soxan

               nerx-e šakkar be-šekast

In both these cases the mustazād element follows the
complete bayt; very often it is attached to each miṣrāʕ:

har laḥže be-šakli: bot-e ʕayyɑ:r bar ɑ:mad

             del bord o nehɑ:n šod

har dam be-lebɑ:s-e: degar ɑ:n yɑ:r bar ɑ:mad

            gah pi:r o javɑ:n šod

gɑ:hi: be-del-e: ṭi:nat-e ṣalṣa:l foru: raft

             ḍavvɑ:ṣ-e maʕɑ:ni:

gɑ:hi: ze tak-e: kahgel-e faxxɑ:r bar ɑ:mad

            z-ɑ:n pas be-janɑ:n šod

            (Moulavi)

kas ni:st ke taqri:r konad ḥɑ:l-e gedɑ:-rɑ:

            dar ḥaẓrat-e šɑ:hi:

k-az ḍolḍol-e bolbol ce xabar bɑ:d-e ṣabɑ:-rɑ:

            joz nɑ:le va ʔɑ:hi:

har cand nayam lɑ:yeq-e dargɑ:h-e salɑ:ṭi:n
                 nu:mi:d nayam ham

k-az ru:-ye taraḥḥom be-navɑ:zand gedɑ:-rɑ:
                 gɑ:hi: be-negɑ:hi:

        (Ebn Ḥesɑm Heravi, d.737/1336-7)

In all the above examples the mustazād element has a
separate rhyme of its own; in the following modern example
by ʕešqi the rhyme is the same as that of the main miṣrāʕ:

ʔei majles-e cɑ:rom be-xodɑ: nang-e bašar bu:d
               di:di: ce xabar bu:d

har kɑ:r ke kardand ẓarar ru:y-e ẓarar bu:d
               di:di: ce xabar bu:d

ʔi:n majles-e cɑ:rom xodemɑ:ni:m samar dɑ:št
               vallɑ:h ẓarar dɑ:št

ṣad šokr ke ʕomr-aš co zamɑ:ne: be-gozar bu:d
               di:di: ce xabar bu:d

(d) <u>qiṭʕa</u> (pl. <u>qiṭaʕāt</u>, <u>muqaṭṭaʕāt</u>).

The term qiṭʕa (fragment) is applied to any piece of
verse, from two to 170 couplets in length (but generally
short), which cannot be classified as a <u>qasīda</u> or a <u>ḡazal</u>
owing to the absence of the rhyme in the first <u>miṣrāʕ</u>.
It would normally deal with a single topic. The term <u>naẓm</u>
is sometimes used for a <u>qiṭʕa</u> in <u>ḡazal</u> form, but differing
from this form in choice of subject.

A single verse used in quotation, or as an epigram, is
called <u>fard</u> (<u>mufrid</u>). A single rhymed couplet is <u>muṣarraʕ</u>.
A single hemistich has the Persian title <u>miṣrāʕ-i āzāda</u>.

(e) <u>tamām-maṭlaʕ</u>.

In this purely Persian form all the hemistichs rhyme

with the same rhyme throughout the poem.

(f) rubāʕī (pl. rubāʕīyāt).

The rubāʕī is the shortest and one of the most discussed
of the Persian verse-forms, and for full details reference
may be made to the writings of Christensen, Rempis, Bausani,
and others.   Here it is necessary to deal only with the main
characteristics, which may be categorised under the headings
of form, metre and rhyme-scheme.

The word rubāʕī originally implied nothing more specific
than a verse of four lines, and appears not to have been
distinguished from the dūbaytī (verse of two bayts) and the
tarāna (poem of freshness and youth, a term surviving, as we
have seen, from pre-Islamic times).   Owing to the fragment-
ary nature of the early Islamic Persian verse that is extant,
it is difficult to pin down precisely the beginnings of the
form.   We cannot necessarily assume that every verse of
four lines is a complete quatrain, and not merely part of
a longer poem.   The verse by Maḥmud Varrαq already quoted
has all the earmarks of the form, though it is not in the
conventional rubāʕī metre, but in 2.1.11, which still
survives as the first choice for the popular quatrain,
known as the dūbaytī to distinguish it from the rubāʕī
proper.

    negā:ri:nα: be-naqd-e: jα:nt nadham

    gerα:ni: dar bahα: ʔarzα:nt nadham

    gereftastam be-jα:n dα:mα:n-e vaṣlat

    deham jα:n az kaf u: dα:mα:nt nadham

The best-known practitioner of this form was the darvish
poet Baba Taher Ꞁoryan of Hamadan (fl. 5th/11th cent.), most
of whose verses are in dialect.

The rubāꞀī proper is since classical times still
further marked by its distinctive metre, 5.1.13/3.3.13, the
use of which has already been fully discussed. It is interesting to compare the relative use of these two patterns in
early Persian poetry with the figures given in Chapter IV
on the basis of a more general survey. A check of 172
rubāꞀīyāt attributed to the earliest poets up to Manucehri
shows that 51 keep to 5.1.13 throughout, 59 use 3.3.13 once,
45 twice, and 15 three times, while only two follow 3.3.13
throughout. This gives a percentage of 70.6% to the
Pattern 5 metre, as against 58.5% in the general survey.
Too much importance must not be attached to these figures,
but they do suggest that the 5.1.13 is the older and more
popular.

Perhaps the most surprising feature of the rubāꞀī metre
is the fact that, in spite of its easily assimilated rhythem,
it is confined in use almost exclusively to the quatrain
form. The qualification "almost" is necessary because, as
Mojtaba Minovi has shown,[36] poets have been known to experiment with it in other forms. However even this indefati-
gable scholar has only been able to turn up five examples,
and one of these indeed, a qaṣīda by Farroxi, should, in

spite of Šams-e Qeis's classification to the contrary,
rather be scanned as 4.4.13.   Of the other four examples,
the best known is a musammaṭ by Manucehri, while the others
include a qiṭʕa by ʕeinol-qozạt Hamadạni (492/1099-525/1131),
a qiṭʕa by Abu Ṭaher Xạtuni (fl. 500/1106), and a qaṣīda by
the little-known poet Jamạloddin Abol-maḥạsen Yusef b. Naṣr,
of unknown date but quoted in a 7/13th century work.

There is very little evidence even of the rubāʕī being
used as a component in a stanzaic poem.   Minovi quotes four
examples, but two of these are acknowledged prosodist's
tours de force, a fact that in itself proves the rarity of
the device;   while the others seem rather to be collections
of independent quatrains grouped according to subject-matter.

The third feature that distinguishes the rubāʕī is the
rhyme-scheme.   While the majority (some 70%) of rubāʕīyāt
composed by classical poets follow the scheme characteristic
of all monorhyme forms - a common rhyme for each of the first
two hemistichs and at the end of every subsequent bayt), a
solid minority preserve the rhyme throughout all four hemistichs.   It has been suggested that the four-rhyme form is
the earlier, but there is very little evidence one way or
the other.   The two oldest extant complete rubāʕīyāt, by
Šahid Balxi, have three rhymes, while one by his slightly
later contemporary Abu Šakur has four.   Of 37 complete
rubāʕīyāt attributed to Rudagi, 12 have four rhymes and
25 three.   Scattered verses by other poets up to the
middle of the 5th/11th century show 15 four-rhyme and 17

three-rhyme quatrains.   However all of these are of somewhat dubious authenticity.   When we come to those 5th/11th
century poets whose rubāʿīyāt have survived in substantial
numbers, we find that the figures lean heavily towards the
four-rhyme type: Farroxi - 37 aaaa, 1 aaba; Qaṭrαn -
130 aaaa, 21 aaba; ʿonṣori - 59 aaaa, 8 aaba; Azraqi -
88 aaaa, 20 aaba; Abolfaraj Runi - 43 aaaa, 5 aaba; Masʿud
Saʿd Salmαn - 399 aaaa, 8 aaba; Amir Moʿezzi - 149 aaaa,
28 aaba.

Some modern poets have devised variant forms of the
rubāʿī - the ṭulāṭī with three hemistichs, the xumāsī or
panjgāna with five, and the sudāsī (šišgāna) with six.

goftam magar-at peste nehα:n dar dahan-ast
sang-am be-dahα:n zad ke ce jα:y-e: soxan-ast
goftam bali ʔi:n javα:b-e dandα:n-šekan-ast
                              (ɑyati - 1290/1873- ?)
ʔandi:še-ye to: garce bovad dorr-e xošα:b
tα:bα:n našavad tα: ke nayα:yad be-ketα:b
gar tabʿ našod be-dast-e mardom na-fetα:d
bar ru:ye zami:n cehre-ye roušan nagošα:d
cu:n barq-e jehande ʔast o cu:n naqš bar α:b
                              (Afsar - 1297/1879-1360/1941)
xα:hi: ke ʔasα:s-e vahm bar bα:d šavad
ʔα:ʔi:n-e xodα:y saxt-bonyα:d šavad
ʔavval bα:yad ʿaqi:de ʔα:zα:d šavad

har mard ze ja:n-e xi:š ʔeiman gardad

har mazhab o maslaki: mobarhan gardad

ta: ʔa:nke ḥaqa:yeq hame roušan gardad

(Afsar)

III. STANZAIC (a) tarjīʕ-band.

Several stanzas, all of the same metre and usually in
the ḡazal-form of 5-10 verses, are linked by a recurring
bayt (wāsiṭa, band-i šiʕr)using the same rhyme as the first
stanza, or sometimes having an independent rhyme. Normally
each stanza (with the exception of the wāsiṭa) has a
different rhyme.   The stanzas may also be muṣarraʕ (all
hemistichs rhyming), but this variety cannot be mixed with
the other form.

(b) tarkīb-band.

This form is identical with the tarjīʕ-band, except that
the wāsiṭa differs for each stanza.   Normally there is a
common rhyme for the wāsiṭāt, but this does not seem to be
necessary;   Xaju has a tarkib-band in which each stanza
consists of five bayts with their own rhyme (including the
muṣarraʕ first bayt) and one bayt (the wāsiṭa) which is also
muṣarraʕ and has an independent rhyme not repeated.

rang-e: šafaq negar ke co xorši:d roušan-ast

k-az xu:n-e cašm-e ma: falak a:lu:de-da:man-ast

...koni:	...an-ast
...raʕd	...an-ast
...to-st	...an-ast
...xorrami:	...an-ast

qoṭb-e: molu:k o na:ṣer-e donya: va di:n nama:nd

farmɑ:nde-ye: ʔakɑ:ber-e ru:-ye: zami:n namɑ:nd

              *

    ...šešdari:m   ...ari:m
    ...gahi: ...ari:m
    ...kaši:m   ...ari:m
    ...cašm-hɑ: ...ari:m
    ...havɑ:š   ...ari:m
    ...ɑ:m dar gozašt   ...ɑ:m dar gozašt

Masʕud Saʕd Salmɑn has a tarkīb-band in which each stanza has
its own independent rhyme, including the wāsiṭa.

The Persian term for the stanza in these two forms is
tarjīʕ-xāna, tarkib-xāna.   No special metre is prescribed;
those found include 2.1.16, 2.1.11, 2.3.16, 2.4.15, 3.1.15,
3.1.11, 3.3.07(2), 3.3.14, 3.4.11, 4.1.15, 4.4.07(2), 4.5.11,
4.7.02/09, 4.7.14, 5.1.11, 5.1.10, 5.3.16.

(c) musammaṭ.

The couplet basis is abandoned, the stanza consisting of
a number (ranging from three to ten) of hemistichs, all
rhymed, but the rhyme usually changing at a fixed point in
the stanza.   The following rhyme-schemes are typical:

    aaabb, cccbb, dddbb,......
    aaabb, cccdd, eeeff,....

sometimes

    aaaaa, bbbbb, ccccc,......

The musammaṭ is classified according to the number of
hemistichs in the stanza (which must remain constant throughout the poem).

    murabbaʕ (four lines):

The rhyme-scheme is normally aaab, the rhyme of the
fourth line (and sometimes the line itself) remaining
constant throughout (the former is murabbaˤ mukarrar, the
latter murabbaˤ muzdawij).

muxammas (five lines):
The rhyme-scheme may be either aaabb or aaaab.

musaddas (six lines):
The rhyme-scheme may be either aaaabb, aaaaab, or rarely
aaaabc (in this last case the rhymes of the two final lines
remain constant throughout all the stanzas).

Similar rules obtain for the muṭallaṭ, musabbaˤ,
muṯamman, mutassaˤ, and muˤaššar, which are less common.

musammaṭāt have been found in the following metres:
1.1.11, 1.3.10, 2.1.16, 2.1.11, 2.3.16, 2.4.11, 2.4.15,
3.1.15, 3.3.14, 3.4.11, 4.1.16, 4.4.15, 4.4.13, 4.5.11,
4.6.15, 4.7.14, 4.8.08(2), 5.1.10, 5.1.13, 5.6.07(2),
6.1.16.

murabbaˤ

bi:zɑ:ram az piyɑ:le: v-az ʔarḍavɑ:n o lɑ:le:
mɑ: vu: xoru:š o nɑ:le: gonji: gerefte tanhɑ:...
                                           (Kesɑʔi)

musaddas

xi:zi:d o xaz ɑ:ri:d ke hengɑ:m-e xazɑ:n-ast
bɑ:d-e: xonak az jɑ:neb-e xɑ:rezm vazɑ:n-ast
ʔɑ:n barg-e razɑ:n bi:n ke bar ɑ:n šɑ:x-e razɑ:n-ast
gu:ʔi: be-maṣal pi:rahan-e: rangrazɑ:n-ast
dehqɑ:n be-taˤajjob sar-e ʔangošt gazɑ:n-ast

k-andar caman u: bɑ:ɖ na gol mɑ:nd o na golnɑ:r....

(Manúcehri)

taḍmīn: another poet's dazal may be expanded into a

musammaṭ by prefixing to each couplet a number of hemistichs,

each of which rhyme with the first hemistich of the original

couplet.   This device is also known as tarbīʕ, taxmīs,

tasdīs, etc., according to the form that is constructed in

this way.   In the following example by Xɑju the asterisked

lines are from a qaṣīda by Sanɑʔi:

  bi: ṭalab dar nażar nayɑ:yad yɑ:r

  bi: ṭarab barg-e gol namɑ:yad xɑ:r

  hast maqṣu:d-e mɑ: ʔaz i:n goftɑ:r

  *ṭalab ei ʕɑ:šeqɑ:n-e xoš-raftɑ:r

  *ṭarab ei ni:kovɑ:n-e ši:ri:n-kɑ:r

  bi:-navɑ:-ʔi:m o ʔaz navɑ: fɑ:reɢ

  dardmand-i:m o ʔaz davɑ: fɑ:reɢ

  tɑ: be-kei xaste v-az šafɑ: fɑ:reɢ

  *dar jahɑ:n šɑ:hedi: va mɑ: fɑ:reɢ

  *dar qadaḥ jorʕe-ʔi: va mɑ: hošyɑ:r

The dīwān is a formally arranged collection of a poet's

writings, disposed generally under the headings qaṣāʔid,

tarkības, ḍazalīyāt, qiṭaʕāt, rubāʕīyāt, though other

categories may be included.   Since the 7th/13th century it

has been the practice to arrange the poems in each section

in the alphabetical order of the last letter of the rhyme

(sometimes known in this connection as the radīf), and some-

times further grouped within each letter according to the

buḥūr used.   According to Neẓami, the dīwān should begin
with ḥamd (praise of God), naʕt (praise of the Prophet),
munājāt (prayers for the poet himself), madḥ-i sulṭān (praise
of the patron), sabab-i taʔlīf (the poet's purpose in com-
piling the diwan), and sitāyiš-i suxan (praise of poetry
and speech).

The kullīyāt are a less formal and more comprehensive
"collected works", in which, in addition to the sections
mentioned above, there may well be classifications according
to subject-matter - madāʔiḥ, marātī, zuhdīyāt, qalandarīyāt,
mawāʕiẓ, ṭayyibāt (muṭāyabāt), hazalīyāt, xabītāt, xamrīyāt,
muwaššaḥāt (acrostics), mulammaʕāt (macaronic poems),
badāʔiʕ, taḍmīnāt, muḍḥikāt, etc.   matnawīyāt, unless they
are very long, will often be included.

Bibliography

(a) References in the Text.

1. Wright, Grammar of the Arabic Language, Vol. II, pp. 368-90.
2. Quoted by Xanlari, Vazn-e Šeʕr-e Farsi, p. 70.
3. Weil, Grundriss und System der altarabischen Metren, p.24.
4. Wright, op.cit., pp. 358-68; Noeldeke, Delectus Veterum Carminum Arabicorum, pp. 234-6.
5. Agha Ahmad Ali and H. Blochmann, A Treatise on the Rubáʕí, p. 8.
6. Guyard, Theorie nouvelle, JA VIII, p. 102.
7. Daudpota, The Influence of Arabic Poetry, p. 73.
8. Weil, op.cit., p. 78n.
9. al-Jāḥiż, Kitāb al-Bayān wa l-tabyīn, Vol. I, p. 295.
10. Moḥammad Qazvini, Bist maqale-ye Qazvini, Vol. I, p. 35.
11. Benveniste, JA (1930), Vol. II, pp. 193-225; ibid., JA (1932), Vol. II, pp. 245-293; Mary Boyce, The Manichaean Hymn-Cycles in Parthian, pp. 45ff; Henning, "A Pahlavi poem"; Tavadia, "A rhymed ballad in Pahlavi"; Shaked, "Specimens of Middle Persian verse"; Tafaẓẓoli, "Andarz i Wehzād Farrox Pērōz".
12. Mary Boyce, JRAS (April 1957), p. 31.
13. A. Bausani, Storia della Letteratura Persiana, p. 243.
14. N. Marr, Hazare-ye Ferdousi (The Millennium of Ferdousi), p. 195 (Pers.).
15. Christensen, Les Gestes des Rois, pp. 48, 53.
16. C. Rempis, ZDMG 105 (1955), pp. *64*-*65*.
17. Tarix-e Sistan, pp. 35-37.

18. Adib Ṭusi, Našriye-ye Daneškade-ye Adabiyat-e Tabriz,
    V 2 (1954), pp. 138-168.
19. Ibn Xurdādbih, Muxtārāt min kitāb al-lahw wa'l-malāhī,
    p. 16; Šafiʕi Kadkani, "Kohnetarin namune-ye šeʕr-e
    farsi", p. 26; Lazard, "The New Persian Language",
    p. 605.
20. Rajaʔi, Poli miyan-e šeʕr-e hejaʔi va ʕaruzi-ye farsi,
    pp. xliii-xlvi.
21. Gilbert Lazard, Les premiers poètes persans, Vol. I, p.10.
22. Henning, "The Disintegration of the Avestic Studies",
    pp. 52-4; Hertel, Beitraege zur Metrik, pp. 77-8.
23. al-Bīrūnī, Tahqīq mā li l-hind, p. 65; translation,
    p. 135.
24. von Wilamowitz-Moellendorf, Griechische Verskunst,
    p. 336n.
25. Rypka, Iranische Litteraturgeschichte, pp. 92-93, 297;
    ibid., History of Iranian Literature, pp. 92, 309.
26. M. Ishaque, Modern Persian Poetry, pp. 87-90.
27. ʕ. Ahmad Baxtyari, "Šarh-e hal-e Farroxi Baxtyari", p.494.
28. Avicenna, Maxārij al-hurūf, p. 42.
29. Noeldeke, "Das Iranische Nationalepos", pp. 188-9.
30. Lazard, op.cit., Vol. I, p. 46.
31. Christensen, op.cit., p. 55.
32. Vaṭvaṭ, Hadayeqos-sehr, p. 79.
33. Habib Yaḋmaʔi, ʕelm-e Qafiye, p. 14.
34. Blachère, "The Ghazal in Arabic Poetry", p. 1028;
    Brockelmann, Geschichte der Arabischen Litteratur,
    Supplementband I, pp. 30, 82.
35. Mirzoev, Rudaki va enkešaf-e ḋazal, pp. 71-2.
36. Minovi, Panzdah Goftar, pp. 335-7.

(b) Editions used for the Statistical Survey in Chapter IV.

Adib Pišavari: Divan, ed. ʕali ʕabdorrasuli (Tehran, 1933).
Adibol-mamalek: Divan, ed. Vahid Dastgerdi (Tehran, 1933).
Ašraf: Divan-e Sayyed Hasan Ḋaznavi Ašraf, ed. Taqi Modarres
    Razavi (Tehran, 1949).

Amir Moˁezzi; Divan, ed. ˁabbas Eqbal (Tehran, 1939).

Ouhadi: Divan, ed. A.S. Usha (Madras, 1951).

Iraj Mirza: Kolliyat-e Divan-e Iraj Mirza, ed. Xosrou Iraj
(Tehran, N.D.).

Baba Feqani: Divan, ed. Soheili Xansari (Tehran, 1937).

Parvin Eˁtesami: Divan-e Qasayed va Masnaviyat-e Xanom
Parvin Eˁtesami (Tehran, 1941).

Pur Daˀud: Purandoxt-name - Divan-e Pur Daˀud, ed.
D.J. Irani, (Bombay, 1928).

Jami: Divan, ed. H. Pežman (Tehran, 1938).

Hafež: Divan, ed. Mohammad Qazvini and Qasem Qani (Tehran,
1941).

Xaqani: Divan, ed. ˁali ˁabdorrasuli (Tehran, 1937).

Rudagi: Ahval o ašˁar-e Abu ˁabdollah b. Jaˁfar Mohammad
Rudagi Samarqandi, Vol. III (Tehran, 1940).

Runi: Divan, ed. Mahmud Mahdavi Damqani (Mashad, 1968).

Saˁdi: Kolliyat, ed. Mohammad ˁali Foruqi (Tehran, 1942).

Sanaˀi: Divan, ed. Modarres Razavi (Tehran, 1941).

Šuride: Qazaliyat-e Šuride-ye Širazi, ed. Hasan Ehsan Fasihi
(Tehran, 1946).

Saˀeb: Kolliyat-e Saˀeb-e Tabrizi, ed. Amiri Firuzkuhi
(Tehran, 1954).

Tarzi Afšar: Divan, ed. M. Tamaddon (Rezaˀiye, 1930).

ˁaref: Divan, ed. Rezazade Šafaq (Berlin, 1924); ˁaref-name-
ye Hazar, ed. M.R. Hazar (Širaz, 1935); Jeld-e dovvom-e
Divan, ed. Hadi Haˀeri Kuruš (Kerman, 1942).

ˁašeq: Divan, ed. Hosein Makki (Tehran, 1939).

ˁobeid Zakani: Kolliyat, ed. ˁabbas Eqbal (Tehran, 1953).

ˁorfi: Divan, ed. Mohammad Hamed (Cawnpore, 1915).

ˁešqi: Kolliyat-e mosavvar-e ˁešqi, ed. A.A. Salimi (Tehran,
1945).

ˁattar: Divan, ed. Saˁid Nafisi (Tehran, 1960).

ˁonsori: Divan, ed. Yahya Qarib (Tehran, 1944).

Qaˀani: Kolliyat (Bombay, 1860).

Qatran: Divan, ed. Mohammad Naxjavani (Tehran, 1954).

Kamaloddin Esfahani: Kolliyat (Bombay, 1889).

Lameᶜi: Divān, ed. Saᶜid Nafisi (Tehrān, 1940).
Laᶜli: Kolliyāt-e Divān, ed. Moḥammad ᶜali Ṣafvat (Tabriz, 1943).
Masᶜud Saᶜd Salmān: Divān, ed. Rašid Yāsemi (Tehrān, 1939).
Manucehri: Divān, ed. Moḥammad Dabir Siyāqi (Tehrān, 1947).
Moulavi: Ketāb-e jazabāt-e elāhiye - Montaxabāt-e Kolliyāt-e Šamsoddin Tabrizi, ed. Asadollāh Izad-gošasb (Eṣfahān, 1940).
Naṣer Xosrou: Divān, ed. Āqā Moḥammad Kāzem Širāzi (Calcutta, 1926).
Neżāmi: Ganjine-ye Ganjavi - Divān-e qaṣide va ġazal-e Ḥakim Neżāmi Ganjavi, ed. Vaḥid Dastgerdi (Tehrān, 1939).
Homām: Divān-e Homāmoddin Tabrizi, ed. Moʔayyed Sābeti (Tehrān, 1954).

(c) General Bibliography.

Abū Dīb, Kamāl, Fī'l-bunyat al-Īqāᶜīya li'l-šiᶜr al-ᶜarabī (Beirut, 1974).
Adib Ṣaber Termedi, Resāle-i dar bāb-e ouzān-e šeᶜr-e ᶜarabi va fārsi, ed. Mojtabā Minovi. Supp: Majalle-ye Dāneškade-ye Adabiyāt-e Tehrān IX 3 (Tehrān, 1961).
Adib Ṭusi, "Moṣallasāt-e Šeix Saᶜdi", Našriye-ye Daneskade-ye Adabiyāt-e Ṭabriz, VII, pp. 175-189 (Tabriz, 1956).
   "Šeᶜr va šāᶜeri dar Irān", NDAT IV 1/2, pp. 38-48 (Tabriz, 1951).
   "Tarāne-ha-ye Maḥalli", NDAT V 1, pp. 48-101, V 2, pp. 138-168 (Tabriz, 1953-54).
   "Yak pišnehād-e tāze dar fann-e ᶜaruẓ", NDAT XII 3, pp. 360-395, XII 4, pp. 461-502 (Tabriz, 1960-61).
ᶜalī b. al-Jahm, Dīwān (Damascus, 1949).
Aliev, R.M., Innovation in Contemporary Persian Poetry (Moscow, 1963).
Amir Jāhed, Moḥammad ᶜali, Divān-e Amir Jāhed (Tehrān, 1954).
Amir Xosrou Dehlavi, Bahr-e Ṭavil (Khairabad, 1875).
Arnold, E.V., Vedic Metre in its historical development (Cambridge, 1905).

Asadi Ṭusi, Abu Manṣur Ꜥali b. Aḥmad, Loḡat-e Fors,
    ed. Ꜥabbas Eqbal (Tehran, 1940).
Avicenna, Maxārij al-ḥurūf, Vol. I, ed. and trans.
    P.N. Xanlari (Tehran, 1954).
Axavan-e Sāles, Mahdi, "NouꜤi vazn dar šeꜤr-e emruz-e farsi",
    Peyam-e Novin, V 9-12, VI 1-2 (Tehran, 1963).
Ꜥayyuqi, Varqe va Golšah, ed. Z. Ṣafa (Tehran, 1964).
Azraqi, Divan, ed. Ꜥali Ꜥabdorrasuli (Tehran, 1955); ed.
    SaꜤid Nafisi (Tehran, 1957).
Bahar, Mohammad Taqi, "ŠeꜤr dar Iran", Majalle-ye Mehr, V
    1-5 (Tehran, 1937).
"ŠeꜤr-e Farsi", Peyam-e Nou, II 5. Reprinted in: Iraj
    Afšar, Naṣr-e farsi-ye moꜤaṣer, pp. 111-19 (Tehran, 1951).
Tarix-e taṭavvor-e šeꜤr-e Farsi (Mašhad, 1955).
"Yak qaṣide-ye Pahlavi", Soxan, II 8, p. 577 (Tehran, 1945).
Barkešli, M., Musiqi-ye doure-ye Sasani (Tehran, 1947).
    and Musa MaꜤrufi, Radif-e musiqi-ye Iran (Tehran, 1963).
Bausani, Alessandro, "Di una possibile origine dell'
    accentuazione sull' ultima sillaba in persiano moderno",
    Oriente Moderno XXVII, 4-6, pp. 123-30 (Rome, 1947).
see Pagliaro, A.
Baxtyari, Ꜥ. Aḥmad, "Šarḥ-e ḥal-e Farroxi Baxtyari",
    Armaḡan, VI 7/8, pp. 491-5 (Tehran, 1925-6).
Benveniste, E., "Le Memorial de Zarēr", Journal Asiatique,
    221, pp. 245-293 (Paris, 1932).
"Le Texte du Drakht asūrīg et la versification pehlevie",
    JA, 217, pp. 193-225 (Paris, 1930).
"Une apocalypse pehlevie, le Zamaspnāmak", Revue de
    l'histoire des religions, CVI, p. 337 (Paris, 1932).
al-Bīrūnī, Tahqīq mā li l-hind, ed. E. Sachau (London, 1887);
    trans. E. Sachau (London, 1910).
Blachère, R., "The Ghazal in Arabic Poetry", Encyclopedia of
    Islam, Vol. II, pp. 1028-33 (London/Leiden, 1965).
Blochmann, H., and Agha Ahmad Ali, A Treatise on the Rubáꜥí
    entitled Risálah i Taránah (Calcutta, 1867).
The Prosody of the Persians according to Saifi, Jami and

other writers (Calcutta, 1872; repr. Amsterdam, 1970).

Boyce, Mary, The Manichaean Hymn-Cycles in Parthian (London, 1954).

"The Parthian gōsān and the Iranian minstrel tradition", Journal of the Royal Asiatic Society, 1/2 (London, 1957), pp. 10-45.

Braginskii, I.S., Ocherki iz istorii tadžikskoi literatury (Stalinabad, 1956).

Iz istorii tadžikskoi narodnoi poezii (Moscow, 1956).

Brockelmann, Carl, Geschichte der Arabischen Litteratur (Weimar, 1898; Berlin, 1902; Leiden, 1937, 1938, 1942).

Browne, E.G., Literary History of Persia, Vol. II (London, 1906; repr. 1928, etc.).

Christensen, Arthur, Critical Studies in the Rubá'iyát of 'Umar-i-Khayyám (Copenhagen, 1927).

Les Gestes des Rois dans les Traditions de l'Iran antique (Paris, 1936).

Recherches sur les Rubā'iyāt de 'Omar Ḥayyām (Heidelberg, 1905).

Choeroboscus, Georgius, Exegesis in Hephaestionis enchiridion, ed. Guglielmus Hoerschelman. In: Schoell and Studemund, Anecdota Varia, Vol. I (Berlin, 1886).

Clinton, Jerome W., The Divan of Manūchihrī Dāmghānī: A critical study (Minneapolis, 1972).

Clarke, Samuel, Tractatus de Prosodia Arabica (Oxford, 1661).

Daudpota, U.M., The Influence of Arabic Poetry on the Development of Persian Poetry (Bombay, 1934).

Daryuš, Parviz, Namune-ha-ye šeʕr-e nou (Tehran, 1945).

De Sacy, Grammaire Arabe, Vol. II, pp. 615-661 (Paris, 1831).

Doulatšah, Tazkeratoš-šoʕara: The Tadhkiratu 'sh-Shu'ará... ed. E.G. Browne (London & Leiden, 1901).

Elwell-Sutton, L.P., "The Foundations of Persian Prosody and Metrics", Iran,XIII, pp. 75-97 (London, 1975).

"The Persian Metres", Akten der XXIVsten Int. Orient. Kongress Muenchen, pp. 307-9 (Wiesbaden, 1959).

"The Rubā'ī in Early Persian Literature", Cambridge History

of Iran, Vol. 4, pp. 633-57 (Cambridge, 1975).

Ewald, Heinrich, De metris carminum arabicorum libri duo
    (Brunswick, 1825).

Grammatica critica linguae arabicae (Leipzig, 1833).

Faqir, Mir Šamsoddin, Hadayeqol-balaqat (Calcutta, 1814).

Farroxzad, Foruq, Tavallodi Digar (Tehran, 1963).

Javedane (Tehran, 1968).

(ed.), Az Nima ta baʕd (Tehran, 1968).

Farzad, MasʕUd, ʕaruẓ-e Ḥafeẓ (Tehran, 1971).

ʕaruẓ-e Rudagi (Tehran, 1970).

Concise Persian Prosody (Coventry, 1966).

Mabna-ye riyaẓi-ye ʕaruẓ-e farsi (Tehran, 1966).

Majmuʕe-ye ouzan-e šeʕr-e farsi (Tehran, 1970).

Persian Poetic Metres - A Synthetic Study (Leiden, 1967).

The Metre of the Robàà‹ii (Tehran, 1942).

Ferdousi, Šahname, 10 vols. (Tehran, 1934-36); 9 vols.
    (Moscow, 1960-71).

Ferguson, Charles A., "Word Stress in Persian", Language,
    XXXIII 2, (Baltimore, 1957).

Foruq, Mahdi, "Talfiq-e šeʕr va musiqi", Majalle-ye Musiqi,
    17-32 (Tehran, 1957-58).

Freytag, Georg Wilhelm, Darstellung der Arabische Verskunst
    (Bonn, 1830; repr. Osnabrueck, 1968).

Garcin de Tassy, Joseph, Rhétorique et Prosodie des Langues
    de l'Orient Musulman (Paris, 1848; repr. 1873; repr.
    Amsterdam, 1970).

Gauthiot, Robert, "Notes sur le rythme du vers epique persan",
    Mem. de la Soc. de Linguistique de Paris, XIV, pp. 280-5
    (Paris, 1906).

Geiger, W., and H. Kuhn, Grundriss der Iranischen Philologie,
    Vol. II (Strassburg, 1896-1904).

Geldner, Karl, Ueber die Metrik des juengeren Avesta
    (Tuebingen, 1877).

Gibb, E.J.W., History of Ottoman Poetry, Vol. I, pp. 70-124
    (Leiden, 1900).

Gladwin, Francis, Dissertations on tne Rhetoric, Prosody and

Rhyme of the Persians (Calcutta, repr. London, 1801).

Gudarzi, Faramarz, "Nažari be-mostazad dar šeʕr-e farsi",
    Honar va Mardom, 140/1, pp. 36-42 (Tehran, 1974).

Guyard, Stanislas, "Theorie nouvelle de la métrique arabe",
    JA, VII, pp. 413-479, VIII, pp. 101-252, 285-315 (Paris,
    1876); "Note sur la métrique arabe", JA, X, pp. 97-115
    (Paris, 1877).

Hamidi, Mahdi, ʕaruz-e Hamidi (Tehran, 1963).

Heidar, Divan, BM Or. 28 (Rieu II p. 623a).

Henning, W.B., "A Pahlavi Poem", BSOAS, XIII 3, pp. 641-8
    (London, 1950).

    "Die aelteste persische Gedichthandschrift", Akten der
    XXIVsten Int. Orient. Kongress Muenchen, pp. 305-7
    (Wiesbaden, 1959).

    "Persian poetical manuscripts from the time of Rudagi",
    A Locust's Leg, pp. 89-104 (London, 1962).

    "The Disintegration of the Avestic Studies", Trans.
    Philological Society, pp. 40-56 (London, 1942).

Hertel, J., Beitraege zur Metrik des Awestas und des
    Rgvedas (Leipzig, 1927).

Hodge, Carleton T., "Some aspects of Persian style", Language,
    XXXIII 3 (Baltimore, 1957).

Ibn ʕabd Rabbih, al-ʕiqd al-farīd, Vol. IV (Cairo, 1928).

Ibn Xurdāḏbih, Kitāb al-masālik wa l-mamālik, Bibliotheca
    Geographorum VI (Leiden, 1889).

    Muxtārāt min kitāb al-lahw wa'l-malāhī, ed. Iqnāṭiyūs ʕabd
    al-Xalīfa (Beirut, 1961).

Ishaque, M., Modern Persian Poetry (Calcutta, 1943).

    Soxanvaran-e Iran dar ʕaṣr-e hazer, 2 vols. (Calcutta,
    1933-37).

al-Jāhiż, Kitāb al-bayān wa l-tabyīn (Cairo, 1932).

Jamaloddin, ʕali, ʕaruz-e torki (Istanbul, 1874).

Jhaveri, Krishnalal Mohanlal, Outline of Persian Prosody with
    Figures of Speech (Bombay, 2nd ed., 1922).

Kamkar, Taqi Vahidiyan, "Takye va vazn-e šeʕr-e farsi",
    Rahnema-ye Ketab, XIV 4/5/6, pp. 242-8 (Tehran, 1973).

Kei Ka?us b. Eskandar, Qabusname, ed. Saꞓid Nafisi (Tehran,
    1934);   ed. Reuben Levy (London, 1951).
Köprülü, Fuat, "Arap arûzunun diğer islâmî edebiyatlara
    tesiri. I. Acem arûzu", İslâm Ansiklopedisi, 8, 9,
    pp. 635-643 (Istanbul, 1942).
Krymskii, A., Istoriya Persii, yeya literatury i
    dervišeskoi teosofii (Moscow, 1906-9, repr. 1914-17).
Kurylowicz, J., L'accentuation des langues indo-européennes,
    pp. 438-451 (Krakow, 1952).
Lazard, Gilbert, Les premiers poètes persans, 2 vols.
    (Tehran/Paris, 1964).
    "The rise of the New Persian language", Cambridge History
    of Iran, Vol. 4, pp. 595-632 (Cambridge, 1975).
Levy, R., "Mathnawi", Encyclopedia of Islam, Vol. III,
    pp. 410-12 (Leiden/London, 1936).
Lorenz, Manfred, "Zum Versbau in modernen Ossetischen",
    Wiss. Zeitschr. d. Humboldt-Universitaet zu Berlin, XIV,
    pp. 593-99 (Berlin, 1965).
Mackenzie, D.N., "Pashto Verse", BSOAS XXI, pp. 319-33
    (London, 1958).
Marr, N., "Vazn-e šeꞓr-e Šahname", Hazare-ye Ferdousi (The
    Millennium of Firdausi), pp. 195 (Pers.) (Tehran, 1944).
Meillet, A., "La déclinaison et l'accent d'intensité en
    perse", JA, pp. 254-77 (Paris, 1900).
    Les origines indo-européennes des métres grecs (Paris,
    1923).
Meredith-Owens, G., "Arūd II", Encyclopedia of Islam, Vol. I,
    p. 677 (Leiden & London, 1958).
Minovi, Mojtaba, Panzdah goftar (Tehran, 1963).
Mirzoev, Abdulgani, Rudaki va enkešaf-e ġazal (Stalinabad,
    1957);   Russian translation: Rudaki i razvitiye gazeli
    (Stalinabad, 1958).
Moꞓin, Mohammad (ed.), Bar-gozide-ye šeꞓr-e farsi (Tehran,
    1952).
Moqarrebi, Moṣtafa, "Enteqad az ꞓaruz-e Hamidi", Rahnema-ye
    Ketab, VI 10/11, pp. 780-7 (Tehran, 1964).

Moʕtamed, A.F., De la métrique (Tehran, 1962).
   Logistique de l'harmonie métrique (Tehran, 1963).
Moulavi, Jalaloddin Rumi, The Mathnawi, ed. trans. & comm.
   R.A. Nicholson, 8 volumes (London & Leiden, 1925-40).
   Kolliyat-e Šams ya Divan-e kabir, ed. Badiʕozzaman
   Foruzanfar, 10 vols., (Tehran, 1957-67).
Namune-ha-ye šeʕr-e azad (Tehran, 1963).
Nima Yušij, Maxula (Tabriz, 1966).
   Maneli (Tehran, 1957).
   Šeʕr-e man (Tehran, 1966).
Noeldeke, T., "Das Iranische Nationalepos", Grundriss der
   Iranischen Philologie, Vol. II, pp. 130-211 (Strassburg,
   1896-1904).
Nyberg, H.S., "Ein Hymnus auf Zervān im Bundahišn", ZDMG,
   LXXXII, pp. 217ff., (Wiesbaden, 1928).
Pagliaro, A. and A. Bausani, Storia della Letteratura
   Persiana (Milan, 1960).
Qazvini, Moḥammad, Doure-ye kamel-e bist maqale-ye Qazvini
   (Bombay, 1928, Tehran, 1934; repr. Tehran, 1953).
Raduyani, Moḥammad b. ʕomar, Tarjomanol-balaǧe, ed. Ahmad
   Ɑteš (Istanbul, 1949).
RajaʔI, Aḥmad ʕali, Poli miyan-e šeʕr-e hejaʔi va ʕaruži-ye
   farsi dar qorun-e avval-e hejri: tarjame-ye ahangin az
   do jozv-e Qorʔan-e Majid (Tehran, 1974).
Rempis, Christian, Beitraege zur Ḥayyām-forschung (Leipzig,
   1937).
   "Die aelteste Dichtung im neupersisch", ZDMG CI, pp. 220-48
   (Wiesbaden, 1951).
   "Die metrik als sprachwissenschaftliches Hilfsmittel im
   Alt-iranischen", ZDMG, CV, pp. *64*-*65* (Wiesbaden,
   1955).
Rudagi va Zaman-e ʔu, ed. Abdulgani Mirzoev (Stalinabad,
   1958).
Rueckert, F., Grammatik, Poetik, und Rhetorik der Perser
   (Vienna, 1827-8; repr. Osnabrueck, 1966).

Rypka, Jan, Iranische Litteraturgeschichte (Leipzig, 1959);
    English ed: History of Iranian Literature (Dordrecht,
    1968).
"La metrique du Mutaqārib", Hazɑre-ye Ferdousi (Tehrɑn,
    1944).
Ṣafa, Ẕabiḥollɑh, Tɑrix-e adabiyɑt dar Irɑn, 2 vols. (Tehrɑn,
    1956-7).
Safiʕi Kadkani, "Kohnetarin namune-ye šeʕr-e fɑrsi: yaki az
    xosravɑnihɑ-ye Bɑrbod", Ǆreš, VI, pp. 18-28 (Mašhad,
    1963).
Salemann, Carl, and Valentin Shukovski, Persische Grammatik
    (Berlin, 1889).
Šams-e Qeis, al-Moʕjam fi maʕɑyire ašʕɑre l-ʕajam, ed.
    Moḥammad Qazvini and Modarres Raẕavi (Tehrɑn, 1935).
Seifi, ʕaruẕ-e Seifi, ed. H. Blochmann (Calcutta, 1867; in
    The Prosody of the Persians..., Calcutta, 1872, repr.
    Amsterdam, 1970).
Šehɑb Toršizi, Divɑn, BM Suppl. 353 Or. 3318.
  M. Bahɑr, "Šehɑb-e Toršizi", Armɑǧɑn, XIII (Tehrɑn, 1932).
  Mohiṭ Ṭabɑṭabɑʔi, "Šehɑb-e Toršizi", Armɑǧɑn, XIII (Tehrɑn,
    1932).
Shaked, S., "Specimens of Middle Persian verse", W.B. Henning
    Memorial Volume, pp. 395-405 (London, 1970).
Tafaẕẕoli, A., "Andarz i Wehzād Farrox Pērōz containing a
    Pahlavi poem in praise of wisdom", Studia Iranica I,
    pp. 207-17 (Paris, 1972).
Talât, Ahmet, Türk Şiirlerinin Vezni (Istanbul, 1933).
Taqizɑde, H., "Šɑhnɑme-ye Ferdousi", Hazɑre-ye Ferdousi
    (Tehrɑn, 1944).
Ṭāriq al-Kātib, Muḥammad, Mawāzīn al-šiʕr al- ʕarabī bi-
    stiʕmāl al-arqām al-tināʔīya (Baṣra, 1971).
Tɑrix-e Sistɑn, ed. M. Bahɑr (Tehrɑn, 1935); Russian
    translation by: L.P. Smirnova (Moscow, 1974).
Tavadia, J.C., "A didactic poem in Zoroastrian Pahlavi",
    Indo-Iranian Studies, (Santiniketan, 1950).
"A rhymed ballad in Pahlavi", JRAS (1955), pp. 29-36

(London, 1955).

Tavallali, Feridun, Rehą (Tehran, 1950).

Ṭusi, Naṣiroddin, Meʕyarol-ašʕar (Tehran, 1901).

Vaṭvaṭ, Rašidoddin, Ḥadayeqos-sehr, ed. ʕabbas Eqbal (Tehran, 1930).

Vaziri, Ali Naqi, "Eṣlaḥat-e adabi", Majalle-ye Mehr, V 10-11 (Tehran, 1937-8).

Veṣal Širazi, Golšan-e Veṣal, ed. Rouḥani Veṣal (Tehran, 1941).

Von Wilamowitz-Moellendorf, Griechische Verskunst (Berlin, 1921).

Weil, Gotthold, "Arūḍ I", Encyclopedia of Islam, Vol. I, pp. 667-77 (Leiden/London, 1958).

"Der Grundriss des Systems der altarabischen Metra", Akten der XXIVsten Int. Orient. Kongress Muenchen, pp. 274-6 (Wiesbaden, 1959).

Grundriss und System der altarabischen Metren (Wiesbaden, 1958).

Wright, W., A Grammar of the Arabic Language, ed. W. Robertson Smith and M.J. de Goeje (Cambridge, 1894-6, repr. 1933).

Xaju Kermani, Divan-e ašʕar, ed. Aḥmad Soheili Xansari (Tehran, 1957).

Xaleqi, Ruḥollah, Naẓari be-musiqi, 2 vols. (Tehran, 1937, repr. 1954; 1938).

Sar-gozašt-e musiqi-ye Iran, 2 vols. (Tehran, 1955-6).

Xanlari, Parviz Natel, "Dar vazn-e šeʕr-e farsi ce kar-e taze-i mitavan kard?", Soxan, VI 10 (Tehran, 1955).

Taḥqiq-e Enteqadi dar ʕaruẓ-e farsi (Tehran, 1948).

"Vazn-e nou", Soxan, VI 11 (Tehran, 1956).

"Vazn-e šeʕr", Soxan, V 7-9 (Tehran, 1954).

Vazn-e šeʕr-e Farsi (Tehran, 1958).

Yaḡmaʔi, Ḥabib, ʕelm-e Qafiye (Tehran, 1955).

Zonis, Ella, Classical Persian music: an introduction (Cambridge, Mass., 1973).

Index of technical terms

Ṭ

ṭarafān 44.

ṭams 19,27-28,32,38.

ṭawīl 13,41,49,53,66-69,72-73,90.

ṭayy 18-19,23,25,27,30-31,33-34,
    36,43,47,50-51,235.

ṭayyibāt 260.

ʿ

ʿajz 40,44.

ʿarūḍ 40,43,52,55,57,69,79,93,
    98-99,106,108,110,112-113
    115,118,178,239,241.

ʿarīḍ 186.

ʿaṣb 20-21,23,26-28,30,33-34,49.

ʿaḍb 17,20,22,25,27-28,30,34.

ʿaqṣ 20,27-28,30,36.

ʿaql 17,20,23,26,28,30,34.

ʿilla 14-15,22,25,27-28,39,
    46-52,59,62-64,234.

ʿamīq 186.

Ḍ

ḍāya 43.

ḍarīb 41,66,78,104,117,119.

ḍazal 163-167,184,245-246,249,
    251,256,259.

ḍulū 238.

ḍinna 4,214.

ḍayr sālim 13-15,42.

____ murdaf 236.

____ muʾassis 236.

F

fāṣila 9.

____ ṣuḍrā 9,12.

____ ʿuẓmā 9.

____ kubrā 9.

fatḥa 208,229.

fard 251.

farʿ 13,15,29,33,63.

faṣl 43.

Q

qāṭiʿ 186.

qāfiya 226-227,231,236,238.

____ maʿmūla 238.

qabḍ 17,9-20,23,26-29,34,
    37,43,47,49-50,59.

qarīb 41-42,66,77-78,101,
    106-107,109,119.

qaṣr 20-21,24,27-29,31-32,
    35-37,62-64,234.

qaṣm 20,27.

qaṣīda 70,163-167,223-224,
    237,242,246-249,251,259.

qatʿ 16,20,24-25,27-31,34-
    35,37,47-49,62,64.

qiṭʿa 163-167,242,251,259.

qaṭf 20,27,49.

qalb 215.

qalandarīyāt 260.

qalīb 186.

qayd 229-230,233.

K

kāmil 13,41,48,53,66-69,
    72-73,81,239.

kabl 21,27-28,47,51.

kabīr 186.

kasf 21,25-27,31-32,35-37,
    51,235.

musattar 186.
mustazād 115,249-251.
mustatīl 186.
mustaʕmal 186.
musajjaʕ 242.
masx 19,21.
musaddas 40-42,44-45,47-54,56,
    70,89-98,100-111,113-118,
    258.
maslūx 19.
musammaṭ 242,257-259.
mušākil 41,66,78,102-103,
    116,119.
muštarik 186.
maštūr 42.
mušaddad 5.
mušaʕʕaṭ 17,63.
maškūl 19,55,79,89,111-112.
miṣrāʕ 2,14,16,27,39-40,46,
    65,124,226,238,243,245,
    249-251.
____-i āzāda 251.
miṣraʕ 39.
muṣarraʕ 241-242,249,251,256.
maṣnūʕ 186.
muḍāriʕ 41,43,50,56,63-64,66,
    69,73-74,77-78,105-108,
    116-117,119.
muḍhikāt 260.
muḍmar 16,53.
mutāyabāt 260.
maṭlaʕ 40,124,242,245,249.
maṭmūs 19,105,107,109.
muṭawwal 16.

maṭwī 19,44-45,52,54-56,70,
    76-78,91,99-101,103-104,
    108,110-115,117-118.
muʕāqaba 39,43-44.
____ ṭarafayn 44.
muʕarrā 39.
muʕaššar 258.
maʕṣūb 20,53.
maʕqūl 20.
maʕkūs 186.
maʕlūl 14.
muʕammam 186.
muʕayyan 186.
mufrid 251.
maqbūḍ 20,53,55,58,60,99,
    101,109-110,112,114,116.
muqtaḍab 41,44,66,73-74,77-78,
    108,112,117,248.
maqṣad 247.
maqṣūd 247.
maqṣūr 20,45,54,56,63-64,89.
maqṭaʕ 245.
maqṭūʕ 20,53,63-64,70,93-94,
    98,109,115,239.
maqṭūf 20,53.
muqaffā 242.
makbūl 21,101.
mukarrar 42.
maksūf 21,45,54,56,91,103-
    104,106,110,113,118.
makšūf 21.
makfūf 21,52,54-56,60-61,64,
    76-78,89,97-99,102-103,
    105-110,112.

Index of proper names